For Madeleine, Martine, Eleanor, Bill, Janice, and Dianne

For Jay, Kalli G, and Anupa

USING FORCE TO PREVENT ETHNIC VIOLENCE

An Evaluation of Theory and Evidence

David Carment
and Frank Harvey

Praeger Studies on Ethnic and
National Identities in Politics
John F. Stack, Jr., Series Adviser

Westport, Connecticut
London

Library of Congress Cataloging-in-Publication Data

Carment, David, 1959–
    Using force to prevent ethnic violence : an evaluation of theory
and evidence / David Carment and Frank Harvey.
        p.   cm.—(Praeger studies on ethnic and national identities in politics, ISSN 1527–9901)
    Includes bibliographical references and index.
    ISBN 0–275–96979–7 (alk. paper)
    1. Ethnic relations—Political aspects.   2. Ethnic relations—International cooperation.
3. Political violence—Prevention.   4. Social conflict—Political aspects.   5. Conflict
management—Political aspects.   6. Conflict management—International cooperation.
I. Harvey, Frank P.   II. Title.   III. Series.
GN496.C35   2001
305.8—dc21   99–086108

British Library Cataloguing in Publication Data is available.

Library of Congress Catalog Card Number: 99–086108
ISBN: 0–275–96979–7
ISSN: 1527–9901

First published in 2001

Praeger Publishers, 88 Post Road West, Westport, CT 06881
An imprint of Greenwood Publishing Group, Inc.
www.praeger.com

Printed in the United States of America

The paper used in this book complies with the
Permanent Paper Standard issued by the National
Information Standards Organization (Z39.48–1984).

10 9 8 7 6 5 4 3 2 1

USING FORCE TO PREVENT ETHNIC VIOLENCE

Contents

Acknowledgments

The authors are grateful to several organizations and people who helped to bring the volume to completion. We would like to thank the Security Defence Forum of the Department of National Defence of Canada for two very generous grants to our respective home institutions, for a special projects grant to Frank Harvey, and for its support in providing travel assistance to Bosnia for both of us. We would also like to thank the Social Sciences and Humanities Research Council of Canada for its support in our research. Both authors were recipients of NATO Fellowships provided by the Royal Society of Canada and NATO. These fellowships allowed both of us to conduct several interviews with key NATO personnel over the course of the Bosnian and Kosovo crises. David Carment would also like to thank the *Policy Planning Division* of the Department of Foreign Affairs and International Trade Canada and the International University of Japan where portions of this volume were written. Frank Harvey is very grateful to the Faculty of Arts and Social Sciences at Dalhousie for teaching release associated with the Burgess Research Award.

The authors would like to thank the excellent scholars who read and supplied valuable insights on various chapters in this volume: Dean Oliver, Dane Rowlands, Patrick James, Paul Huth, Denis Stairs, John Patterson, and Dan Middlemiss. The authors are especially indebted to Troy Joseph, Shannon Leah Smith, and Kevin Hamilton for their excellent editing and contributions to the final version of the book. We are also very grateful to Troy Joseph for his excellent statistical work and commentary on various chapters, Heather Edwards for her very able editing of earlier drafts, and Karen Garner, Mike Elliot, Rasheed Draman, Susan Ampleford, and Hasit Thankey for excellent service as research assistants.

Portions of an earlier draft of chapter 2 appeared in the *Canadian Foreign Policy Journal* (Winter 1999) as an article co-authored with Karen Garner titled: "Conflict Prevention and Early Warning: Problems and Pitfalls." Some of the insights presented in chapter 3 are based on David Carment's work with Dane Rowlands presented in "Three's Company: Game Theory and Third Party Intervention" in *Journal of Conflict Resolution*, Winter 1998. Chapter 7 is a much revised version of a chapter by Carment that appeared in A. Schnabel and H. G. Erhart, eds., *The Southeast European Challenge: Ethnic Conflict and the International Response* (Hambourg: Nomos Verlagsgeselleschaft, 1998). Some of the Bosnia case material used throughout this volume appears in Harvey, "Deterrence and Ethnic Conflict: The Case of Bosnia-Herzegovina, 1993–1994," *Security Studies* (Spring, 1997). An earlier draft of Chapter 5 appeared as "Deterrence Strategies and Conflict Prevention: States vs. Institutions" in H. Adelman and Susanne Schmeidl, eds., *Early Warning and Early Response*, Columbia University Press, Columbia International Affairs Online, 1998. Portions of chapters 1 and 8, particularly the material on evolutionary theory, also appear in Harvey. "Primordialism, Evolutionary Theory and Ethnic Violence in Bosnia: Opportunities and Constraints for Theory and Policy," *Canadian Journal of Political Science* 33 (March, 2000).

1

Introduction

The emergence of ethnic strife in the 1990s coincided with a perceived decline in the Westphalian foundations upon which the Cold War system was based. At the same time, as domestic violence has been unleashed, the restraints that restricted intervention by multistate coalitions and organizations have been relaxed. The internationalization of ethnic strife intensifies the search for solutions even further by provoking the passions of ethnic brethren in neighboring states, challenging the legitimacy of current borders, and raising the spectre of ethnic cleansing, genocide, and state failure.

Much is to be learned about how regional and international security organizations can prevent destructive ethnic conflict and manage cases in which violence already is at hand. Since the momentum of crisis escalation has become faster than ever, there exists simultaneous pressure for help in numerous regions. The need to coordinate diplomatic and military strategies—now more crucial—occurs in a larger and more diverse international system. Although some conflicts have been successfully brought to a close, state failures and genocides have created new, and in some cases unprecedented, demands for solutions.

The outlook is not promising, to say the least. Evidence from the most recent cases of protracted ethnic violence in the former Yugoslavia, for example, appears to confirm suspicions that international and regional organizations are not easily mobilized to handle ethnic conflicts before they become violent. The question is, why? What does the evidence suggest about when and under what conditions third parties should intervene in coercive and noncoercive ways to prevent ethnic tensions from escalating out of control, or how to manage crises when they do? Are we any closer to understanding the conditions under which deterrent and compellent threats will succeed and fail, or how the credibility, resolve, and capability of third parties can be enhanced to prevent an ethnic war from escalating and spreading?

Unfortunately, the academic and policy communities are not well equipped to provide persuasive answers to pressing questions about the onset, escalation, and resolution of contemporary conflicts characterized by ethnic rivalry. Most of the work in the field, according to the most skeptical, continues to focus on theories of international relations and international conflict and crisis management that have been generated from decades of Cold War analysis. Since most of these conventional models, frameworks, and methodologies were derived from unrealistic assumptions about the behavior of states in an outdated international system, they have become either obsolete or, worse, irrelevant (Whitworth 1994; Cox 1992). Such critics argue that research on coercive diplomacy, deterrence, and crisis management and other so-called "dominant concerns of the past" are no longer useful for understanding "new" threats to peace and security.

Deterrence, for example, is a relatively abstract "realist" theory derived from analysis of the behavior of independent states in "anarchy," and since both anarchy and states are becoming obsolete, state-centric, rationalist models such as deterrence cannot possibly offer any insights into post–Cold War problems of ethnic conflict. Ethnic violence, critics claim, is more likely a product of primordial hatreds or deeply entrenched religious and political divisions that do not lend themselves well to rationalist models of interstate relations or crisis bargaining. By implication, the tremendous amount of time and energy spent on trying to understand the protracted nature of ethnic conflict through the prism of mainstream international relations theory will not yield important results (or any cumulative knowledge of ethnic violence, for that matter).

The problem with this line of argument is that its proponents rarely specify the precise impact "change" has on the theories and models they criticize and dismiss. Their claims tend to be sweeping generalizations about how change, in and of itself, is sufficient to render obsolete particular research programs, without offering a careful study of this proposition. There is a tendency in scholarship on international relations, as Holsti (1985) observed more than a decade ago, "to develop theoretical innovations on the basis of recent diplomatic developments . . . before these developments have assumed the character of long-term trends or patterns of behaviour." After all, the process of change is not boundless; some things change more than others. But the impact of these relatively stable (unchanging) forces is rarely considered by scholars who are prepared to dismiss as obsolete the findings from years of research into interstate conflict and war.

Although the international system has undergone significant change, analysis of international politics must take into account that a great deal of global activity today, particularly with respect to questions of war and peace but not limited to them, will continue to be a product of structures and strategic processes specified in traditional research programs. Scholars should avoid the trap of rejecting important paths to knowledge because of the pressure to offer something new in the wake of change.

With this in mind, the challenge of this book is to develop a conceptual framework for advancing basic research on questions about coercive diplomacy and the management of ethnic violence. We pursue this objective in two ways. First, we aim to uncover and evaluate theoretical knowledge about the causes of violent ethnic conflict, using case material and quantitative assessments. Second, we apply these assumptions against recent instances of conflict prevention, management, and resolution. If successful, the results should help us anticipate the future behavior of ethnic rivals and possibly enhance the prospects for crisis management through regional and international organizations, an especially important project in an era of unprecedented ethnic tensions. More importantly, if it is possible to illustrate the explanatory and predictive power of these time-honored theories regarding questions of war and peace in a contemporary setting, an important contribution to current debates in the field will be made.

The remainder of this introductory chapter reviews key concepts and approaches in the literature in an effort to set the stage for the analysis of the prevention, management, and resolution of intrastate ethnic conflict in subsequent chapters. This review serves as the basis for exploration of ethnic management practices and their evaluation in each subsequent chapter. An in-depth study of conflict in the former Yugoslavia (focusing on NATO's role in Bosnia and Kosovo) is used throughout the book to illustrate and evaluate these practices.

This study is concerned with the use of force as an instrument of coercive diplomacy in situations where violence is already at hand. But we are also interested in situations in which threats to use force are elicited to either mitigate an escalating conflict or stem the recurrence of violence in postconflict situations. Findings from case study material drawn from the crises in Bosnia and Kosovo are reinforced with evidence drawn from aggregate research, formal modeling, and statistical methods. Therefore, the book represents a more integrated approach to the subject that promises a greater degree of reliability in comparison with other studies on the subject.

In the second chapter, we examine the role of early warning and its precise link to conflict prevention. The guiding question is, how do we detect ripe moments and turning points in conflict escalation so we can stem, prevent, mitigate, and channel conflictual behavior before it becomes violent? This chapter argues that identifying patterns of interaction can help us understand how and when the conditions of escalation and de-escalation occur. If one party can be induced to reduce its conflictual behavior, it is possible that the other side will reciprocate. International efforts can then be employed as leverage to induce a "hurting stalemate" or to influence the behavior of one of the participants.

The debate over coercive diplomacy, centering on the scope, timing, and intensity of force required to achieve a mediated settlement, is the focus of the third and fourth chapters. The key problem tackled in chapter 3 is making coercive diplomacy more effective in conflicts involving armed groups that operate outside the control of recognized political authorities and that resist traditional peacekeeping efforts (e.g., Bosnia-Herzegovina, Kosovo). We illustrate our points with a focus on NATO's preventive capacity applied first in Bosnia and then in Kosovo.

Chapter 4 provides a more detailed account of coercive strategies used by NATO in Bosnia and Kosovo. The chapter introduces a distinct approach that recommends identifying separate deterrence and compellence encounters within a single crisis, thus expanding the pool of evidence that would be appropriate for testing a wide range of theoretical propositions.

In chapter 5 we investigate, quantitatively, the question of whether and how perceptions of commitment, credibility, and resolve are influenced by (a) the *type of intervener* (states versus international organizations), (b) the *type of conflict* (ethnic versus nonethnic), and (c) the *location of the dispute* (interstate versus intrastate). Several propositions are tested against crisis data. The findings indicate, among other things, that (a) ethnic and intrastate crises are more violent than their counterparts, and (b) multistate coalitions are more likely than unilateral interveners, and unilateral interveners more likely than international organizations (IOs) to control hostilities in both ethnic and intrastate crises. The implications are discussed in the context of growing opposition to unilateral intervention into ethnic crises.

Chapter 6 examines NATO's peacebuilding role as it pertains to both immediate and long-term efforts such as the rapid deployment of a coalition of forces to respond to state failure and insurgencies on the one hand, and the provision of security guarantees for beleaguered states on the other. NATO's role in the Bosnian and Kosovo crises indicates that the institution has a well-developed capacity to carry out immediate postconflict peacebuilding tasks.

In chapter 7 we assess the effectiveness of third-party techniques in the termination and resolution of intrastate ethnic conflict. The key question is, when are pacific and coercive forms of third-party intervention likely to lead to conflict termination? Using outcome indicators that link both the decisiveness and formality of outcomes, we evaluate the impact third parties have on conflict termination. Consistent with the results from previous chapters, the findings indicate that the settlement and resolution of intrastate ethnic conflict is more difficult in the absence of coercive efforts.

The final chapter reviews the contributions and limitations of the preceding chapters. The chapter concludes by pointing to a way out.

UNDERSTANDING ETHNIC CONFLICT

For a variety of reasons outlined below, there are some fundamental misconceptions about the causes of ethnic conflict and, more importantly, what to do about them. Indeed, in the last decade, academics and policy makers have made a concerted and often unjustified search for novel approaches to managing ethnic conflict. This is because in the absence of any hard evidence to the contrary, policy makers, analysts, and ordinary citizens were left to assume the worst: the last decade of the twentieth century would mark the beginning of a downward spiral into global anarchy.[1]

In fact, in the latter half of the twentieth century, repression of minorities and ethnic conflict went hand in hand. For example, between 1945 and 1980, ethnic rebellion and nonviolent protest among ethnic groups gradually increased. As new, institutionally weak and divided states emerged on the geopolitical map in the 1960s, the upward trend in violent ethnic conflict began. The trend has been most closely associated with decolonization and contention for state power in Africa and Asia. However, the collapse of the Soviet Union and the communist countries of Europe has since provided the basis for ethnic rebellions in these transitional states.[2]

By 1998, the total number of ongoing very serious conflicts (those with 1,000 battlefield fatalities or more) had declined in absolute terms either because of military defeat, government concessions, or some form of concerted third-party intervention. Some long-standing conflicts were either successfully mediated or at least came to a truce during which the ethnic cleansing and warfare were discontinued. Among the most notable settlements were those in Bosnia, Northern Ireland, and the Philippines. These successes contrast with governments' failed attempts to end internal wars in the Sudan, Burma, India, Iraq, and Sri Lanka.

Nevertheless, public concern about the extreme cases—those involving a combination of refugees and displaced persons, state failure, and spillover to neighboring states—remains at the forefront of the development of ethnic conflict management policy and analysis. For every civilized divorce Czech-style there have been many more armed conflicts. In extreme cases, ethnic conflicts, violence, and spillover appear to be inextricably intertwined *and* unstoppable.

In brief, the rapid development of ethnic conflict management theory and policy during the past decade has occurred against the backdrop of some basic misconceptions about the nature and sources of ethnic conflict. The first of these has been general confusion over root causes. Indeed, the label "ethnic conflict" itself reveals very little about what underlies intergroup tensions. It is still widely believed that ethnic conflicts are distinct from other forms of conflict in both form and content. This outlook assumes on the one hand that all identity-based disputes possess similar underlying causes, and on the other that it is identity that makes these conflicts distinct. In essence, this perspective holds that ethnicity is no more than a primordial sentiment reactivated in the modern context. On an abstract level, nationalist upheavals and ethnic conflicts are problems about human rights, participation, justice, and distribution. However, the manifestation of these issues becomes ethnic because that is the basis for exclusion or repression.

LIMITATIONS TO UNDERSTANDING ETHNIC CONFLICT

Scholars who seek to explain ethnic conflict and violence are confronted by three distinct sets of empirical puzzles. Each puzzle is drawn from the perspectives of evolutionary psychology, sociobiology, or cultural selection theories:

1. *Macro*, or long-term selection processes associated with basic human preferences for individual or group survival, ethnic identity, or kinship affiliations (e.g., van den Berghe 1981; Johnson 1986, 1987, 1997; Warnecke, Masters, and Kempter 1992; Bennett, Hanley, and Orbell 1997; Salter 1997);

2. *Intermediate* selection mechanisms associated with the fitness and adaptability of specific cultures, religions, or belief systems in different regions of the world—e.g., the former Yugoslavia (Silverman and Case 1997; Hislope 1997); the former Soviet Union (Moses 1997); and

3. *Micro*, or short-term selection processes and fitness mechanisms that account for the escalation and/or duration of ethnic hatreds, violence, or war at a particular point in time (Hislope 1997).

Much of the literature on evolutionary theory addresses ethnicity from the perspective of the first two puzzles, whereas comparatively less time has been spent addressing micro-evolutionary questions about the timing, escalation, and duration of ethnic violence. This empirical gap is, of course, entirely understandable—an evolutionary perspective furnishes a very useful framework for studying biological, sociocultural, and systemic change and transformation over relatively long periods of time, whereas explanations for specific choices, events, or behaviors tend to focus on environmental stimuli in the context of standard social scientific models. In brief, research on cultural selection provides an excellent source of information about why and under what conditions certain beliefs (and hatreds) survive, but the link to ethnic violence is not as well developed.

PRIMORDIALISM, EVOLUTIONARY THEORY, AND
ETHNIC CONFLICT

The dominant "evolutionary" explanation for ethnic conflict is often referred to as *primordialism*. Proponents argue that people's ethnic and religious identities "have deep social, historical, and genetic foundations," and that the motivation for ethnic and kinship affiliation comes from these subjective, psychological forces internal to the individual and related to basic human needs for security and, more importantly, survival (Geertz 1973; Isaacs 1975; A. Smith 1981; van den Berghe 1981; Horowitz 1985; Stack 1981, 1986, 1997; Johnson 1997). Individuals are bound to an ethnic group by virtue of some "absolute import attributed to the very tie itself" (Geertz 1973, 259). There is something fundamental about the nature of ethnicity, in other words, that ties individuals together and provides a sense of communal anchorage and protection lacking in other forms of organization.

It is true that shared historical experiences and cultural traits are likely to strengthen ethnic identities, but the pressure such forces exert on individuals and groups is likely to vary from individual to individual and from group to group.[3] As Holsti points out (1985, 12),

Everyone identifies groups to which they do not belong as the "Other." But this does not allow us to make predictions about resulting attitudes, much less about behavior. Some people embrace the "Other" to the point of engaging in rapturous admiration of their culture, learning their language, promoting their political system(s)—in general, integrating. Other people adopt racist and belligerent attitudes towards the "Other," but probably not to all relevant "Others."

The point here is that there is a great deal of variability in both attitudes and behavior resulting from the acknowledgment of "difference." In fact, as Holsti points out, most multicultural communities throughout the world coexist peacefully, including Bosnians, Serbs, and Croats.[4] As Reynolds et al. observe (1986, 271),

Even if ethnocentrism and group conflict have their origins in our evolutionary past, and even if our genes predispose us to make in-group/out-group distinctions and behave accordingly, we can hope at least that through greater knowledge and understanding we can substantially overcome those tendencies.

With respect to human social behavior, *selection, adaptability*, and *fitness*, all essential features of the evolutionary processes, are not linear as they generally are in biology. This is especially relevant to explaining ethnic conflict, since changing environmental conditions can reverse (in very short periods of time when compared with genetic evolutionary processes) the fitness and adaptability of cultural preferences.

Indeed, the vast majority of ethnic leaders respond to incentives, threats, and coercion in fairly predictable ways. If we are to assume that the leaders who orchestrate acts of terror are acting independently of their environment, the analysis, and by extension the prevention and management, of ethnic strife would be almost impossible. Given the correct set of incentives, the most violent of ethnic militia leaders is open to negotiation.

This is because, as irrational as it may appear, ethnic violence plays an important role in ensuring ethnic group solidarity. Ethnic conflict appears to be irrational because it leads to undesirable social outcomes over the short term, such as destruction of property and economic decline. Yet however costly and irrational it appears in human and material terms, violence is a means of regulating behaviors and maintaining social order. In short, a collectivity will pursue violence if it safeguards advantageous and long-term political and economic outcomes.

Performance expectations are one way to ensure mobilization, cohesion, and stronger support. Violence serves a functional and positive role for an ethnic elite and their followers. Leaders will use violence if it is a means of increasing cohesion among the group. From the perspective of an ethnic militia leader, the long-term gains from a dispute (such as territorial consolidation, enhancement of political power, and increased ethnic homogeneity) can be dramatically enhanced if a conflict can be controlled. For elites who play on the fears of their constituency, the benefits of escalation are obvious.

One might ask why "ethnic" ties are more important than others when satisfying needs—presumably one could accommodate a desire for security in several ways that have little to do with cultural or ethnic traits (e.g., political, class, occupational, or functional identities). The answer, from an "evolutionary" perspective, is that ethnic ties are inherently more potent as an organizing (and, by implication, evolutionary) force than, say, ties based on class or occupation (Horowitz 1985; Johnson 1987). Elegant explanations for why ethnic bonds are more important are part and parcel of evolutionary approaches (van den Berghe 1981; Masters 1989; Spriggs 1996; Johnson 1997). As Spriggs points out (1996, 2), "since the battle being fought was for the survival of 'self,' the enemy became the 'non-self,' the 'other.' These 'others' were not of your immediate genetic line. The easiest method of determining 'others' was to see, to hear, and to smell them." Johnson (1997, 6) makes a similar argument—phenotypic matching of an organism's physical and behavioral characteristics (e.g., language, dialect, customs, diet) "is probably the most important kin recognition mechanism for humans . . . because there is often a correlation between genotype and phenotype—those who are related are more similar phenotypically than those who are not, at least on average." In sum, humans bond to one another for evolutionary reasons that enhance reproductive success (Johnson 1997, 4).

From this perspective, enhancing reproductive success is the key to evolutionary explanations of ethnic conflict. The war in Bosnia escalated as the groups' affinities were challenged and their existence threatened. Memories of the Croatian slaughter of Serbs during World War II played an important role in the Serbian decision to mount such an intense offensive (Midlarsky 1997, 29). The war also took place amidst the economic collapse of Eastern Europe, creating additional threats from "others" and greater incentives to fight for security.

Research on evolutionary theory, phenotype matching, and kinship affiliations is extremely useful for understanding the root causes of patriotism, nationalism (both ethnic and nonethnic), xenophobia, and even racism. But it cannot explain ethnic war—that particular subset of human social interaction that involves a high level of intergroup violence and hostility. Nor can it account for variations in the scope, severity, and timing of ethnic violence more generally.[5] In fact, ethnic conflict is a dynamic process in which at least five stages of escalation can be clearly identified and acted upon. These include a latent stage (lasting years or decades) in which differences between ethnic groups are made salient but there is no overt conflict; an onset phase whereby a "trigger" creates the conditions for violence; a peak point leading to large-scale confrontation between groups and leading to repression or domination; a de-escalation phase, including perhaps some form of third-party involvement; and finally, a termination phase resulting in the resolution or transformation of the conflict. Ethnic conflicts can last months, years, or decades. The most salient are protracted conflicts, fluctuating in intensity over the course of several decades and involving entire communities.

Stronger explanations for this variability focus on environmental forces, some of which underscore the prominent role played by ethnic elites in the mobilization process. Examples include Barth 1969, Bell 1975, Rothschild 1981, Nagel and Olzak 1982, Olzak 1983, Neilson 1985, O'Sullivan-See 1986, Zald and McCarthy 1987, and Mason 1994. These "instrumentalists" posit that ethnicity is a resource that becomes politicized by ethnic elites in the competition for power, prestige, and authority (Rothschild 1981). In fact, ethnicity enhances the ability of group leaders to mobilize support by "facilitating identification of potential supporters," thereby making it easier to detect and sanction free riders (Mason 1994, 9). Ethnic elites often intentionally promote feelings of cultural and economic inequality for political gain in hopes of establishing a strong, unified base for action. The strategy often involves tapping economic grievances and reframing them in the discourse of ethnonationalism (O'Sullivan-See 1986).

Others conceptualize the mobilization of ethnicity in the language of pluralism and in the competition over scare economic and political resources (Furnivall 1948; Gellner 1964; M. Smith 1965; Hechter 1975; Despres 1967, 1976; Horowitz 1985). Where culturally divergent groups inhabit a common society, there is a "structural imperative" in which one group becomes subordinate to another (M. Smith 1965, 62). This is especially common when ethnic cleavages are reinforced by differences in class and status (Hechter 1975; Valdez 1994), or when labor markets are divided along ethnic lines (A. Smith 1981, 1986). The inequalities often result in exploitation, discrimination, and blocked mobility for members of subordinate groups, which create the grievances, feelings of relative deprivation, and, by implication, the motives for ethnic mobilization and violence (Gurr 1970, 1991). Pluralism promotes ethnonational sentiments by making the "ascriptive basis of ethnicity a functional and effective vehicle" for promoting individual and group interests (Stack 1986, 6).[6]

Waltz's explanation for the relative importance of "structure" in explaining international politics is appropriate here. Waltz uses the analogy of our desire for wealth and prosperity to argue that we might all want a million dollars (for security, survival, and so on), but a very small fraction of the population is prepared to rob a bank to achieve that objective. If the police were to go on strike, however, the number of bank robbers and robberies would increase.

Similarly, individuals and groups may be persuaded by ethnic elites to hate and fear members of "other" groups, but the probability of war, violence, ethnic cleansing, and genocide depends on the opportunities and constraints that present themselves to the warring factions and their leaders. In fact, the analogy of a police strike is quite appropriate when accounting for the escalation of ethnic violence in Bosnia. Although cultural traits can account for the motivations behind demands for political, social, or territorial separation based on distinct national identities, and can explain why each side may end up fighting, the approach is less successful at establishing whether the violence is a product of animosities produced by the fears associated with ethnic differences, or international forces and environmental stimuli.

CONCLUSIONS

With respect to policy, preferences for solutions to ethnic conflict depend on the explanations we accept for the violence. If one emphasizes root causes (for example, ethnonationalism, elite mobilization, primordialism, relative deprivation), the list of solutions would include partition, power sharing, democratization, constitutional entrenchment of ethnic or minority rights, proportional division of key offices, mutual vetoes, and so on.

The problem is that few theories of ethnic conflict provide appropriate guidelines on what third parties, such as NATO, can do when fighting breaks out, when territory is lost, or when the death toll increases by tenfold, creating yet another generation of fear and hatred. The purpose of this volume, therefore, is to identify third-party strategies to prevent, manage, and resolve ethnic conflict at different stages of conflict intensity.

NOTES

1. These views find reinforcement in the image of ethnic violence as an irrational, spontaneous, unmanageable, and contagious phenomena leading to the breakup of the current state structure. In one forceful statement on the theme, Daniel Patrick Moynihan argued, in his book *Pandemonium* (Oxford: Oxford University Press, 1993), that by the mid-twenty-first century there would be close to 300 states in the international system.

2. Source: "Minorities Report 1 Ethnopolitical Conflict in the 1990s: Patterns and Trends" by Ted Robert Gurr, Department of Government and Politics, University of Maryland, College Park, and Michael Haxton, Minorities at Risk Project Center for International Development and Conflict Management, April 1996.

3. Ethnonationalism has also been interpreted as a defense against the forces of modernization—that is, contemporary conditions of rapid social and technological change, intrusive state institutions, impersonal bureaucracies, an absence of political consensus, and so on—that tend to create a sense of "anomie" and a "loss of identity" (O'Sullivan-See 1986). Under these conditions, people may rediscover their ethnicity as a way of establishing the emotional security that comes from communal association (Rothschild 1981). Valdez (1994) applies a similar thesis to the case of Yugoslavia, claiming that

Serbian efforts to prevent democratization and market reforms were essentially antimodernizing.

4. There are anomalies that do not mesh with expectations about the almost automatic grouping of individuals on the basis of ethnicity, even when faced with a common threat from the "other" ethnic group. The division among gangs in the United States is not based on the phenotypic matching of skin color, probably the most potent phenotype. Instead the divisions are almost entirely territorial, with only the color of one's clothes identifying which side one is on—red or blue. The rivalry between the Bloods and the Crips suggests that a somewhat different set of forces are at play in this particular ethnic battle.

5. The Minorities at Risk project has identified 268 politically significant national and minority peoples making up 17.7 percent of the world's population. There are three main clusters of these politically active ethnic groups. The first of these clusters consists of national peoples, including regionally concentrated peoples with political autonomy; national minorities, which comprise segments of transnational peoples; and indigenous groups. It is the regionally concentrated ethnic nationalists that have been involved in the bulk of protracted conflicts since 1989. The majority of these groups reside in Central and Eastern Europe and Asia. Minority peoples make up the second cluster and reside in all regions save the Middle East. Finally, there are religious sects that dominate the Middle East and parts of Asia.

6. Selection cannot explain nonadaptive cultural traits, such as altruism and heroism, without reference to some alternative explanation derived from a theory of group selection, or some other standard social science theory that emphasizes the importance of environmental forces. When this happen there will be a paradigm shift away from the standard social science model—in which the individual is viewed as a learning machine, and behavior is a product of learning and culture—toward an evolutionary psychology model, in which the individual is viewed as having a cultural and evolutionary history, and the mind is composed of learning devices that have evolved and been selected for the purposes of solving specific problems.

2

Early Warning and Conflict Prevention: Theory and Practice

INTRODUCTION

Early warning is not just about fact finding, theory building, and model development. Early warning is also about anticipating and responding to prevent such events from occurring. Therefore, early warning systems are not confined to analyzing a crisis, but also relate to the capacities and response strategies for dealing with a crisis (Adelman 1996). To convince themselves that action is necessary, strategists must know the costs of not being involved coupled with the likelihood that a conflict will escalate. Early warning is necessary only if decision makers can be persuaded that accurate information is useful to finding an appropriate fit between strategy, the problem at hand, and the resources available. Decision makers can then develop an active and effective response to the specific conflict based on a combination of factors. These would include the salience of the conflict, the potential for a larger regional conflict, the resources available, and the available alternatives (which might include doing nothing).

RISK ASSESSMENT AND EARLY WARNING

The complexities of our era suggest that analytical capacity alone is insufficient to manage today's problems. There is a need to gather and sort additional information more effectively. The collection and analysis of intelligence is now more than ever heavily influenced by the shifting needs of policy makers. The central problem for decision makers in this transitional era is coping with unprecedented and rapid change. Transitional change has three distinct elements. First, the international system is in an unstable disequilibrium punctuated by frequent and dynamic disruptions.[1] This means that the characteristics and requirements of foreign policy analysis are much different than they were during the Cold War. The analytical requirements of today's foreign policy focus on managing dynamic patterns of change and not on system stability. The net result is that states experience greater fluctuations in their foreign policies—a kind of zigzagging effect—marked by a continuous search for innovation and flexibility in maintaining stable international relations.[2] Accordingly, foreign policy ideas and strategies have a relatively short shelf life. Security concerns move constantly: states engulfed in intrastate crisis and civil war can move to the top of public attention and the policy makers' agenda with lightning speed, and just as readily disappear if the crisis is contained or resolved by truce, humanitarian intervention, or other means.

Second, and following from the first point, there is a greater tendency for states to act out of sync with one another. As the system as a whole is unable to cope, states tend to fall back on local and regional patterns of political authority.[3] In extreme cases, the result can be destabilization of individual states, loss of control by the center, or worse, defining of state interests along narrow bands of parochial sensibility. Overall, this means that the legitimacy and authority of the current system are undergoing a transition. The resulting tension is inextricably woven into a worldwide crisis of authority in which current norms cannot keep pace with changes in the issues and actors that seem to be evolving at a much faster pace.

Finally, there is a tendency for domestic patterns of behavior of even a modest magnitude to have a greater and often destabilizing impact on the system. This dynamic interaction means that the distinction between foreign and domestic affairs is becoming increasingly obscure. The ramifications for policy planning are straightforward. Strategy selection and strategy change are now determined almost wholly by the preferences and values of domestic constituencies, including nongovernmental organizations (NGOs), interest groups, and ordinary citizens. Decision makers must first consider the long-term ramifications that their foreign policies engender among their constituencies. This means that the foreign policy agenda shifts constantly from one based on clearly defined national interests to one based on a mix of domestic interests and domestic values.

To some extent, domestic factors can have a constraining effect on foreign policy by decreasing the attraction of strategies that involve risks. This linkage is especially important at a time when many front-line workers abroad are no longer soldiers and diplomats but volunteers, peace builders and aid workers, working in societies in transition and in zones of conflict where human rights are often trampled and ordinary lives are increasingly at risk.

The demand that such profound changes place on decision makers and analysts has been compared to kayaking in rapids. There is "a premium on strategic timing and the ability to think beyond the next bend or, in other words, to be able to draw conclusions from a complex array of individual observations about how a system's dynamics may be about to undergo radical change."[4]

The decision maker's need for information clearly requires enhanced analytical and organizational abilities. The end of the Cold War has not diminished the importance of intelligence gathering, but rather has made the process more difficult because of increased complexity in nontraditional areas such as transnational ethnic politics and violence, the environment, demographics, and social migration.

Unfortunately, there is no direct route through which informational analysis can bypass the political constraints inherent in any decision-making process. By itself, intelligence lacks the rapidity necessary to be a truly effective weapon in crisis situations.[5] Technological change has ensured the trend toward more rapid escalation of crises. Decision makers are pressured to decide in progressively shorter time intervals. At peak points within a crisis, ad hoc forms of consultation often take precedence over established procedures. Consequently, the *analysis* of events requires constant and permanent updating not just by area experts but by all those involved in policy formulation.

Such an approach has two implications. First, it means that the analysis of events and intelligence gathering no larger fit neatly into compartmentalized and modular frameworks of responsibilities (if they ever did). Second, it means that to cope with events as they unfold, "just in time" strategies of information gathering and analysis become crucial. Long-term planning tends to take a back seat to more medium-term and short-term contingency planning.

Second, there is the problem of weak signals leading to problems of interpretation. Errors in predicting outcomes become greater as we move further in time from the onset of a crisis. The signals are inevitably clearer as a crisis looms, but this is of less benefit to a decision maker. Additionally, with the complexity of today's conflicts, analysts need to think about alternative sequences of events—not just one or two, but many—and far enough ahead to anticipate a likely chain of events.

These problems mean that analysts must establish a time frame appropriate to the issue at hand. In this sense, conflict analysis is like peeling an onion, in which each layer reveals progressively longer time lines: long-term fundamental dynamics relating to structural causes and consequences, midterm behavioral patterns, and current events such as looming humanitarian crises. For example, warning must come years in advance to respond strategically to structural problems (development, institution building, establishing infrastructure) but only a year or two or less when escalation is imminent and when the tasks are to engage in preventive diplomacy, dialogue, and mediation.[6] At different levels of aggregation, early warning has been extolled as a tool for overcoming some of these decisional constraints. Although it is fair to say that early warning does offer the opportunity to surmount some of the obstacles noted above, it is also true that the term *early warning* is used too loosely and is at risk of becoming an outdated cliché. Bereft of its theoretical import, early warning has been used to explain everything from risk assessment to forecasting. Properly understood, forecasting and risk assessment are complementary but distinct modes of analysis and can be distinguished from early warning in several important respects.

Forecasting is about the likelihood that an event will happen. By itself it has no strategic connotation or purpose. Forecasting can be either passive (about events over which we have no control) or active (about events over which we have some control).[7]

To be relevant to policy, forecasting needs to take on three additional qualities. It must be diagnostic, by which emphasis is on describing how and why things work as they do. It must also take the form of a conditional generalization—that is, in situation x, if one does y, one should expect z. Finally, policy-relevant forecasting must be prescriptive, offering explicit recommendations to policy makers faced with certain kinds of problems.[8] Policy-relevant forecasting (or risk assessment) has traditionally referred to the chance or probability that some event will occur, and has been associated with the word *gravity*, used to describe the event's consequences. More formally, risk means an expected value arrived at by multiplying consequences by the probability that they will occur. Risk indicates probabilities about consequences.

Risk assessments rely on the field monitoring of indicators of specific types of behavior, monitoring indicators of related factors, and the proximate causes or systematic analysis of events through predictive models.[9] Collectively, their objective is to combine monitoring of indicators with diagnosis, using theoretical findings and index construction to develop knowledge of certain causes that produce specific effects.[10] The effect can be either a danger, such as crisis, war, or genocide, or an opportunity, such as investment or the victory of a democratic government.[11]

Not surprisingly, as we move from passive to policy-relevant forecasting, the effects of forecasting are more consequential. The need for accuracy is paramount. First, since resources and lives are at stake, it is important that risk assessments be as reliable as possible.

Second, since risk assessments precede early warning, accurate diagnosis has consequences for effective strategies. Assessments identify background and intervening conditions that establish the risk for potential crisis and conflict.[12] They concentrate on high-risk situations before they become crises. They also provide a context for interpreting the results of on-the-ground monitoring.[13]

Third, risk assessments can overcome misperceptions of high risk. For example, extensive media coverage leads people to overestimate the risk of international violence and to place undue importance on human-produced crises. The main impediments to communicating reliable risk assessments of human-produced crises are twofold. First, there may be conflicting and competing risk assessments of identical problems. Second, decision makers may choose to ignore the advice they are given, not so much because they doubt the forecast's veracity, but because the proposed action may not generate much political capital.

ETHNIC CONFLICT AND EARLY WARNING

A central deficiency in current approaches to early warning on ethnic conflict is that they focus almost exclusively on micro-level interactions between state centers and minorities. Domestically based political models and variables are central to this approach. The units of analysis are usually the group or the individual. As a consequence, the resulting patterns of behavior and inferences tend to underemphasize the importance of other actors and structural forces external to an ethnic conflict, be these individual states, neighboring ethnic groups, regional or international organizations, or social and international structures.

Knowledge of the ways in which socioeconomic and political factors impact the dynamics of conflicts may also be lacking. If the conflict is latent, it may be difficult to identify potential harmful consequences. In addition, there may be many factors triggering a particular dispute, making it difficult to identify the responsibility of a particular factor or event. The process-based approach concentrates on how interactions between ethnic groups influence conflict-prone behavior (Hardin 1995; Gurr 1994).

Since many of today's conflicts stem from social or economic causes, analysts must know about internal economic and social developments as well as the state of international relations that "co-evolve" with the conflict on the ground. Knowledge of environmental factors (in this context, the role of outside structures that affect the flow of the conflict) is as pertinent as knowledge of the conflict's social or economic causes. Therefore, not one but two dimensions delineate the boundaries of ethnic violence: the domestic and the international. The domestic-related focus is on states at risk of violence during internal political transformation, whereas the international dimension focuses on the role of transnational factors and outside actors. Of course, the two are interrelated. In this chapter we briefly assess some of the domestic and international factors that affect the flow of a conflict and its propensity to become violent. In subsequent chapters we detail the role of a specific international factor—namely third-party intervention (with an emphasis on NATO).

Violent ethnic conflict most often occurs when the state becomes the principal instrument for advancing ethnic group interests. Frequently, the existence of an ethnic political movement depends on an elite with skills and resources to sustain a movement. Ethnic identities are evoked in certain structural circumstances to advance the material and political interests of actors whose primary purposes are not ethnic. Subsequent myth making and the dredging up of past events become symbols around which ethnic groups coalesce. These symbols make interethnic violence appear just, honorable, and legitimate.

UNDERSTANDING INTERNATIONALIZATION

When there is an ethnic challenge from within, internationalization is sure to follow. In general, the most basic international dimension of ethnic conflict emanates from disputes over territory and transnational ethnic linkages (Carment and James 1998). Here, the concern is that claims to territory by a minority in one state may lead to demonstrations of solidarity by a neighboring ethnic majority state. There are two types of linkage: external support for secessionist-type conflicts involving large territorially concentrated minorities, and irredentist-type efforts at retrieving territorially concentrated minorities. Irredentism entails a claim to the territory of an entity—usually an independent state—where an ethnic ingroup is a numerical minority. The original term *terra irredenta* means "territory to be redeemed." Either an ethnic nation-state or a multiethnic plural state may seek redemption. The territory to be redeemed is sometimes regarded as part of a cultural homeland or historic state (or as an integral part of one state). This claim is based on transnational ethnic affinities.

The problem is particularly acute when "hypernationalist" leaders pressure governments to take assertive measures (Kaufman 1998; Ryan 1998). Even if the extremists do not want violence, they may not be in a position to restrain strident and highly committed followers. Thus, for a state to pursue an irredentist claim or involvement in secessionist strife, ethnic affinities provide opportunities to be exploited, which increases the likelihood of interstate conflict, crisis, and even war.

In brief, nearly all ethnic conflicts with origins inside a state have an important international dimension (Heraclides 1991; Chazan 1991; Midlarsky 1997). In turn, the actions of states external to a conflict greatly influence a conflict's dynamics and resolution. Depending on the motivations of the external actors, external involvement can cause an ethnic conflict to spread through encouragement and diffusion, or it can prevent it from spreading by concerted efforts of suppression. In a complex and interdependent world, of course, a myriad of international factors can reverberate negatively or positively. The factors delineated below are highly visible characteristics and focus exclusively on the affective dimension.

Moreover, mutual interests are strongest for those groups that have high international ethnic affinities *and* where the "other group" is seen as an enemy of the supporting state. The "other group" or "out group" can, in this instance, be the state center or an ethnic minority. If affinities are not promising for a convergent mutual interest, a state is less likely to pursue an ethnically oriented foreign policy strategy, and the group or state in question is less likely to pursue ethnically based support. Future escalation is unlikely unless these identities change.

Intimately linked with transnational ethnic affinities is the concept of ethnic cleavage (Shih 1991). Cleavage refers to the degree of divided political loyalties among the ethnic groups within a state. For example, ethnic groups that aspire to self-determination but that are willing to work through existing political institutions and procedures would be characterized as having a lower level of cleavage than those who seek to transform the political status quo through force and/or external assistance. For intervening states, cleavage provides an opportunity to be exploited.

For the state in question, cleavage is an obvious domestic constraint. Cases where loyalties are divided occur within a state that has weak system maintenance functions, weakened institutions, and political parties based on ethnic groups. In this instance, the elites of an ethnic group pursuing secessionist policies will actively seek external support and goods, as will the state-center. Low levels of cleavage between ethnic groups occur within a state that has developed strong institutions, political capacities for the management of ethnic tensions, and cross-cutting cleavages that weaken the capacity for mobilization on the basis of ethnicity.

When divided loyalties exist in combination with high ethnic affinities, the outcome is potentially explosive. Protracted conflict and future escalation are probable. All parties may seek to exploit the potential gains that can be garnered from these external links. The situation is set for an ethnic group to be very receptive to external support and intervention and, indeed, actively seek it. Though interstate conflict is more likely, states may be inhibited in using force in such situations. For a state already seriously divided, using force against another state may not be possible.

The case of Yugoslavia demonstrates how transition states are particularly susceptible to interelite competition and rivalries. During periods of political upheaval, soldiers who remain on the sidelines will have difficulty putting ethnic affiliations aside. The inability of newly elected governments to manage intrastate ethnic tensions becomes a prime reason for the armed forces to support ethnic leaders who promise to address their concerns.

Despite the move to internationalize, most ethnically based conflicts remain regional affairs. This is because the particularities of ethnic conflicts tend to make them self-limiting. In the post–Cold War era, claims that give rise to ethnic violence have expanded across borders insofar as there are kindred groups who might be interested in providing support. In essence this means that most conflicts do not spread globally. Even neighboring states that might have every reason to undermine a rival generally can show surprising restraint in expressing unconditional support for an ethnic group's claims.

It should be emphasized, moreover, that few if any of the world's most protracted conflicts have proven salient enough to attract major power interest beyond belated efforts at peacekeeping and postconflict reconstruction. In the post–Cold War era, most ethnic conflicts are not directly connected to broader patterns of competitive international relations as was the case during the Cold War. As a consequence, there has been a fundamental shift away from supporting proxy wars—a major source of conflict escalation—toward mutual reconciliation and conflict prevention.

To be sure, some ethnic conflicts have carried on from their Cold War roots. The Arab-Israeli wars, the irredentist conflict between Turkey and Greece over Cyprus, and the Indo-Pakistan rivalry over Kashmir are examples of high-stakes ethnically based disputes that persist in varying degrees of open hostility despite the absence of superpower rivalry. At the same time, however, the absence of a superpower rivalry dominating the international system has contributed to the winding down of insurgencies in Latin America, Southeast Asia, and Africa.

Finally, there is a trend toward multilateral intervention into intrastate conflicts. As subsequent chapters will show, in those cases where there is a serious possibility of the spillover of violence across borders, third-party coalitions (NATO in particular) have, by and large, proven effective in limiting their expansion through a combination of diplomatic intervention, embargoes, and preventive measures such as the deployment of troops in areas of potential diffusion.

POLICY IMPLICATIONS

Early warning information is still highly dependent on the national intelligence accumulation and evaluation systems of individual states. However, a number of carefully orchestrated projects have been undertaken in the field of early warning by academics with financial support from their governments. Because of a larger resource base from which to draw, partnership arrangements are better equipped to get over two hurdles. The first hurdle is obtaining the necessary quantity and quality of intelligence in a reliable and accurate fashion, an informational problem. The second hurdle is avoiding misperception, an analytic problem. The primary analytic problem is avoiding misperception or other faulty analysis of the likelihood of a conflict's diffusion.

Consistent with the preceding analysis, there are two complementary but distinct prevention strategies encompassed in risk assessment and early warning. The first is to rely primarily on early warning networks for the analysis of impending conflicts. This option would see individual states rely to some extent on global networks for their informational analysis. Such capacity is slowly falling into place. For example, the International Organization for Migration (IOM) has established an emergency response unit to respond to refugee-related humanitarian emergencies, and the Food and Agricultural Organization's (FAO) Global Information and Early Warning System (GIEWS) has been assigned to constantly monitor the global food supply-and-demand situation and alert the international community to countries or regions threatened by serious food shortages.[14]

The strengths of the network approach is in potential cost savings and information distribution through an institutional division of labor. Having access to many eyes and ears could, in practice, surmount the two previously mentioned hurdles. The inclusion of NGOs in the information-gathering process could potentially overcome faulty analysis of the likelihood of diffusion and/or escalation of a conflict or complex emergency.

A consortium of NGOs and states is still very much a conduit for the informational system of individual governments, and for this reason it is still dependent on the intelligence-gathering assets of individual countries. This in itself is not a weakness, but there is always the potential for some countries to withhold information on sensitive political issues. A global entity that is capable of monitoring politically generated catastrophes currently exists.

Since the call for preventive action by former United Nations Secretary General Boutros Ghali in 1992, the UN interagency arrangement for humanitarian early warning (HEWS) was created to assist humanitarian operations. It is not, however, equipped to detect or analyze political and military warning signals. The UN lost its capacity to analyze political early warning information when it disbanded the Office for Research and Collection of Information (ORCI). Since the loss of ORCI the UN does not and will not in the foreseeable future have the capacity for political early warning. This point was made abundantly clear in the Joint Evaluation Report on the Emergency Response to Genocide in Rwanda:

More simply, the UN lacks a system for drawing on existing information sources, in the region and outside, from specialists in state agencies, academic institutions, rights monitoring agencies, and the various agencies of the UN itself. The UN lacks a specialized unit, without operational responsibilities, for analysing such information and translating that analysis into evolving strategic options that can be channelled directly to the Secretary-General.[15]

A fundamental deficiency of the early warning network option is that the early warning required to respond to human-generated disasters is really late warning, a response to crises that are already at an advanced stage of escalation and violence. The inherent risk for policy makers in this approach is that at the height of a crisis, policy options are rapidly and significantly constrained and significantly narrowed to operational responses (usually military and humanitarian) such as those detailed in subsequent chapters. The Carnegie Commission's report on "Preventing Deadly Conflict" recognizes this as a fundamental stumbling block to the development of more effective long-term, structurally oriented, conflict prevention policies.[16] Late response, with the attendant likelihood that a strategy will be less than successful, is the strongest ammunition against developing more coherent forward-looking approaches. Critics are quick to claim that early warning rarely succeeds, but the evidence they cite to support this argument are situations in which action is taken to treat the symptoms rather than the underlying causes.[17] Although the Carnegie Commission's report does highlight the need for the short-term treatment of impending crises, the report also emphasizes attitudinal change among policy makers toward more effective long-term conflict prevention strategies.[18]

It is within the latter context that a second policy option can be understood. More specifically, individual states must more fully integrate their risk assessments into strategic and contingency planning to develop coherent, sustainable, and long-term structurally oriented policies on conflict prevention. Under this schema, according to Michael Lund, prevention would consist of

policies and institutions that are taken deliberately to keep particular states or organized groups within them from threatening or using organized violence, armed force, or related forms of coercion, such as repression, as the means to settle interstate or national political disputes, especially in situations where the existing means cannot peacefully manage the destabilizing effects of economic, social, political and international change.[19]

Ultimately any measurement of success in Lund's approach, with its focus on the long-term maintenance of peace, depends heavily on a clear sense of the international and domestic structural factors responsible for violence.[20] In this context, a blend of analytical skills—those that combine in-depth analysis with regional and country expertise—in addition to those that can identify and explain dynamic patterns of behavior through quantitative analysis are necessary. A comprehensive quantitative risk assessment approach may be unable to identify the precise points at which specific events are likely to occur,[21] but combined with the appropriate country-specific information and field reports, accuracy in prediction is likely to be much greater.[22] Such an approach requires the identification of common patterns and indicators as well as the development of models.

Therefore, the purpose of subsequent chapters is to identify patterns of ethnic violence, to develop models based on those patterns, and finally, to evaluate the impact that third-party efforts have on the reduction of that violence. We pursue these objectives in two ways. First, we identify specific behaviors and their interactions that feed into creating ethnic violence. Second, we evaluate the impact that third-party efforts have on altering those patterns of behavior, placing emphasis on the coercive dimensions of conflict prevention. The challenge, as the following chapters will show, is whether the consequences of success and failure of third-party efforts can be properly understood so that preventive strategies can be rendered more effective for future conflict management.

NOTES

1. Michael Brecher, *Crises in World Politics: Theory and Reality* (Oxford and New York: Pergamon Press, 1993); Kumar Rupesinghe, "Towards a Policy Framework for Advancing Preventive Diplomacy" (paper presented at conference, Towards a Common Agenda for Conflict Prevention, Oslo, May 1995).

2. Albrecht von Muller and David Law, "The Needs of Researchers: Crisis Management and Conflict Prevention in a Historic Transition Period," *Information Technologies and International Security* 30, no. 95 (1995): 27–38.

3. Ibid.

4. Ibid., 28.

5. Gabriel Ben Dor, "Intelligence and Early Warning: Lessons from a Case Study," in *Synergy in Early Warning Conference Proceedings*, ed. S. Schmeidl and H. Adelman (15–18 March 1997, Toronto, Canada), 10–15.

6. Mary O. McCarthy, "Potential Humanitarian Crises: The Warning Process and Roles for Intelligence," in *Synergy in Early Warning Conference Proceedings*, 15–16.

7. Dipak Gupta, "An Early Warning About Forecasts: Oracle to Academics," in *Synergy in Early Warning Conference Proceedings*, 375–396.

8. Alexander George and Jane Holl, "The Warning-Response Problem and Missed Opportunities in Preventive Diplomacy: Discussion Paper" (Carnegie Commission on Preventing Deadly Conflict, Washington, DC, Carnegie Corporation of New York, 1997).

9. Ted R. Gurr, "Early Warning Systems: From Surveillance to Assessment to Action," in *Preventive Diplomacy: The Therapeutics of Mediation*, ed. Kevin M. Cahill (proceedings of a conference at the United Nations, New York, 23–24 April 1996).

10. Ibid.

11. Daniel Frei and Dieter Ruhoff, *Handbook of Foreign Policy Analysis* (London, Martinus Nijhoff, 1989).

12. Janie Leatherman and Raimo Vayrynen, "Structure, Culture and Territory: Three Sets of Early Warning Indicators" (paper presented at the International Studies Association 36th Annual Convention, Chicago, 21–25 April 1995).

13. Will Moore and T. R. Gurr, "Assessing Risks of Ethnopolitical Rebellion in the Year 2000: Three Empirical Approaches," in *Synergy in Early Warning Conference Proceedings*, 45–70.

14. Other UN-based early warning bodies include: the WMO/IAEA Convention of Early Notification of Nuclear Accidents; the UN System-Wide Earthwatch; HazardNet for disasters; the Epidemiological Early Warning System (NEWS) for health concerns; and the Global Early Warning System for displaced persons (GEWS).

15. Howard Adelman and Astri Suhrke, *Joint Evaluation of Emergency Assistance to Rwanda* (Chr Michelson Inst. Norway, 1996). Volume 2 on early warning, 35.

16. Jane Holl et al. *Carnegie Commission on Preventing Deadly Conflict: Final Report* (Washington, D.C., Carnegie Corporation of New York, 1997). Web-based text is available at <http://www.ccpdc.org/frpub.htm>, chapter 3.

17. See, for example, S. J. Stedman, "Alchemy for a New World Disorder: Overselling Preventive Diplomacy," *Foreign Affairs* (May/June 1995).

18. Effective preventive strategies rest on three principles: early reaction to signs of trouble; a comprehensive, balanced approach to alleviate the pressures, or risk factors, that trigger violent conflict; and an extended effort to resolve the underlying root causes of violence. Jane, Holl et al. *Carnegie Commission on Preventing Deadly Conflict: Final Report*. Executive summary, 1997.

19. M. S. Lund, "Early Warning and Preventive Diplomacy," in *Managing Global Chaos: Sources of and Responses to International Conflict*, eds. Chester A. Crocker and Fen Osler Hampson (Washington, DC: USIP, 1996): 379.

20. This view is shared by the Swedish Ministry of Foreign Affairs, whose own report, *Preventing Violent Conflict: A Study* (Stockholm: Norstedts Tryckeri AB, 1997), proposes early conflict-prevention strategies as the cornerstone of Sweden's developmental assistance programs. Key recommendations include strengthening civil society, strengthening of regional security arrangements, efforts to address religious and cultural conflicts, and strengthening early warning mechanisms.

21. Gerald Schneider and Patricia Weitsman, eds., *Enforcing Cooperation: Risky States and Intergovernmental Management of Conflict* (London: Macmillan), chapters 1 and 2.

22. With the rise of new communications technology, including Web-based technologies, risk analysis based on quantitative and qualitative approaches could be more fully integrated into foreign policy decision making in real time. Political risk models would be updated continually and cross-referenced with other modes of analysis such as qualitative assessments and field reports from either field officers or NGOs. See, for example, <http://www.carleton.ca/cifp>.

3

The Theory and Practice of Coercive Diplomacy, Part 1

INTRODUCTION

In general, credible and effective diplomacy requires, among other things, early warning information, an analysis of the interests and values that stand to be threatened, and an appropriate fit between strategy, the problem at hand, and resources available.[1] In its most robust form, coercive diplomacy includes a full range of political, diplomatic, and military instruments. Arguably, such a comprehensive list is beyond the scope of any single state. Yet there are instances when, with the appropriate major power backing and organizational support, state violence has been reduced, conflict ameliorated, and crises managed. These are instances when the possibility of uncontrolled violence is sufficient for the Western powers to feel compelled to support the use of force.

SCOPE, TIMING, AND INTENSITY

The debate over coercive strategies focuses on the scope, timing, and intensity of force required to achieve an end to the violence. One of the key problems is determining how much force should be used in conflicts involving armed groups and authorities who resist traditional efforts at mediation and peacekeeping (e.g., Bosnia and Kosovo). In essence, the use of force and threats to use force by regional organizations are improvised techniques that have a weak legal basis and are not addressed as such in the UN Charter (Durch 1993).

The "rules" surrounding coercive diplomacy have been built by practice over the years and are covered in chapter 7 of the charter. The UN Security Council has, by its actions, established a broad body of de facto principles for coercive action, but no measures exist to specifically delineate how regional organizations, and NATO in particular, should act. In general, Security Council resolutions and agreements between the UN and individual nations are the legal basis for the initiation and implementation of coercive action. In turn, regional organizations such as NATO may be mandated by the UNSC to take on a specific coercive role. At this point, a coalition of forces under NATO guidance may have the de facto right to use force once the Security Council labels events as aggression (although that term is not as clearly defined in the charter as it could be), and any state that has ratified the charter agrees to this interpretation by the Security Council.

This latter point has some bearing on managing conflicts when there exists no cogent international law or UN doctrine on how to conclude agreements with substate actors (Ryan 1998). In essence, the ad hoc nature of coercive action by regional organizations will always engender a great deal of resistance from regime leaders, self-appointed warlords, demagogues, and insurgents who perceive intervention as proto-imperialism or at least as an infringement on their authority (Kaufman 1998). In principle, state sovereignty does not permit forceful intervention by regional organizations (A. James 1998; Haglund and Pentland 1998). However, coercive action may be appropriate in situations in which states lose their ability to regulate a conflict either to events that occur outside their control (such as famine brought on by environmental change) or through spillover effects (such as refugee flows) (Kaufman 1998).

More often than not, intrastate ethnic conflicts are brought on by bad governance (Carment and James 1998). This has two implications. First, states that fail to regulate internal behavior—that is, failure to abide by constitutive norms established by the UN Charter—are, in principle, at risk of intervention. Second, disunity and lack of cohesion within the ranks of the adversaries make it difficult for the various factions and third parties to engage in any meaningful form of negotiations. Ethnic leaders often lack both the power and authority to enforce their decisions and concessions (Kaufman 1998). For third parties, there is a need to lay the political groundwork before committing forces (Ryan 1998; Haglund and Pentland 1998).

Since most of the interventions in the post–Cold War era have been undertaken either in the midst of civil war or prior to the outbreak of violence, it is vital to understand how this newer breed of intervention influences the matrix of tradeoffs that an organization must consider before resorting to force. These tradeoffs include a consideration of costs, credibility, and outcomes.

First, in an intrastate ethnic conflict situation, a third party must not only decide when and how to intervene but must also assess the costs associated with escalation.[2] The most basic challenge a multilateral force faces is identifying the degree of force an intervention requires to ensure that basic objectives are achieved at minimal cost.[3] Thus, third parties must frequently confront the dilemma of whether to commit to a high-intensity operation when the political and economic stakes are low or nonexistent (Carment and Rowlands 1998). To suggest that a third party can induce a peaceful settlement in an ethnic conflict by engaging in a costly intervention misses the point. Proclaimed salience cannot generate the sustained credibility that is often necessary to bring an end to an ethnically based conflict. Third-party intervention works only when the belligerents believe that the third party is there to enforce a settlement between ethnic groups into the indefinite future. In the absence of precommitment mechanisms, salience is the only means of establishing this political credibility (Lake and Rothchild 1996).

Second, by presenting a credible military threat, a multilateral force seeks to convince all conflictual parties that violence will not succeed. International force is brought to bear not to defeat but to neutralize the local forces and to reduce the expected gains of continued fighting (Ruggie 1994). The political objectives are to prevent local forces from becoming preeminent and to persuade combatants that they have no viable alternative but to reach a third-party-assisted negotiated settlement. The intended military effect is to deny victory to any one ethnic group to create the military stalemate on which negotiated settlements often depend. To ensure credible effectiveness, coalition forces must not only decide whether to escalate their intervention, but also consider the degree of coercion to apply (Carment and Rowlands 1998; Ruggie 1994).

Third, and related to the issue of credibility, are the third party's tradeoffs in influencing outcomes. Intervention can, in principle, alter the internal balance of ethnic power and possibly engender some degree of political stability. At the least it may lead groups to moderate their demands (Lake and Rothchild 1996). For example, at some point in the conflict, ethnic leaders must choose either a settlement imposed on them by third parties or a negotiated solution. For the belligerents, these choices must be preferable to continued fighting. Ethnic leaders must be able to persuade their supporters to accept an alternative, and they must enforce their followers' observance of it.

Third-party efforts to reduce continued fighting focus on moderating claims to political or territorial autonomy or some combination thereof. In an objective sense, since ethnic groups differ in their size, political power, economic wealth, demographic patterns, and territoriality, expected gains can encompass any one or more of these issue areas. In reality, however, territorial and political disputes are the most difficult to resolve (Posen 1993). With respect to territorial gains, secession or irredenta or some combination of both is at stake (Kaufman 1998; Carment and James 1997).

When the evaluation of the costs, credibility, and outcomes leads to intervention, a multilateral coalition will still need to react to developments in-theater (Carment and Rowlands 1998). In favorable circumstances the warring parties may choose to cooperate with third parties to reach a peaceful solution, thereby facilitating the task of the intervention force. In other cases, however, one or more of the disputants may decide to resist the pacification efforts of the intervening force and attempt to prolong the conflict. In this case there is no peace to keep, and third parties are faced with three options: withdraw, acquiesce to the aggressors, or escalate the conflict through the judicious use of force (Carment and Rowlands 1998).[4]

In the sections below we evaluate how NATO came to choose the third option, first in Bosnia and then in Kosovo.

BOSNIA

Was NATO's forceful intervention in Bosnia appropriate? Was it successful? The answer to both questions is a qualified yes. To understand why this is so, it is first necessary to analyze the Bosnian conflict within the context of the larger Yugoslav war. As in Bosnia, two factors provided an indication of whether latent animosities would become violent in Yugoslavia. The first turned on the question of who controlled the military, the economy, and the political institutions.[5] The second process was the development of more particularist identities and competing visions of the future among Yugoslavia's various ethnic group leaders. The latter process was under way in the decade immediately after Tito's death, as the confederal structures instituted under his power gradually ceded more and more power to the republics. The subsequent inability of the leaders of these republics to develop a national policy consensus can be traced to the rise to power of Serb nationalist leaders and the failure of the other republics to pursue policies that would balance this domination. Reformists who held fast to the view that Yugoslavia's constitution and economy could be restructured along existing political arrangements were discredited by their failure to respond to Yugoslavia's economic collapse.

In prewar Bosnia, the convergence of interests among Croatian, Muslim, and Serb leaders resembled a balance of power system, characterized by a shifting pattern of flexible coalitions. Eventually, this balancing broke down and Bosnia moved from a state based on an equilibrium engendered by decentralized constitutional arrangements to one in which coercion became the main instrument of control.

Of Yugoslavia's five crisis theaters (Bosnia, Croatia, Kosovo, Macedonia, and Slovenia), Bosnia Herzegovina is the most complex.[6] Bosnia is the one state in which Slav Muslims make up most of the population. Although the Muslims are a numerical majority (44 percent of the population), they never possessed the equivalent political clout and military power of their numerically smaller Serbian and Croatian counterparts. At the onset of the crisis, Bosnia was led by a coalition government composed of representatives of all three ethnic groups. Operating outside of this coalition, the Serb Democratic Party of Bosnia (SDS), a Serb breakaway group led by Radovan Karadzic and armed with equipment from the Yugoslav National Army (JNA), had already proved successful in stalling any political solution to the future of Bosnia. This stalling tactic was aided by the fact that the majority of the JNA was stationed in Bosnia-Herzegovina prior to the conflict, and that the republic was the site of most of the JNA's weapons factories.[7]

As the conflict in Croatia wound down in January 1992, the SDS declared an independent "Serbian Republic of Bosnia-Herzegovina" made up of regions that the SDS had taken over during the summer of 1991.[8] On 20 December 1991, the Bosnian government formally requested recognition, promising to establish autonomous territories in areas where members of a minority formed a local majority. Bosnian Serbs were not satisfied with this proposal and proclaimed an independent Serbian republic on 2 January 1992. On 25 January 1992 the Bosnian National Assembly, boycotted by the Serbs, announced that a referendum on independence would be held at the end of February. In response, the Portuguese presidency of the European Community (EC) stated that the EC would recognize Bosnia if the referendum was in favor of independence. On 6 April Bosnia declared independence. Around the time of the referendum on Bosnia's future, Serbs and Croat forces began fighting in key regions of Bosnia. Serbian guerrilla forces threw up roadblocks around Sarajevo and other cities and began a process of orchestrated terror against dissenters.

Justification for these actions was presented as a response to a threat of Muslim fundamentalists in Bosnia, who were seeking to perpetrate genocide against Serbs, an argument that pervaded the Belgrade media. After all, in their view, the Serbs had not agreed to independence according to the principle of three constituent nations.[9] The real concern for Yugoslav leader Slobodan Milosevic was in controlling the unpredictable zealotry of the Bosnian-Serb leadership to reduce the possibility that their "ethnic cleansing" would bring outside military intervention. This could be best achieved by having a controlling interest in the Bosnian conflict and by staking claim to much of Bosnia.

When an overwhelming number of Bosnians chose independence in that state's 2 March 1992 referendum, the act had the simultaneous effect of triggering foreign policy crises for both Croatia and Serbia and signaling a shift in the winds of the larger Yugoslav war. In the referendum, Muslims, Croats, and Serbs outside of Serb-controlled areas voted overwhelmingly for a "democratic" independent Bosnia, an act that suited neither the interests of Croatia's leader Franjo Tudjman nor those of Milosevic.[10] For example, by portraying itself as the sole arbiter of Serbian politics in and outside of Serbia, Milosevic's party, the Serbian Socialist Party (SPS), could justify its continuation and the preservation of the existing power structure. Since Serbia itself is only 65 percent Serbian, bringing the 30 percent of Bosnian Serbs into the political fold meant the SPS would be able to increase the total Serbian proportion substantially (aided by the expulsion of Albanians from Kosovo). A key ingredient in Milosevic's ability to consolidate his power within Serbia was his ability to appeal to nationalist sensibilities and control the hypernationalism of his allies in Bosnia. Milosevic's SPS was the source of supply for the Serb's mobilizing efforts in Bosnia, providing them with money, weapons, and strategic advice (Glenny 1993).

In response to the disintegrating situation in Yugoslavia, the UN Protection Force (UNPROFOR) was established in early 1992. UNPROFOR was established as an interim measure to create the conditions of peace and security required for the EC-initiated negotiation of an overall settlement to the Croatian crisis. Eventually, the operation evolved into a traditional disengagement mission in Croatia, a humanitarian support mission in Bosnia and Herzegovina, and a small observation mission in Macedonia. While UNPROFOR's tasks multiplied, mainly in response to the rapidly deteriorating situation in Bosnia and Herzegovina, the resources at its disposal lagged behind, and the political process on which it relied for authority and direction all but disintegrated.

From the beginning of the conflict there was never a situation in Bosnia in which a conventional mission would have been adequate. Heavy weapons were operated and used by groups that were not members of any regular army of a recognized government. These weapons were used on a large scale against civilians in clear violation of international humanitarian laws (Kaufman 1998; Fortmann, Martin, and Rousel 1998).

During the lifetime of UNPROFOR, the UN was concerned with the United States' unwillingness to participate in a conventional operation. From the outset of the Yugoslav crisis, the U.S. administration considered most options except sending troops to Bosnia. Even with the 1995 decision to deploy the NATO Implementation Force (IFOR), there was little political backing inside the American political setting for the use of ground troops.[11] Since the outbreak of the conflict in Bosnia, there was always much greater support to use air strikes as a negotiating "tool" to force the Serbs to the bargaining table. This choice had considerable impact on peacekeepers already on the ground. Differences in strategy were most acutely felt in November 1994 when UN peacekeepers were detained by Bosnia-Serb forces in retaliation for the NATO bombing of Serb-controlled airfields.

UNPROFOR's half-measures may have extended the conflict. Most certainly the biggest issue was the changed mandate.[12] The decision to move UNPROFOR away from the principle of impartiality added confusion and ambiguity to an already complex mission. Peacekeepers and civilians were placed at considerable risk (A. James 1998).

For example, to ensure safe havens for civilians ensnared in the conflict, NATO, at the request of the UN Security Council, implemented plans for the military enforcement of a non-fly zone. On 19 February 1993, UN peacekeepers were given the mandate to use force if necessary to defend themselves under chapter 7 of the UN Charter. NATO made several announcements, including the one of 22 April 1994 that if any Bosnian Serb attacks involving heavy weapons were carried out on UN-designated safe areas, these weapons and other Bosnian Serb military assets would be subject to NATO air strikes.

Without NATO support, a politically viable outcome would not have been possible in such a short time. For example, on 15 December 1995 the United Nations Security Council—acting under chapter 7 of the charter of the UN—adopted Resolution 1031, which authorized the member states of NATO to establish the NATO IFOR under unified command and control, and composed of ground, air, and maritime units from NATO and non-NATO nations to ensure compliance with the relevant provisions of the Dayton Peace Agreement.

KOSOVO

During the crisis in Bosnia, the Kosovo Liberation Army (KLA) was formed as a small radical group in late 1992 and early 1993. At the time it was composed mostly of a small number of Kosovar Albanians who were members of an activist radical leftist organization in the early 1980s, the LPK, or Levizja Popullore e Kosoves (the Popular Movement). The LPK consistently claimed that the only way toward independence for Kosovo was through violence (Judah 1999b, 20).

The first acknowledged armed attack by the KLA occurred in May 1993 in Glogovac, resulting in the death of two Serb police officers and the wounding of five. When the Dayton Peace Accords were signed without any representation for and by the Kosovars, there began large-scale questioning of the utility of the nonviolent path (Troebst 1999, 89).

It is at this point that the KLA began to grow from the small group of like-minded individuals. The Kosovar leader Ibrahim Rugova called for Albanians living abroad to send 3 percent of their earnings to the alternative "governmental" structures he and the LPK had set up in Kosovo. Some chose to divert their share to the KLA's "Homeland Calling" fund instead (Hedges 1999, 31). Newspapers in the Albanian diaspora began printing statements from KLA members, as well as their ads for donations, as the name of the KLA slowly spread (Hedges 1999, 31).

Over time, the organization began to take responsibility for killing Serb police officers, Serb civilians, and Kosovars they called "collaborators" (ICG 1998b). In 1997 the KLA received a large influx of firearms (mostly guns) from the military arsenals of Albania, which were easily looted and transported out of the country in the wake of the collapse of Albania's government. By November 1997 the KLA had managed to force Serbian police vehicles to pull out of the Drenica region. The KLA then set up checkpoints, keeping the Serb police out of the area for some time (ICG 1998a).[13]

On 23 February 1998, U.S. Special Envoy to the Balkans Robert Gelbard made a statement that "the KLA is without any question a terrorist group," and insisted that the United States denounce such terrorist activity in Kosovo. Milosevic took this as a signal that he would not be opposed should he take any action he wished against the KLA (Hedges 1999, 36) (also, Sebak 1998: "Gelbard's words were interpreted in . . . Belgrade as a green light for a security forces operation against the KLA"). Two weeks later Serb special police attacked Prekaz, a small village enclave of some well-known KLA fighters, decimating the town with antiaircraft cannons and killing almost 100 people, including women and children who were not KLA fighters. This action in particular ignited the uprising and a buildup of the KLA.

Although Federal Republic of Yugoslavia (FRY) forces claimed to have "destroyed the core" of the KLA at this time, more independent reports noted that the actions appeared to have "swelled their ranks beyond belief" (Sebak 1998). Tim Judah, a reporter who spent time with the KLA, noted that "following violent events in the Drenica region [in late winter/early spring 1998] the KLA suddenly found itself in command of an uprising" (1999a). Others concurred: "no one disputes the fact that since the first Serbian operation against them in March, the KLA's influence has grown" (Lungescu 1998). British Foreign Secretary Robin Cook was quoted as saying that Milosevic's tactics had backfired, leaving the KLA in control of more territory, with greater strength and more money (Lungescu, 1998).

As talks among the "international community" (e.g., NATO, UN, the Organization for Security and Cooperation in Europe [OSCE]) and Belgrade bogged down, the KLA used the brokered cease-fire to "improve its training and command and control, as well as to acquire more and better weapons" (Tenet 1999). In November, after recovering a fair amount of ground, the KLA announced its plans to set up a "civilian authority in those parts of the Serbian province under its control" (BBC World News, 6 November 1998).[14]

As early as 17 October 1998, KLA statements indicated that they viewed NATO as an ally, and that they seemed to believe NATO also saw them that way. On this date the KLA issued a statement that rejected an agreement between Milosevic and U.S. envoy Richard Holbrooke that called for 2,000 OSCE observers to move into Kosovo following a measured pullback of Serbian troops and "demanded that the UN and NATO force the withdrawal of Serb forces from all their positions." They asserted that "the KLA is the decisive factor (from the Albanian side) which must lead the talks between Pristina, the international community and Belgrade" and offered "universal cooperation to the Alliance intending to establish peace and democracy" (BBC World News, 18 October 1998). Such statements continued in November, as the KLA indicated that "the guerilla movement could develop into a Kosovo Security Force under a NATO 'equip and train program' similar to one in Bosnia" (Bugajski 1998). At this time, their confidence also had them announcing plans to set up a civilian government, signaling their defiance to Milosevic and Serbs, as well as to Rugova.

There is little doubt that NATO credibility was on the line at these and subsequent talks. For example, on 6 October 1998, in an opening address at the International Monetary Fund (IMF) Annual meetings, U.S. President Bill Clinton stated that "NATO is prepared to act if President Milosevic fails to honor the United Nations resolutions. The stakes are high. The time is now to end the violence in Kosovo" (as quoted by the U.S. Information Agency 1998). In addition, Ambassador Thomas Pickering, U.S. undersecretary of political affairs, explicitly tied the threat of force to the need for the ethnic Albanians' autonomy in Kosovo: "[that the threat of NATO air strikes in Kosovo is] designed to bring about . . . an early and very significant negotiation coming to a rapid conclusion on an autonomy settlement for the Kosovars, on an interim basis solution which Ambassador [Christopher] Hill has put forward" (as quoted by the U.S. Information Agency 1998).

Some, such as *New York Times* journalists Elaine Sciolino and Ethan Bronner, argued that the KLA managed to "snare" two weeks of mediated talks held in February at Rambouillet castle in France—negotiations that were supposed to secure some measure of autonomy for Kosovo as a means of avoiding further bloodshed. Judah (1999a), after conducting interviews with KLA spokespeople and members, concluded that the KLA—while viewing NATO as an ally and recognizing their need to have NATO on their side—would nevertheless "make sure that NATO troops are brought in to enforce any deal, because their presence will mean that the Serbs will no longer be able to fight—and defeat them."

By the beginning of January 1999, U.S. Secretary of State Madeleine Albright, in particular, used rhetoric that was stronger and of a different quality. Her language demonized Milosevic, and repeatedly stated that he "only understands the language of force" (Hirsh and Barry 1999, 40). Hirsh and Barry argue that she may have changed in order to "sell the bombing to the White House and Europeans" (40).

Upon the January massacre in the village of Racak, two senior NATO officers were sent to Belgrade with warnings that it would face air strikes if it did not comply with the cease-fire agreed on in October 1998. Days afterward, on 19 January, Albright presented a new plan to the White House. From it came threats of bombing again, but for the first time it included demands that Milosevic accept NATO troops in the FRY, under the enforcement of a deal that would also see him withdraw his forces from Kosovo, granting it broad autonomy (Sciolino and Bronner 1999, 13). Two days later, Albright asserted that NATO "can't take force off the table because that's all President Milosevic seems to understand. We hope it doesn't have to go that far but that's why it remains a live option" (U.S. Information Agency 1999). On the same day, U.S. Defense Department spokesman Kenneth Bacon announced that NATO forces were at forty-eight-hour alert, stepped up from the previous four-day alert in place since October 1998.

On 28 January 1999, in a rare statement issued at both the fighting ethnic Kosovar Albanians and the Serb regime, NATO allies announced that they were ready to use force immediately unless both sides committed to talks in February. But the following day, Clinton announced, "The Contact Group has now approved the terms of an interim agreement that would do just that, by protecting the rights of all people of Kosovo and giving them the self-government they clearly deserve. . . . To that end, the international community has sent a clear message to the authorities in Belgrade: the time for denial and delay is past. NATO is united and ready to act if you don't" (U.S. Information Agency 1999).

When the Rambouillet peace talks faltered (and eventually failed), Albright provided continuing assurances to the Albanians of U.S. support, even allowing the deadline to pass in order to get them on board. The *New York Times* stated that she "implored" them to sign (18 April 1999, A13). She gave them a two-week pause to bring the deal home for discussion. Then, in her statements to the press, she blamed only Milosevic for the delays: "The Kosovar Albanians have negotiated with discipline and a unity of purpose. Belgrade, in contrast, has taken every opportunity for evasion and delay. The Serb delegation bears the lion's share of responsibility for the difficulties we have experienced today" (Albright, 20 February 1999, as quoted by the U.S. Information Agency).[15]

In a statement made at the same time, U.S. Defense Secretary William Cohen stated that the purpose of NATO air strikes would be "to reduce the military assets posing the most immediate threat to the Kosovars" (U.S. Information Agency 1999). In support, Javier Solana, NATO secretary-general, also spoke of NATO air strikes in concrete, planned terms: "The European Allies will provide most of the troops. But U.S. involvement is crucial. It will demonstrate in the most concrete way the essential transatlantic unity of purpose without which we simply cannot solve problems like Bosnia and Kosovo" (U.S. Information Agency 1999).

On 20 March 1999, international monitors were evacuated from Kosovo by the OSCE, a sure sign of impending violence. A last-ditch diplomatic effort was launched, with Richard Holbrooke sent to Belgrade to talk to Milosevic. The FRY remained intransigent, and persisted in its refusal to accept any agreement that allowed the deployment of NATO troops to Kosovo. NATO Commander General Clark was quoted as being bothered by the fact that with "each day without strikes" the Serbs were sending in more troops to Kosovo (Hirsh and Barry 1999, 39). Milosevic's actions didn't seem to be giving NATO any justification not to bomb, and the ethnic Albanians, and the outside world, would certainly have been able to discern the bias toward their stance at this point. This was punctuated by statements made by U.S. Defense Department spokesman Kenneth Bacon that seemed to indicate that NATO was viewing the Kosovar Albanians as victims and the KLA as a protector force in the region: "The Kosovar Albanians want attacks against them to end, and they want the Serbs to stop shooting Kosovar Albanian fathers and their sons, and killing their wives and daughters, and . . . to stop burning their villages and destroying their houses. Although the KLA has put up some resistance, the Serb forces are moving in with considerable brutality at this time. [Any NATO air strikes would seek] to arrest the ability of the Serbs to brutally attack the Kosovar Albanians" (U.S. Information Agency, 23 March 1999).[16] At the same time as he implicitly praised the ethnic Albanian team, the OSCE chairman argued that "continuing fighting in Kosovo showed the necessity of NATO deployment" (BBC World News, 2 March 1999). Such statements seemed to signal to Belgrade the insistence of the international negotiators upon this element of the peace plan, and to the Kosovar Albanians that NATO would stick to guarantees to support them.[17]

By the beginning of April, the KLA already appeared to be marshaling its resources while waiting for NATO's air strikes to weaken Yugoslavia's military capacity (Partos 1999). At the same time, the KLA intensified its attacks on the FRY forces. In response, FRY authorities implemented a "clear and burn" campaign of villages, which served only to strengthen the resolve of the KLA and to drive new recruits to it.

After the signing of the peace agreement between NATO's force in Kosovo (KFOR) and the FRY in the spring of 1999, KLA fighters quickly moved into the towns and cities left by the withdrawing Serbs, "[i]n a bid to establish authority ahead of the arrival of incoming NATO troops," and began setting up administrative centers (ICG 1999g). Essentially the KLA was acting to establish itself as a government, as it had indicated it would upon the implementation of a peace agreement back in March. This was as much a notice to other political factions in Kosovo, such as Rugova's Democratic League of Kosovo (LDK), as it was to the FRY and NATO. KLA soldiers also took control of a border crossing into Albania, erecting an Albanian flag in place of a Yugoslav one (ICG 1999g).

Initially, KLA soldiers were reluctant to disarm, and some had to be forcibly disarmed by U.S. Marines. Kosovo leaders believed the KLA could make the transition from a liberation army to the form of an (armed) national civilian guard working alongside NATO and the UN-controlled civil administration (ICG 1999g). On 20 June 1999, the KLA signed an arms-surrendering agreement with NATO because it "had a genuine interest in cooperating with NATO," as they could not have won their concessions against Serbia without the organization (ICG 1999g). By late 1999, many members of the KLA who had previous experience with political administration, most notably with the LPK, began to set up local administration structures, bolstering hopes that the KLA would quickly transform itself into a political party (ICG 1999g).

POLICY IMPLICATIONS: A PRIMER FOR NATO

Understanding how coercive action is to be properly executed requires some understanding of its effectiveness in Bosnia and Kosovo. These are the barriers that prevented NATO from mounting a completely successful strategy in Bosnia and a more successful one in Kosovo. Some of these impediments are specific to the Bosnian and Kosovo cases, but most are endemic to conflict management in a post–Cold War world. The ability to generate the international consensus required to mount an effective and credible threat is becoming increasingly limited. In the case of Bosnia and less so in the case of Kosovo, divisions within

NATO forced many of the organization's retaliatory threats to be diluted. For example, during the Bosnian crisis the Europeans were reluctant from the outset to use air strikes against the Serbs, fearing retaliation against their peacekeepers. Initially, Britain and France agreed to participate in the use of force only if the United States refrained from introducing air power in the region. This policy was reversed during the Kosovo crisis; the British became the strongest supporters of force against the Milosevic regime. In Bosnia the presence of British and French troops on the ground gave those countries what amounted to a veto over U.S. policy. Since there were no ground troops in harm's way at the height of the Kosovo crisis, the potential for a split among the allies was theoretically reduced. In contrast during the Bosnian crisis, the split created by continued European rejection of several key U.S. demands (e.g., lifting the arms embargo against the Muslims) had a debilitating effect on the peace process.[18] As Weiss observed (1994, 123):

Inadequate military and humanitarian action, combined with half-hearted sanctions and a negotiating charade, constituted a powerful diversion. They collectively impeded more vigorous western diplomatic and military pressure to lift the arms embargo for Muslims to help level the killing field.

As a consequence, the United States was in the difficult position of having to negotiate with the Bosnian Serbs, Serbia, Croatia, Bosnia, Europeans, Canadians, Russians, NATO, and the UN, each of which had its own agenda and special concerns. As domestic pressures in each capital became paramount, no single group of leaders had the power to generate consensus on key issues (Lieber 1994). As the Bosnian crisis extended over months, then years, divisions within (and between) the White House and Congress grew. Initially, chairman of the Joint Chiefs of Staff Colin Powell and Secretary of State Warren Christopher constantly pushed for a more restrained and cautious approach to the crisis, whereas Les Aspin, Madeleine Albright, and National Security Council Adviser Anthony Lake were convinced that air strikes were needed to control the fighting.[19] It was only after Congress began to demand that the Clinton administration clearly outline official U.S. policy that the "lift and strike" strategy was promoted (Berdal 1994).[20]

But of all the alternatives considered, there was never any real commitment to send U.S. ground forces to the region. The exclusion of this option from the outset gave European and Serb leaders the impression that there never would be a moral imperative pushing the Americans to become more formally involved. As Secretary Christopher stated, "Bosnia may be a human tragedy but it does not affect our vital security interests except as we're concerned about humanitarian matters and except as we're trying to contain it" (from Berdal 1994, 37). Even when there was a moral imperative to respond (as occurred in the aftermath of the 5 February market bombing), the American public remained highly sensitive to casualties and continued to reject the idea of deploying American troops. Clinton was placed in a position of having to "reconcile two conflicting aspirations: demonstrating resolve while avoiding measures that would place American lives as risk" (Berdal 1994, 37). The Bosnian dilemma was particularly damaging to Clinton because there was never any real political capital to be gained, even if the policy succeeded. Unlike Republicans, Democrats consistently rank foreign policy low on their list of priorities come election time (Lieber 1994).

In essence, the protracted nature of the fighting in Bosnia was a direct consequence of strategic decisions by political and military officials. Ethnic difference accounted for only a part of the mutual hatred underlying the fighting; the war was really waged with specific objectives in mind—for example, territory, economic and political control, access to key waterways, and transportation and trade routes.

In contrast, a much stronger commitment to enforce intense and protracted air strikes and bombing raids to deter fighting in Kosovo set the stage for a fairly short bombing campaign. One important benefit of this kind of swift and fairly intense retaliation is that it quickly eliminates the threat that triggered the deployment, so that sustained pressure from the public to leave is satisfied without facing the prospect of withdrawing with the threat left hanging.[21] As they did when assessing potential failure in Bosnia, skeptics offered up Vietnam as a warning against a bombing campaign in Kosovo. But the analogy in both instances is inaccurate and misleading, since the United States attempted to win the Vietnam war, not stop the fighting.[22]

The potential benefits of the intense bombing campaign go well beyond Bosnia and Kosovo, as Clinton himself has acknowledged: "I think we have an interest in standing up against the principle of ethnic cleansing. If you look at the turmoil all through the Balkans, if you look at other places where this could play itself out in other parts of the world, *this is not just about Bosnia* [emphasis added]."[23] Indeed, all of the important lessons from Bosnia appeared to have been applied in the Kosovo case. As in Bosnia, NATO faced a dilemma: how to establish short-term commitments to quick solutions to complex problems with only a minimum risk of casualties. To be sure, NATO leaders showed much greater single-mindedness and unity in the lead-up to the bombing campaign in Kosovo. But NATO's response to the crisis in Kosovo also exemplified the extreme measures (such as tacit support for the KLA) to which allies must go to achieve unity of purpose.

However, most important among the immediate lessons taken from Bosnia and applied in Kosovo was that the United States and its allies needed to develop a policy of extended conventional deterrence based on a comprehensive set of guidelines to prevent ethnic violence from escalating out of control. This lesson is discernible in the behavior of NATO toward the escalating violence in Kosovo. Since policy failures in Bosnia had a direct impact on the probability of success in Kosovo, establishing a strong and credible reputation for responding (without hesitation) to control the violence was a crucial factor in NATO's decision to use force in Kosovo. Indeed, several specific strategies were used in Kosovo, all of which are consistent with (and indirectly supported by) the evidence from the Bosnian case.

For example, NATO attempted to use both general and immediate deterrent threats against Serb forces that were "asymmetrical in application, intense and overwhelming in (their) offensive, with a capability for punishment as well as denial."[24] Air strikes against Serb targets in Yugoslavia and Kosovo were in theory tailored to the "values of the targeted regime," and "were disproportionate in order to convey the seriousness of challenging US interests." These measures were, in theory, intended to help NATO establish a stable deterrent threat by codifying commitments and resolve against Serb aggression in Kosovo.[25]

More generally, the NATO attacks on Serb forces in Kosovo and Serbia required an enthusiastic shift in Western rhetoric toward bombing campaigns for humanitarian purposes. A crucial component of the policy on Kosovo, and an important reason why the shift was successful, was an aggressive publicity campaign to sell a "human security strategy" to the public. Publicizing the effects of ethnic cleansing, refugee flows, and gross systematic human rights violations provided U.S. and European officials with the ammunition to convince the public of the merits of a more assertive and expanded role for NATO in the management of conflict at the century's end. In the following chapter, drawing on evidence from Bosnia and Kosovo, we detail the key characteristics of NATO's deterrence and compellence strategies.

NOTES

1. For a full description of these terms and policy recommendations see Luc Reychler, "The Art of Conflict Prevention: Theory and Practice" in *The Art of Conflict Prevention*, ed. Werner Bauwens and Luc Reychler (London: Brassey's Atlantic Commentaries, 1994), and *U.S. Intervention in Ethnic Conflict*, ed. Fred Wehling (University of California IGCC Policy Paper No. 12, 1995). Contributions by John Steinbruner, George Kenney, Michael Klare, and Michael Mazarr.

2. Ethnic conflicts are still approached too much as purely political problems exclusive to one state. They should be put in their regional context as political problems that have the potential for diffusion to neighboring countries. Whether it is through refugee flows or violent interstate disputes, ethnic conflicts affect entire regions, not just single states (Lake and Rothchild 1996).

3. Since under Chapter 6 operations, peacekeepers act as observers and are inserted only after a settlement is achieved, it becomes clear why credibility will be difficult to maintain. Peacekeepers are not there to enforce the provisions of an accord and lack both the commitment to and capability of such a process. A second hybrid situation falls under the general rubric of a Chapter 6 mandate but is applied in situations where operational but not tactical consent is obtained. That is, the host state has invited peacekeepers in, but there remain "pockets" of resistance within the host state. In these situations peacekeepers use force to protect themselves, the flow of humanitarian assistance, and ordinary citizens caught in the cross fire. Such operations are called Chapter

6½ operations—aggravated or robust peacekeeping. Second-generation operations are characterized by emphasis on humanitarian aspects, refugees on a massive scale, more comprehensive peace plans, a basic recognition of the concept of peacebuilding, and a generally broader application of military capabilities and expertise.

4. To understand these differences it is useful to briefly identify those principles that have traditionally guided peace operations in the past. These are principles that have determined classical UN Chapter 6 peacekeeping operations including impartiality, consent, and the use of force only for self-defense. These "conventional" standards are most effective in the management of disputes between member states of the international system—conflicts in which peacekeeping is essentially observation, the belligerents are safely separated, and the peacekeepers themselves are not vulnerable to attack. This type of peacekeeping most often occurs after a cease-fire is obtained and when force and interposition are deemed unnecessary (i.e., no need for armed troops or buffer). In essence, impartiality works best where intervention is needed least: where the belligerents have already learned through bitter experience and sheer exhaustion that they are ready for the negotiating table.

5. The 860,000-strong Territorial Defense Force was designed to counter outside attack and would be joined by the 200,000-strong regular armed forces. As Slovenia and Croatia prepared to secede, the Serb-dominated army handed out heavy weapons, including artillery, to Serb irregulars. Though the United Nations imposed an arms embargo in 1991, the number of weapons showed no signs of drying up. Major external suppliers of arms included Germany (arms manufactured in both East and West Germany), and many weapons from the United States (from a 1951–57 aid program), Czechoslovakia (pistols), and Russia (tanks) (*Globe and Mail*, 14 July 1992).

6. During the years of Turkish rule, the majority of the area's Christians were converted to Islam. In 1870, Bosnia fell under Austro-Hungarian occupation, became a full part of the empire in 1908, and was incorporated into the new Kingdom of Serbs, Croats, and Slovenes in 1918. In 1946, it became one of Yugoslavia's six socialist republics.

7. *New York Times*, 3 March 1992, A9.

8. In an agreement reached 18 March 1992, Bosnian-Muslims, Serbs, and Croats agreed to a plan that would transform Bosnia-Herzegovina into an independent country divided into three ethnically defined regions (*New York Times*, 19 March 1992). On 7 April the agreement fell through as air strikes on predominately Croatian-held territory were ordered by the JNA (*New York Times*, 8 April 1992). At the same time, Bosnia mobilized its guard and reserves, and President Alija Itzebegovic (a Bosnian-Muslim) assumed command of the guard (*New York Times*, 4 April 1992).

9. In 1971 Tito had elevated the Muslims to the status of Yugoslav "nation." In Bosnia-Herzegovina three constituent "nations" were said to coexist. Before any constitutional changes regarding secession could be made, all three communities in Bosnia would have to agree, which they did not.

10. It is important to note that a year earlier on 18 March 1991, Croat, Serb, and Bosnian-Muslim leaders met in Lisbon and agreed to a set of ethnically based cantons that might have turned Bosnia into the entity envisioned in the Vance-Owen plan eighteen months later. Under pressure from Serb hard-liners, Bosnian leader Itzebegovic renounced that agreement.

11. On 3 May 1994, President Bill Clinton signed Presidential Decision Directive 25 (PDD-25), a policy directive outlining the administration's position on reforming multilateral peace operations. PDD-25 sets forth several stringent requirements that must

be satisfied before the United States will participate in future international coercive diplomacy operations and suggests ways in which the UN could improve its management of such operations. The directive defines "command" of United States armed forces and "operational control" of those forces, distinguishes the two, and maintains that although the president never relinquishes "command" over United States military personnel, he may place them under the "operational control" of a non-U.S. commander for limited and defined purposes.

12. There still remains a "rift" between the U.S. military and other contributors to coercive diplomacy on the question of the use of ground forces as an impartial element in the coercive diplomacy process. In contrast to the American military, the European states, for example, approach the issue of force from a completely different starting point derived from historical experience.

13. With the violence escalating in early 1998, U.S. intelligence was taken by surprise where the KLA was concerned: "some diplomats argued as late as [spring 1998] about whether the shadowy group really existed" (Hedges 1999, 26). Inside Kosovo itself, ethnic Albanian "president" Ibrahim Rugova argued until relatively recently that the KLA was a Serb ploy to discredit Kosovar Albanians in their movement toward liberation. This may be partially explained by the fact that the KLA was estimated to have numbered only a few hundred until the late winter of 1998 (Hedges 1999, 34; Judah 1999a).

14. Funding to and support for the KLA from the Albanian diaspora increased sharply following the massacre at Racak on 15 January 1999. The slayings are attributed to Serb security forces. By February, the CIA assessed that "the KLA is a more formidable force than the Serbs faced last summer," estimating its ranks at several thousand KLA, plus many thousand "irregulars" (Tenet 1999). The KLA had also grown in its political influence by February. The "rebels" achieved an even stronger role on the ethnic Albanian negotiating team than originally envisaged and hoped for by the international mediators, who had made the suggestion of four seats for KLA representatives. They ended up sending five members to the peace talks (BBC World News, 3 February 1999). As the Albanian Kosovars signaled their willingness to sign an agreement, and NATO and Belgrade continued their posturing over seemingly diametrically opposed views, support grew among the Albanian diaspora overseas. For example, in Yonkers, New York, rallies raised tens of millions of dollars. There were no attempts to curb such open fund-raising, and in fact, many believed "they ha[d] the tacit approval of Washington" (Leyne 1999). Some new arms were reaching Kosovo at this point. They "do not change the military balance [with amassing Serb forces clearly outpowering the ethnic Albanians], but they do give the KLA leadership the self-confidence to play tough in the peace talks" (Leyne 1999). Just prior to the bombing the KLA was estimated to number from 7,000 to 8,000 people (ICG 1999g). They were in possession of automatic guns (approximately 30,000, according to some reports), sniper rifles, rocket-propelled grenades, and antitank weapons (ICG 1999b; Hedges 1999, 37, 39).

15. Upon successfully bringing the KLA on board in agreement to sign, it was thought that perhaps the Serbs would be less intransigent (see NATO's perceptions below) and more willing to negotiate. Chris Hill, one of the Rambouillet mediators, claims that perhaps in this belief, the negotiators would have accepted a force under "any suitable disguise" by this point (Judah 1999, 20). If this is true, in early March, NATO was sending (private) signals that were somewhat more flexible/conciliatory than they had been in January. Milosevic, though, would not engage on the issue. In any case, by 18

March, and with the futile second talks of Rambouillet behind them, diplomatic efforts aimed at securing FRY acceptance of the deal were replaced by warnings to the FRY that NATO action was likely if they did not change their stance (Department of National Defense, 1999).

16. From the following statements it is clear that demonstrating NATO unity and credibility were of utmost importance to its officials. These may provide indicators about NATO's primary motives. All quotes are taken from the U.S. Information Agency. Albright, 23 September 1998: "After today's vote, Belgrade should know that we have the will and unity as well—for thousands of lives are at stake." Albright, congressional briefing, 1 October 1998: "And the purpose of having a credible military threat is to indicate that in the absence of meeting those demands he [Milosevic] faces such a threat." North Atlantic Council, statement issued by President Clinton, 29 January 1999: "The Contact Group has now approved the terms of an interim agreement that would do just that, by protecting the rights of all people of Kosovo and giving them the self-government they clearly deserve. . . . To that end, the international community has sent a clear message to the authorities in Belgrade: The time for denial and delay is past. NATO is united and ready to act if you don't." NATO Secretary General Javier Solana, 15 March 1999: "One lesson that we have learned from Bosnia, and which we are now applying in Kosovo, is that diplomacy can often only succeed when it is backed up with the credible threat of military force." U.S. Special Envoy Richard Holbrooke, 22 March 1999: "The resolve of NATO, the Contact Group, the European Union, the OSCE is clear. The idea that there is disunity is wrong." Solana, on 23 March 1999, announced that there was no alternative to military action and that NATO was united behind that decision.

17. It is also about this time that the KLA named the new "government" for Kosovo, to be put to work upon the implementation of a settlement. This action indicates confidence that in some way there will be a settlement with an improved situation for Kosovar Albanians, as well as the KLA's assumptions that they will be in the best position to provide leadership for ethnic Albanians in Kosovo. Although they included spots for LDK members in their government, as well as members from a total of fifteen political parties, the KLA were the ones deciding upon composition and were in the main leadership positions (e.g., Hashim Thaci, KLA official who took part in the Rambouillet talks as the prime minister).

18. There were serious problems with the policy to begin with; rearming the Muslims threatened to escalate the fighting and provoke an immediate Serbian offensive to win the war to gain advantage before the weapons reached the Muslims. There were also several logistical problems related to delivery and training that would be difficult to overcome.

19. On the utility of air strikes as a deterrent force and the debate in the White House, see Engelberg and Gordon (1994, 1).

20. It has long been argued that during the Cold War, when bargaining efforts were directed against a single opponent over a relatively straightforward set of issues, international politics was less complex. Now that the Cold War is over, demands for international consensus are increasing, but the capacity to generate it is diminishing.

21. Charles T. Alan, "Extended Conventional Deterrence: In from the Cold and Out of the Nuclear Freeze," *The Washington Quarterly* 17 (1994): 203–233. See also Alexander George, *Forceful Persuasion*; Jeffrey Record, "Defeating Desert Storm (and Why Saddam Didn't)," *Comparative Strategy* 12 (1993): 125–140; and Adam Garfinkle, "The Gulf War: Was It Worth It?" *World & I* 6 (1991): 70–79.

22. David Gompert, in "How to Defeat Serbia," *Foreign Affairs* 73 (1994): 30–47, recommended conducting a cold war against Serbia, "one of indefinite duration but certain outcome—while in the meantime using NATO's military power more effectively to ensure that relief reaches Bosnia's innocent victims."

23. *New York Times*, 17 April 1993, A4.

24. Charles T. Alan, "Extended Conventional Deterrence: In from the Cold and Out of the Nuclear Freeze."

25. Lincoln P. Bloomfield, in "The Premature Burial of Global Law and Order," 1994, recommended giving the international community's rule book a "sharper set of teeth" by having the UN Genocide Convention, the Fourth Geneva Convention, and other laws expanded to cover "slow motion genocide" as in Yugoslavia (157).

The Theory and Practice of Coercive Diplomacy, Part 2: Controlling Escalation Through Deterrence and Compellence

INTRODUCTION

This chapter focuses on NATO's deterrence and compellence strategies in Bosnia between 1993 and 1995 and on events between 1998 and 1999 leading up to NATO's intervention in Kosovo. The chapter unfolds in six stages. Stage one reviews the literature on rational deterrence theory and briefly summarizes the key impediments to testing. Stage two introduces a different approach that recommends identifying separate deterrence and compellence encounters within a single foreign policy crisis, thus expanding the pool of evidence that would be appropriate for testing a wide range of theoretical propositions. Stage three presents a case study of fourteen immediate deterrence and compellence exchanges between NATO and UN officials and Bosnian Serb leaders from April 1993 to September 1995. Stage four presents a case study of three immediate deterrence and compellence exchanges between NATO and Yugoslav leaders during the Kosovo crisis from June 1998 to March 1999. Stage five summarizes the findings from both case studies, considers whether the prerequisites for effective use of coercive strategies were met, and assesses whether behavior in these encounters was consistent with the theory's predictions. The last section offers a few thoughts on the contributions of a protracted crisis approach to deterrence theory and testing.

RATIONAL DETERRENCE THEORY: THE DOMINANT TESTING STRATEGY

The most prominent strategy used to produce evidence to evaluate rational deterrence theory recommends identifying cases of immediate deterrence, coding these cases as instances of success or failure, isolating conditions that were present (or absent) during successes and absent (or present) during failures, and, based on these differences, drawing conclusions about why and how deterrence works. In the empirical domain, lack of correspondence in case selection and coding is the key area of difficulty confronting those who apply this *success-failure* framework.[1] The following are among the many coding questions that must be answered prior to making valid judgments about deterrence:

a. Who is the *challenger* and who is the *defender* in the case? Since military-security crises involve a series of interactions and deterrence episodes, with each side (and their respective clients) acquiring and playing both roles at various stages, disagreements about who initiated the crisis are common;[2]

b. Is the retaliatory threat *direct* or *extended*?

c. Is the crisis a *deterrence* or *compellence* encounter (or some combination)?[3]

d. What *class* of deterrent or compellent threat is being issued?[4]

e. Finally, does the case constitute a *success* or *failure* (or some combination of both)?[5]

Case selection is likely to be difficult for researchers who choose to test deterrence theory this way, given the many opportunities available to reject any one case. As revealed by the ongoing debates over case listings, these obstacles cannot be overcome through reference to the historical record; in fact, each side has offered compelling evidence to support their distinct (in some cases contradictory) interpretation of events in almost every crisis.[6]

Although debates over the accuracy of historical accounts are constructive, lingering divisions become counterproductive if very little effort is directed toward producing different testing strategies that lie outside this *success/failure* framework, among alternate sources of empirical evidence and data, or within a wider range of propositions derived from the theories.

This chapter offers an alternative method of testing deterrence and compellence theory that avoids at least some, although not all, of the coding controversies noted above. It does this by rejecting the assumption that a crisis encompasses within it a single, dominant encounter. Instead, each case is viewed as a series of separate and distinct deterrence and compellence exchanges. Dissecting each crisis to reveal different encounters allows for multiple interpretations of any one foreign policy crisis and, more importantly, can account for discrepancies across existing case lists. The approach is expected to provide a fairer test of the theory by specifying the precise time frame and exact sequence within which the appropriately designated threats, counterthreats, and responses

Table 4.1
Empirical Domain of Immediate Deterrence/Compellence Tests

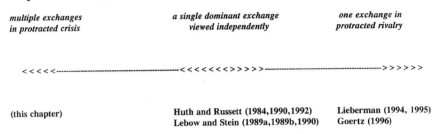

multiple exchanges in protracted crisis	*a single dominant exchange viewed independently*	*one exchange in protracted rivalry*
(this chapter)	Huth and Russett (1984,1990,1992) Lebow and Stein (1989a,1989b,1990)	Lieberman (1994, 1995) Goertz (1996)

were made. Although some crises do not have multiple exchanges, many do. Debates about how to code entire crises (in which both sides may be correct, depending on the time frame) are replaced with potentially more constructive disputes about specific threat/response interactions, thus obligating researchers to track the sequence of events in more precise terms. Since we are no longer faced with having to fit all of this information into a single data point, far more information is made available upon which to judge the strengths and weaknesses of deterrence (Harvey 1997a, 205).

In sum, a protracted crisis approach is important for two reasons: (1) it accounts for anomalies across current data sets (as previously described), and (2) it can provide answers to new questions about deterrence in rivalries. The difference is that the dynamic nature of the deterrence relationship is explored in the context of a single, protracted crisis. The distinction between the three testing strategies appears in Table 4.1.

It is important to note that the effects of *communication, capability, commitment,* and *resolve* on deterrence stability are key conditions of the above noted research programs, all of which serve as essential components of credibility. Breaking crises down into component parts allows for the possibility that the four conditions can change during the same crisis. Credibility, for example, often varies over a relatively short period of time as more states join a defending (or challenging) alliance. Shifts in the level of domestic support for retaliation within a defending state could also improve the capacity of leaders to mobilize forces, thus enhancing the credibility of a deterrent threat—as occurred in the United States following the February 1994 market bombing in Sarajevo. Resolve also varies in crises depending on circumstances; mission creep, for example, often creates additional incentives to become more fully involved in a crisis, notwithstanding the possibility that the economic and military ties between defender and client are minimal to nonexistent. U.S. and European resolve to protect NATO's reputation in Bosnia, for example, increased as the number of failures mounted. Finally, the capacity to communicate retaliatory threats to opponents also changed repeatedly throughout the Bosnian crisis as NATO and UN officials repeatedly eliminated, and then reinstated, the dual key approach to crisis management (described below). In contrast, during the Kosovo crisis, NATO officials demonstrated a much higher commitment to clearly communicating retaliatory threats and showing resolve. The unwillingness of NATO officials to pursue a ground war may also be informed by a desire to avoid a lengthy protracted crisis associated with mission creep as occurred in Bosnia.

It is conceivable that the relative importance of each condition varies across exchanges within the same crisis. For example, throughout most of the first year of fighting in Bosnia-Herzegovina, NATO's willingness to deny the Bosnian Serb military the objectives they sought was never really doubted, until the eighth exchange. It was during this exchange that the Bosnian Serb leadership began to question the ability of UN and NATO officials to coordinate operations for air support, a key component of NATO's retaliatory capability. Several U.S. warplanes, preparing to retaliate against a Serbian attack on French peacekeepers during the first week of April 1994, were unable to respond in time because of communication problems in the chain of command. From that point onward, NATO officials were faced with having to satisfy the capability prerequisite to mount a credible deterrent threat, whereas previously it was only NATO resolve that posed the most difficult problem for peacemaking efforts.

Efforts to identify the presence of *resolve* are especially susceptible to coding problems, unless explored through the prism of protracted crises. Conventional wisdom stipulates that once a challenge takes place and the defender follows through with the retaliatory threat, the case is coded as a failure and the search for evidence ends. But deterrence successes are often achieved as a result of short-term failures, because failures provide the best opportunity for leaders in the defending state to demonstrate resolve, not to mention capability and credibility—all essential requirements for successful deterrence (Lieberman 1995). Evaluating deterrence in the context of protracted crises, therefore, can help to explain otherwise puzzling phenomena and provide a new way to test core hypotheses about deterrence prerequisites.

The relevant question is whether NATO encounters with the Bosnian Serbs in the case of the Bosnian crisis and with FRY forces in the case of the Kosovo crisis constituted specific instances of immediate deterrence or compellence. Huth and Russett's definitions of deterrence and compellence are used to distinguish the two categories of coercive threats.[7]

Compellence: an attempt by policy makers in state A to force, by threat and/or application of sanctions, the policy of state B to comply with the demands of state A, including but not limited to retracting actions already taken.

Deterrence: the threatened sanction is designed to prevent state B from taking actions it is considering but has not already initiated; thus the sanction would be employed only if the target undertook the action that the deterrer had sought to prevent.

Since the objective in each case is to *prevent undesired actions* (either by the threat of sanctions and/or the offer of rewards), both forms of coercive diplomacy can be viewed as essentially similar strategies—preventing undesired actions can take the form of compelling a state to retract or discontinue actions already taken, or deterring a state from taking actions it has contemplated but not initiated.[8]

If retaliatory threats were not initiated, the exchange would be inappropriate for evaluating theory. To qualify as an immediate deterrence or compellence exchange, therefore, an opponent must be considering (or already undertaking) an action that is viewed by opponents as undesirable, and, in response, an attempt must be made to dissuade the challenger from committing the undesired action through the use of one or both of the following: (*a*) threat of sanctions, (*b*) offer of rewards or inducements.[9]

Once a specific encounter was deemed relevant, a judgment was made about success or failure based on the following predictions derived from the theory: a retaliatory threat will succeed if leaders of the deterring state clearly define the behavior deemed to be unacceptable ("The more specific the commitment the more likely it is to be believed" [p. 85]); communicate to challengers a commitment to punish violations ("A commitment has no deterrent value unless its existence is known to an adversary" [p. 86]); possess the means (capability) to defend the commitment by punishing adversaries who challenge it, or by denying the challenger the specific objectives sought through its aggression ("Credible commitments are defensible commitments. The failure to develop the military capability to defend a commitment or retaliate against its challenger encourages an adversary to question your resolve" [p. 88]); and demonstrate their resolve to carry out the retaliatory actions if the challenger fails to comply ("Current commitments are more likely to be taken seriously to the extent that a nation has been resolute in defense of its commitments in the past" [p. 89]).

Resolve is most effectively demonstrated through costly signals—that is, any action, statement, or condition that increases the political, economic, or military costs of the challenge, while lowering the costs of responding to a challenger's probes. Relevant *actions* include the mobilization of military forces; *statements* include public announcements, clear and unambiguous threats of impending retaliation, or explicit ultimatums and deadlines; and *conditions* include domestic and international support for retaliation, positive press coverage, and so on.[10]

If these conditions are satisfied, the expected net costs of the threatened sanction (to the challenger) should be greater than the expected net gain of noncompliance, because the punishment (if carried out) would prevent the challenger from achieving intended goals. If these requirements are met, but the behavior still occurs, that would constitute a failure, both in theory and strategy. On the other hand, if one or more of the conditions are not satisfied, the theory predicts failure in most cases. In other words, even clear and credible threats will fail if the challenger believes that the challenge is worth the risks and political, military, or economic costs incurred by triggering the threatened response.[11]

These are not the only prerequisites discussed in the literature, but they do represent the ones most often cited by critics when describing and testing deterrence. As such, they serve as an excellent starting point for reevaluating their conclusions. Although some critics do not make explicit reference to the identical set of four conditions, the variables they examine are often different representations of the same four.[12]

Kosovo is more clearly a case of compellence because Serb forces were already in Kosovo and fighting was well under way before NATO leaders decided to intervene. During the three exchanges leading up to NATO's bombing campaign, the intention was, among other things, to persuade Milosevic to withdraw his troops from Kosovo. NATO leaders clearly communicated their intentions to achieve this goal with force if necessary. Of course if withdrawal could be achieved without resorting to force, all the better. This is a response much different than that in Bosnia, where leaders debated the merits of using force for almost three years. The use of force was not a credible option in Bosnia until late in 1995. Therefore, the reasons for NATO's initial failure to compel Milosevic to withdraw from Kosovo are somewhat different than those that account for failure in Bosnia. On the other hand, NATO did provide a clearly communicated and credible strategy for compelling FRY forces to withdraw from Kosovo (without ground troops). On the other hand, faced with Milosevic's refusal to pull out, NATO leaders continued to demonstrate their resolve by not wavering from their initial commitment to use force if necessary. Had NATO leaders not shown this resolve and had they stood by as the protracted crisis in Kosovo deepened, the organization's reputation and by extension its credibility as an alliance would have been destroyed. Once the bombing campaign was under way and it was clear that NATO leaders would not waiver, the organization's reputation and credibility were enhanced significantly. The evidence is clear: unambiguous and credible threats of military retaliation are effective ways of stopping wide-scale ethnic violence. In both Bosnia and Kosovo, coercive diplomacy appeared to succeed and fail for all the right reasons.

CASE STUDY: BOSNIA-HERZEGOVINA, 1993–1995

Ethnic conflict theories provide important clues about the root causes of the war in the former Yugoslavia. Although these psychological, social, and historical factors account for the motivations behind demands for political and territorial separation, and can help explain why each side is prepared to fight, only situational variables tied to decisions by political and military officials on all sides of the dispute can explain the protracted nature of the fighting—that is, the escalation, intensity, and duration of the war.[13] Each exchange includes a summary of events, a description of threats and responses, a determination of the severity and credibility of the threat, and an evaluation of the outcome in terms of the theory's predictions. A summary of outcomes is presented in the section following the narratives.

Exchange 1

On 31 March 1993, the United Nations passed a resolution (UNSCR 816) establishing a "no-fly zone" (NFZ) over Bosnia-Herzegovina, which authorized the use of NATO planes to shoot down fixed-wing or rotary-wing aircraft (helicopters) that were in violation of the order. The primary intention was to prevent the commander of Serbian troops in Bosnia, General Radko Mladic, from using airspace over Bosnia for bombing runs on Muslim ground targets. One week later (8 April) NATO formally agreed to enforce the flight ban with jet fighters from the United States, Britain, France, and the Netherlands, and began patrolling the airspace over Bosnia on 12 April.[14]

Unlike in the NFZ established over Iraq, pilots were not authorized to fire on civilian intruders or ground installations before issuing "several warnings" to unauthorized aircraft.[15] With respect to the use of Bosnia-Herzegovina airspace by warring factions for bombing runs, that was stopped as of 12 April. There were no reported violations of the UN Security Council resolution, although no flights may have been planned by the Bosnian Serbs. Activity and operations during the previous weeks, however, indicated that flights would have taken place. Reports from UN observers show that some 500 violations of the UN NFZ resolution had occurred in the previous four months.[16] In any event, the NFZ was not officially violated until ten months later (20 February 1994—see Exchange 8), which led to the downing of four Bosnian Serb planes.

Ironically, the decision by NATO to connect the retaliatory threat to the use of "airspace" gave Mladic more reason to test NATO's commitment to control the war on the ground, since there was no indication (or threat) that NATO planes would be used to "stop" the fighting. On the military front, the violence actually escalated around Sarajevo and Srebrenica with intense artillery barrages beginning *within minutes* of NATO's enforcement of the NFZ. The 123 reported deaths represented the largest number of casualties in a single shelling since Srebrenica had come under attack seven months earlier.[17] In addition to these battles, Bihac was reported to have suffered several casualties from attacks by some 100 Serbian tanks around the same time.

Exchange 2

On 17 April, the UN Security Council passed a resolution (UNSCR 819) to impose the strongest economic sanctions on the Yugoslav Federation to date if SDS President Radovan Karadzic and the Serbian leadership failed to endorse, by 26 April, a draft constitution drawn up by EU mediator Lord David Owen and former U.S. Secretary of State Cyrus Vance that would have seen Bosnia organized into a decentralized federation (the "Vance-Owen" plan). The embargo would amount to total economic and financial isolation of Serbia, and would

1. ban transshipments of any goods through the Federal Republic of Yugoslavia (Serbia and Montenegro);

2. impose stricter controls on barges along the Danube;

3. ban all ships entering the territorial waters of Yugoslavia and create a 12-mile exclusion zone;

4. impound all trucks, ships, aircraft, or rolling stock in other countries; and

5. freeze all Yugoslav financial assets in foreign countries.[18]

The intent was to put direct economic pressure on Slobodan Milosevic to cut all financial and military support for the Serbian Nationalist forces and, in so doing, persuade Karadzic and Mladic to (a) stop the fighting, (b) return to the bargaining table, and (c) give their conditional acceptance to the Vance-Owen peace accord.

From the point of view of satisfying the strategic requirements for compellence, the UN resolution (and NATO blockade around Serbia) fell short for several reasons. First, the threat of economic sanctions was directed against the leadership of the Serb federation, Slobodan Milosevic, and did not affect the ability of Bosnian Serbs to continue their offensive. Second, the list of economic sanctions in the original UN resolution was curtailed by a Russian threat of a Security Council veto. Boris Yeltsin faced a difficult situation at home, most notably an April 25th referendum on power sharing with the Russian parliament. To appease hard-liners who preferred to maintain a strong connection with Serbia, Yeltsin requested that the Security Council hold off on immediate sanctions until the referendum was over. Perhaps most damaging to European efforts to ratify Vance-Owen was an American refusal to "unambiguously endorse" the accord. The United States demanded that the UN resolution only "commend" the plan, ignoring strong appeals from Britain and France to offer unconditional support.[19] Together, these factors undermined the ability of the UN, with only qualified support from the United States and NATO, to mount a credible threat of sufficient intensity (severity) to deny the Bosnian Serbs the political and military objectives they sought. In fact, high-ranking UN officials believed, and publicly stated, that the economic sanction threat would have a negligible effect on the ability of Mladic's forces to continue their air or ground offensives.

The Bosnian Serb leadership did not take the compellent threats very seriously. The day after the UN announcement, the Bosnian Serbs stood firm in their commitment to reject the treaty, threatened to pull out of the negotiations altogether, and "waved off threats of direct military action with an air of both bravado and victimization."[20] The official response to the UN ultimatum came in the form of a vote by the Bosnian Serb parliament on 23 April rejecting the accord.[21] Backed by a mandate from parliament, Karadzic refused to give even a modified conditional acceptance to the peace plan, issued his own warning that the leadership would reject any pressure to sign the accord, threatened retaliatory action in response to the sanction imposed on Serbia, and called for direct negotiations between the three warring parties on territorial issues still in contention. The latter offer was immediately rejected by the Bosnian president, Itzebegovic. On 27 April, one day after the UN deadline, Bosnian Serb forces (approximately 1,000, with ten tanks) mounted a new ground and artillery offensive against the Muslim town of Bihac. The economic sanctions stipulated in the UN ultimatum took effect.[22]

Several things should be considered prior to making judgments about success and failure in this case. In terms of the initial compellent threat to impose a total economic blockade on Serbia unless Vance-Owen was endorsed, the threat appeared to work as predicted by theory. The UN ultimatum was unambiguous, clearly communicated, and tied to a specific deadline. There was a strong commitment to follow through with sweeping economic sanctions if the presidents of Serbia (Slobodan Milosevic), the Republic of Montenegro, and the Yugoslav Federation (Dobrica Cosic) failed to (a) endorse the peace plan, and (b) pressure Karadzic to do the same. The resolve to follow through with the sanctions was bolstered by strong support for the resolution from the Security Council, with abstentions (not vetoes) from Russia and China. The threat appeared to work; from that point on, Milosevic and Cosic expressed strong support for the peace accord and began a campaign to persuade Karadzic to accept it as well.

This particular exchange poses an interesting empirical puzzle for those who prefer to use the dominant testing strategy. Conventional wisdom stipulates that once the defender follows through with the retaliatory threat, the strategy should be considered a failure. Ironically, retaliation did occur in this case (that is, the blockade was carried out), but not because the UN ultimatum lacked credibility (it received strong backing from the United States, Britain, and France) or because resolve was questioned. The threat *successfully* compelled Milosevic and Cosic to endorse the accord and to send a strongly worded letter to Karadzic on 29 April. The letter informed him that, in light of the new sanctions against Serbia, they would be forced to cut off all military and economic aid to the Serbian nationalists.[23] It was Belgrade's subsequent failure to compel Karadzic that accounted for the UN/NATO retaliation. The threat by Milosevic to break economic and military ties with Serbian nationalists was not strong enough to convince the leadership in Pale that it was in their interest to accept the conditions stipulated in the Serbian (or UN) ultimatum. Acceptance of the peace plan was too high a price to pay for the small relief of lifting sanctions. In fact, Bosnian Serb weapons stocks were so extensive by that point that they were actually selling weapons to raise hard cash.

Several events occurred in the last week of April, shortly after the attacks on Bihac, that made Karadzic reconsider his position and return to negotiations. First, the April referendum in Russia gave Yeltsin the mandate he needed to pursue a more active foreign policy in the region, one aimed at compelling the Bosnian Serbs to consider Vance-Owen. At the same time, several high-level NATO meetings were being held to consider a more "assertive peacekeeping" role in Bosnia, which included the use of air strikes to stop the fighting around

Sarajevo and Srebrenica. The pressure had a direct effect on Karadzic, who announced on 30 April that he was now prepared to resume peace talks in Athens. Since the objective of the 17 April UN resolution was to force Karadzic to resume talks on the accord, the exchange was a partial compellence success.[24]

A final point about Exchange 2 should be noted. Coercive threats succeed and fail in time and stages, as George and Smoke pointed out more than twenty years ago.[25] Finding the evidence to illustrate this fact, however, requires detailed examination of exchanges within crises. Without this type of analysis, judgments about the strength of deterrence theory will forever depend on arbitrary selection of evidence from different points in time.

Exchange 3

On 1 May, President Clinton agreed "in principle" to commit American airpower to end the fighting in the Balkans and to protect Muslim "safe havens" from further offensives in Bihac, Gorazde, Gradacac, Brcko, and Tuzla. This time the plans were specific enough to indicate likely targets, including key bridges used for transporting military equipment and other supplies from Serbia to Serbian nationalist territory in Bosnia. The threats, now being directed against Mladic (not Milosevic), became much clearer and more specific in subsequent statements made by Secretary of State Warren Christopher. Three key demands were attached to the warnings: (1) honor the cease-fire, (2) stop shelling Muslim villages, and (3) let the aid convoys continue with their missions. Although U.S. military action at the time was not imminent, Christopher did warn Karadzic that the "clock is ticking"[26] There also was a commitment in principle to lift the arms embargo against the Muslims. The assumption held by U.S. officials was that the same sabre rattling that brought Karadzic back to the table could deter General Mladic from shelling Muslim villages. On 2 May, Karadzic signed the same accord his parliament had rejected a week earlier, agreed to a cease-fire, and formally requested that the United States drop its threats to use military force. One indication that the threat played an important role in the decision was that several Bosnian Serb delegates publicly stated that the prospect of U.S. military air strikes led them to reconsider support for the plan.[27]

This particular exchange is interesting because it illustrates the importance of time when evaluating success and failure. Four days after Karadzic signed the accord, the parliament voted 65–1 (with twelve abstentions) to reject the plan and to hold a second referendum. On that day, Mladic ordered gunners to continue their offensive on several Muslim towns in eastern and western Bosnia. In response to these attacks, the UN Security Council passed a resolution (UNSCR 824) establishing six Muslim enclaves as protected "safe areas": Sarajevo, Tuzla, Zepa, Gorazde, Bihac, and Srebrenica.[28] The resolution, unanimously adopted, stipulated that these areas should be free from any form of military hostility, but it included no specific recommendation regarding how violations would be dealt with.[29] Although Canadian, European, and Russian officials agreed with U.S. demands for tougher action, they rejected the two main U.S. proposals to (a) lift the arms embargo against the Muslims, and (b) expand the air strike mandate beyond the safe havens to enforce a more general cease-fire throughout the region. In both cases, the Europeans and Canadians were concerned for the safety of their peacekeepers, possible targets of Bosnian Serb retaliation. European officials recommended that U.S. troops be stationed in Bosnia to reinforce the credibility of NATO threats, but U.S. representatives on the council rejected that option. The gap between U.S. and European interests appeared to be widening, which hampered NATO efforts to communicate a commitment to respond to acts of aggression and to demonstrate resolve. The problem was compounded even further by a statement from the White House and State Department proclaiming that the United States was doing all it could, and that without European support it was unlikely that tougher actions would be taken to stop the fighting.[30]

U.S. and European actions at this time did not amount to a very credible commitment to retaliate. Without a serious commitment to impose costs on Karadzic and Mladic for violations, the balance of influence in the region remained with them. Although Karadzic "promised" that they would "respect" the UN safe areas, Mladic's forces broke through defense lines that surrounded Zepa, killing more than 500 people in the offensive.[31] The attack had no effect on the approach toward the problem, and as expected, the Bosnian Serb parliament voted, for a third time, to reject Vance-Owen (51–2)—followed by yet another referendum in which 96 percent of the public rejected the plan.

Exchange 4

On 4 June, the United Nations reinforced previous threats by authorizing, through UNSCR 836, the use of airpower (as distinct from air strikes) to stop attacks on Muslim enclaves, and sent additional peacekeepers to the region to help control the escalation in the fighting. The resolution, acting under chapter 7 of the UN Charter, expanded the mandate of UNPROFOR to protect safe areas against attacks, monitor the cease-fire, promote the withdrawal of military units (except for Bosnian government troops), and occupy key points on the ground. The council authorized UNPROFOR to use force if necessary and invited NATO to provide air support. As Major-General John Archibald MacInnis points out, however, close examination of this resolution reveals the presence of some carefully chosen words that, together, undermined the effectiveness of the threat—for example, "to deter attacks against the safe areas" rather than "to defend," and "to promote withdrawal" rather than "to ensure or enforce withdrawal." As for the use of airpower,

[I]t was considered that air strikes would pose grave danger to UNPROFOR personnel and the humanitarian convoys and should, therefore, be initiated with the greatest restraint and, essentially, in self defense. In sum, it was apparent that the extension of the UN-

PROFOR mandate to include a capacity to deter attacks was not to be construed as signifying deployment in sufficient strength to repel attacks by military force.[32]

From the perspective of theory, there were four additional problems with the threat. First, the UN Secretary General recommended that 34,000 additional peacekeeping troops "would be required if deterrence through strength was to be obtained," but that it would be possible to *start* implementing UNSCR 836 with a "light option" of about 7,600 troops "as an initial approach with limited objectives."[33] In UNSCR 844, the council decided to go with the light option. Second, the Russian delegation to the UN was the only co-sponsor of Resolution 844 to agree "in principle" to send additional ground forces to protect the safe areas, a commitment they subsequently withdrew on 12 June despite strong pleas from Britain and France. Third, President Clinton also undermined the credibility of UN/NATO threats with a public statement on 12 June: "On Bosnia, I made a decision. The UN controls what happens in Bosnia, I cannot unilaterally lift the arms embargo. I didn't change my mind. Our allies decided that they were not prepared to go that far this time."[34]

On 18 June the United States began to signal its willingness to consider a Serbian proposal to partition Bosnia into three ethnic regions, and began to pressure Itzebegovic to accept a Serbian-Croatian partition plan giving Serbian nationalists most of the land they acquired through war. U.S. officials began to question publicly whether the Bosnian Muslims were likely to gain back the territory they lost, and whether the United States was capable of doing anything constructive without either European backing or stronger domestic support for a more assertive role. Even European diplomats, who had previously been convinced of the merits of Vance-Owen, began to consider the Serbian-Croatian alternative. To make things worse, UN officials began to state that Western reluctance to carry out previous threats had caused the fighting to worsen.

Karadzic promised, once again, to refrain from attacking the Muslim enclaves, but their forces maintained regular attacks on Sarajevo, Gorazde, Bihac, Tuzla, and Srebrenica throughout June and July. According to a senior policy analyst at NATO, the basic problem with the safe areas was that UNPROFOR never received the required number of troops (34,000) or the necessary equipment to carry out UNSCR 836, which explains why the UN turned to NATO to enforce the resolution from the air.

Exchange 5

Intense fighting continued throughout July, with various negotiated cease-fires all failing to hold. Serb forces intensified their bombardment of Sarajevo and attacked UN peacekeepers and relief convoys on several different occasions. The most significant attack was the shelling of a French-staffed UN base in Sarajevo within hours of a UN-brokered cease-fire. Portions of the official release from the July meeting of the UN Human Rights Commission (Geneva) summed up the prevailing attitude:

We are on the verge of disaster, of collapse. . . . The escalation in fighting, the escalation of attacks on relief convoys, the decline in international financing of our effort, a gap in the food pipeline until mid-September, all this combined with no political breakthrough on the horizon and the international community tightening its restrictions on the entry of people fleeing the fighting, spells disaster for the relief operation.[35]

The increasing level of contempt for international authority fueled calls for Western countries to mount air strikes in support of UNPROFOR and its humanitarian objectives. This prompted President Clinton to express his readiness for U.S. forces to provide air support for strikes against Serb artillery "if asked" by the UN. French Foreign Minister Alain Juppé also called for NATO air strikes to defend UN forces.

On 1 August, the U.S. administration declared that it was now prepared to use airpower "unilaterally" to increase pressure on Mladic to (a) end the attacks on Muslim safe havens, (b) create safe passage for UN relief convoys, and (c) negotiate a peace settlement. More importantly, air strikes would take place without European support. The State Department warned that "the United States, at this point, is determined to act in a more vigorous fashion as it relates to Bosnia."[36] Under pressure from the United States to take a more assertive role, NATO issued its own warning that it would engage in a series of strategic bombing raids against the Serbian military if it did not cease attacks on Sarajevo.[37]

This marked the beginning of a new, more assertive U.S. strategy to mount a credible threat by creating consensus, instead of waiting for it. Also, several attacks on French peacekeepers around this time convinced some European leaders that air strikes could actually prevent, instead of provoke, attacks on their troops. NATO aircraft were deployed to the region and increased patrols over the NFZ, so the threat became explicit. Manfred Wörner, the secretary-general of NATO, issued a formal statement on 2 August stipulating the demands and outlining how the strikes would be coordinated. An unofficial deadline was set for the following Monday, 9 August, when NATO members were to meet to assess compliance with demands and to determine if Bosnian Serb forces "relaxed their grip on the city enough to avert western action."[38]

The immediate response on 2 August was defiance, with Serb leaders issuing public warnings of "dire consequences" and threatening to respond to air attacks with counterstrikes against UN peacekeepers on the ground.[39] This was met with a specific retaliatory threat from both NATO and high-ranking officials of the U.S. State Department stating that air strikes would be used to wipe out the 1,500–2,000 Serbian guns around Sarajevo if UN peacekeepers were attacked. The threat appeared to work; although some of the fighting in other areas of Bosnia continued, artillery attacks on Sarajevo stopped within hours of the

NATO ultimatum. Two days later, Radovan Karadzic emerged from a meeting with UN officers to announce that (a) he and General Mladic had agreed to pull their army back from the hills overlooking Sarajevo (Mount Igmon), (b) they had begun operations to restore electricity, water, and gas services throughout Bosnia, and (c) their forces would no longer restrict relief convoys from reaching Muslims in the city.

On 11 August, the United States reinforced previous NATO threats with a warning to Mladic that heavy artillery "must be removed from Sarajevo by August 13" or face air strikes.[40] Despite some diplomatic maneuvering over timing, weather problems, and a plea by Mladic to have the UN deploy a larger buffer force to protect retreating troops, the threat worked. On 13 August the UN commander confirmed that Mladic had indeed pulled almost all of his troops back from the two mountain regions under dispute, pledged completion of the withdrawal by the next day, and allowed relief trucks and convoys to deliver supplies to Muslims in Sarajevo. This marked the first time since the war began that General Mladic had given up previously occupied territory.

The problem with mounting such an effective deterrent and compellent threat was that Muslim leaders, namely Itzebegovic, began to assume (perhaps prematurely) that the tide was changing in their favor, and that NATO threats could be used to gain major concessions on territory. As U.S. officials regained confidence in the utility of coercive diplomacy, they began to back Muslim demands for territorial concessions. The Geneva talks broke down in August and collapsed by September, setting the stage for continuation of the fighting two months later.

Exchange 6

On 18 October, the Bosnian Serb army renewed its artillery attacks on Sarajevo to force the Bosnian Muslims to accept their partition plan. In response, the United States issued several weak air strike warnings.[41] Unlike the threats in August, no schedule was established nor were the threats backed by official statements (that is, costly signals) from the U.S. State Department or NATO. The attacks on Sarajevo began as minor probes to test NATO's resolve, but increased in number and intensity over the next two months as no retaliatory threat was mounted. Statements by Christopher indicating that the United States would be willing to send food and medicine to the region, *but that no formal military response was being planned*, confirmed that political momentum for U.S./NATO air strikes had diminished. In addition, differences persisted between Western countries over Clinton's advocacy of lifting the arms embargo, and because the United Kingdom, France, and other European Community members continued to oppose air strikes against Bosnian Serb positions.[42]

It was not until 11 January that NATO issued their next warning to stop the siege on Sarajevo, with European and Canadian members voicing their traditional concerns about the possibility of retaliation against their peacekeepers.[43]

Once again, several regulations attached to the plans undermined the threat's effectiveness and potency. UN commanders had to request air strikes and recommend the action to the UN secretary-general, who was then required to issue a formal request to NATO. This dual key approach made it very difficult for UN commanders on the ground to get the air support they needed when they needed it. The Bosnian Serb general ignored the warning and continued to shell Sarajevo throughout January (Sudetic 1994a, A8).

Exchange 7

The most direct and devastating attack on Sarajevo occurred on 5 February in a packed central market, killing 68 and wounding more than 200 civilians. The deaths appeared to galvanize the international community as Western leaders unanimously condemned the massacre. Foreign ministers of France and the United Kingdom stated that the attack was a "turning point," and added that the EU should aim "to bring about the immediate lifting of the siege of Sarajevo by all means necessary, including air power."[44] At their meeting in Brussels on 7 February, foreign ministers of EU member countries—with the exception of Greece—backed the use of air strikes to secure the immediate relief of Sarajevo.[45]

On 9 February, responding to public outrage in the aftermath of the shelling and a UN request for air strikes on artillery and mortar positions around Mount Igmon, NATO issued an ultimatum to the Bosnian Serb leadership. They were to end their siege on the city, withdraw their forces and heavy weapons to positions behind a twenty-kilometer exclusion zone, place all other heavy weapons in the area under UN control, or face direct attacks from NATO bombers. This explicit threat was attached to a firm deadline of 21 February.

Shortly after the threat was issued, General Mladic agreed to an immediate cease-fire and to removal of all heavy artillery from around Sarajevo. According to Lieutenant General Sir Michael Rose, "it was the looming threat of NATO air strikes that caused the Bosnian Serbs to agree to the cease-fire."[46] On 17 February, UN sources confirmed that Serb forces were indeed withdrawing from Sarajevo and that the withdrawal would be completed a day ahead of schedule.[47] In Karadzic's words, "we have been withdrawing convoys and we will withdraw even more. . . . We have made our own desirable deadline. . . . We want to move as quickly as possible."[48] By the 21st, UN officials confirmed that all forces (including the Bosnian Muslims) had withdrawn behind the twenty-kilometer exclusion zone, and gave UN troops unimpeded access to the area to check for violations.

Even as the ultimatum was being met, Clinton continued to demonstrate American resolve by underscoring his intention to follow through with the air strikes should any of NATO's demands not be met. In a televised address, he began preparing the American public for the possibility of direct U.S. involvement in the region to enforce compliance. "Nobody should doubt NATO's resolve. . . . We are determined to make good on NATO's word. And we are prepared to act. . . . Our military goal will be straightforward: to exact a heavy price on those who refuse to comply with the ultimatum."[49]

The Serbian nationalists turned in (or moved to the other side of the exclusion zone) 225 heavy weapons. On the day of the deadline, UN observers agreed that compliance with NATO demands was complete and that air strikes were not needed. There was even some discussion that the Sarajevo experience should be the model for controlling fighting around other safe havens.

As on previous occasions, Serb military leaders waited for the pressure to subside and began to initiate probes to test NATO's resolve. The probes usually occurred when peace talks appeared to be heading in the right direction, which usually meant that European leaders would begin reverting to the "wait and see" strategy so as not to jeopardize the peace process. Unlike previous responses to probes, the immediate retaliation by NATO aircraft on 28 February to violations of the flight ban, in which four Serb warplanes were shot down, was intended as a demonstration of resolve and a commitment to enforce the NFZ.

Exchange 8

Several events happened in April that undermined the stability of NATO's threat and encouraged additional probes by Mladic around the safe haven of Gorazde.[50] On 3 April, U.S. Defense Secretary William Perry stated that "force would not be used to halt the Serb assault on Gorazde."[51] Six days after this statement, Secretary Perry and other high-ranking military officials began to question whether the Sarajevo model should be used to protect other safe havens like Gorazde, given differences in terrain and local grievances. Comparisons to Vietnam implied that U.S. officials were failing to consider all options before stepping up involvement in an area that was not directly tied to American strategic or national interests.

In addition to these political signals, the ability of the UN and NATO to coordinate operations for air support came under criticism. Several U.S. warplanes, preparing to retaliate against a Serbian attack on French peacekeepers during the first week of April, were unable to respond in time because of problems with communication in the chain of command. The original request for air strikes was made by the French commander whose troops were being attacked. His request went to the commander of peacekeeping forces in Bosnia, then to the commander of UN forces in Yugoslavia, and finally (two hours later) to Yasushi Akashi, the special representative of UN Secretary-General Boutros Boutros-Ghali, who had the power to authorize the strikes. The UN official tried for approximately one hour to contact Mladic to inform him of the impending strikes should his forces continue attacking the French troops, and only then requested that NATO planes respond. The three-hour delay allowed Serb forces (and weaponry) to escape without facing air strikes.

The apparent failure of the "dual key" approach weakened UN and NATO credibility and ended a six-week cease-fire, with attacks on Gorazde resuming on 9 April.[52] Another attempt was made to control the fighting around Gorazde, but the threat came from the UN secretary-general, not NATO or the United States, and only warned that the UN was "ready" to order air strikes. No specific deadline was set for a Serbian pullout, nor were any directives issued in the form of ultimatums. The Serbs ignored the warning and continued shelling the city.

On 10 April, two NATO planes mounted a limited bombing attack (three bombs) on Serbian tank and command centers near Gorazde. [53] Shelling slowed down immediately after the air raid while Bosnian Serb commanders assessed the damage. On the morning of 11 April, after a lull in the shelling, the army began another major offensive on Gorazde, which provoked a second (though even more limited) bombing raid by NATO aircraft. Several direct warnings to General Mladic were issued by UN Commander Rose, giving him ten minutes to stop the fighting "or face another air attack." The retaliatory threat was not carried out, and Mladic's forces continued to fire for two more hours.[54]

The overall performance of NATO warplanes throughout this exchange was less than impressive. A total of six bombs were dropped, two of which failed to explode. On 16 April, a British Harrier aircraft was shot down near Gorazde, a French reconnaissance plane was fired upon and forced to land, and UN peace-keepers suffered one death and two injuries in the battle. It was clear from the extent of damage caused by the air raids that they were no more than a "symbolic shot across the bow."[55] Ironically, the strikes were so limited and ineffective that Mladic had reason to believe that further limited damage was sustainable, and that a victory in Gorazde was well worth the costs and risks. It marked the first time that the *capability* of U.S./NATO aircraft to impose unacceptable costs through air strikes, a key component of the deterrence/compellence strategy, was no longer a given. The episode also raised doubts as to the capacity of the UN, through the dual key approach, to provide effective air support to UNPROFOR troops.

On 22 April, NATO issued another ultimatum modeled after the successful Sarajevo exchange (7). This time a personal request by NATO Secretary-General Manfred Woerner (on 23 April) to authorize further air strikes was vetoed by Akashi on 25 April. Russia's acquiescence to the use of force against the Serbs and Russian Foreign Minister Andrei Kozyrev's statements at the time appeared to have some effect: the Bosnian Serb military command "criminally defied the elementary norms of humanity," and "the only alternative to air strikes (was) compliance by the Bosnian Serbs with their commitments."[56] Shortly after the statements were made, the Serbs agreed to a cease-fire and gradually withdrew their forces and weapons behind the exclusion zone once again.

Exchange 9

The cease-fire in place in Bosnia-Herzegovina since late December 1994 (brokered by Jimmy Carter) expired on 30 April.[57] Anticipating the end of the agreement, the Bosnian Serbs' shelling of Sarajevo increased to a rate of approximately 1,000 attacks per day. Lieutenant-General Rupert Smith, the UN Protection Force commander in Bosnia, ordered punitive air strikes against Bosnian Serb forces on 9 April. But this "show of resolve" collapsed after NATO bombers failed to find any target, and the mission was aborted. The bombardment around Sarajevo continued, and on 11 April the Bosnian government banned all outdoor gatherings and closed schools.[58] There was little impediment for the insurgent forces, since at the time, neither NATO nor the Bosnian government was preparing plans for another offensive strike. In two separate incidents (on 13 April and again on 18 April), three French UN peacekeepers were killed (the latest of thirty-three French soldiers to die since the war began in 1992). Five days later, the French prime minister, Edouard Balladur, publicly threatened to withdraw France's 4,530-member UN contingent unless three conditions were met: a stronger international commitment to extending the cease-fire in Bosnia-Herzegovina, improved security measures for UN peacekeepers, and clear and concise rules of engagement in dealing with hostile forces.[59]

The stipulations, however, were not forthcoming. Although the UN Security Council approved Resolution 988 on 21 April, thereby extending international sanctions against Yugoslavia for another seventy-five days, French demands for further international resolve remained idle. Moreover, the force of the resolution was compromised by the call from Chinese Foreign Minister Qian Qichen on 9 April to end the sanctions. A similar sentiment was echoed by the Russian State *Duma* (the lower house of the Russian legislature) on 14 April.[60] On 18 April, Senate Majority Leader Bob Dole fueled the trend when he led the Senate in voting to lift the UN arms embargo against the Bosnian Muslims, in direct opposition to French, British, and Canadian policy.[61] Faced with a mitigated UN commitment and divisions within NATO, and backed by the support of both China and Russia, Bosnian Serb leader Radovan Karadzic forced the closure of the Sarajevo airport on 22 April. Three more French soldiers were killed the very next day.[62]

Exchange 10

Completing an offensive that ended on 2 May, Croatian forces stormed across UN cease-fire lines and reclaimed a significant portion of territory held by Serb forces since 1991. A force of some 7,200 Croatian soldiers was backed by tanks, helicopters, and rocket launchers.[63] The clash over the western Slovenia enclave marked the heaviest fighting between Croatia and the rebel Serbs in nearly two years. Although the Croatian offensive raised the possibility of a return to full-scale war (only two days after the end of the cease-fire mandate), very little direct criticism was leveled against the Croatian government. The response of the international community was exemplified by U.S. State Department spokesman Nicholas Burns, who publicly stated that the United States did not believe "the situation ought to be changed by force."[64] The Bosnian Serbs retaliated with a rocket assault on Zagreb. A total of seventeen rocket-propelled shrapnel-spraying Orkan cluster bombs were fired, killing six people and injuring 175.[65] Although Serb officials claimed that the rockets had been intended for military targets, the U.S. ambassador to Croatia, Peter Galbraith, condemned the attacks as "a repugnant act clearly intended to kill many people."[66] In a related shelling of Karlovac and Sisak (with conventional artillery), 115 UN soldiers and civilian police officers were taken hostage.[67] Although widely acknowledged as an "unfortunate" event, the corresponding deterrent and compellent threats were never intense enough to be perceived by the insurgent forces as potentially costly. Reserved critique, and even ambivalence, pervaded the international community, and in the absence of clear retaliatory threat by the international community, both Croatians and Serbs not only continued fighting, but escalated hostilities.

Exchange 11

There was a pattern of increasing violence throughout April and early May, with the daily number of firing incidents in Sarajevo exceeding 2,000.[68] The fighting was highlighted by the shelling of a crowd of mainly Muslim soldiers and traders in the Butmir suburb of Sarajevo on 7 May. The attack, the worst on Sarajevo since February 1994, killed eleven people and wounded up to forty others.[69] UN military spokesman Lieutenant-Colonel Gary Coward indicated that a number of Serb heavy weapons were located within the twenty-kilometer exclusion zone around the city. Lieutenant-General Rupert Smith responded promptly by ordering punitive air strikes against Serb targets the following day, but his order was countermanded by UN Special Envoy Yasushi Akashi, fearing the vulnerability of UN peacekeepers.[70] Madeleine Albright, the U.S. permanent representative to the UN, and French Foreign Minister Alain Juppé led the criticism of the UN's failure to respond.[71] Mired by controversy and questions about why the UN was maintaining more than 30,000 soldiers in Bosnia and Croatia when they were able to do very little, UN Secretary-General Boutros Boutros-Ghali ordered a fundamental review of UN peacekeeping operations on 12 May. Skeptical of the UN's ability to establish a "credible front," the commander of French UN forces in Sarajevo, Major-General Hervé Gobilliard, instructed his troops to *avoid confrontation* with the forces of both the Bosnian Serbs and the Bosnian government.[72] Once again, faced with a lack of collective resolve, the absence of any retaliatory threats/actions by NATO or the UN for the May 7th assault and violation of the twenty-kilometer exclusion zone, and the defensive stance of the French, Bosnian Serb forces continued shelling the city of Sarajevo. On 16 May, five people were killed and twenty-six wounded in the aftermath of the approximately 800 explosions that were recorded.[73] UN officials considered the fighting to be the worst since 1993.[74]

Exchange 12

Serbian use of heavy artillery in the assault against Sarajevo escalated on 22 May when it was reported that, contrary to the Geneva convention, phosphorous shells were being used. A total of six people were killed and thirty injured.[75] Lieutenant-General Rupert Smith issued a formal ultimatum to both the Bosnian Serb and Bosnian government forces two days later, demanding that all heavy weapons within the twenty-kilometer exclusion zone be removed or surrendered to the UN. Smith warned of impending NATO-led air strikes if the arrangements were not met by noon on 25 May.[76] On the day of the deadline, NATO aircraft, predominately U.S. led, struck an ammunition dump near Pale, destroying two weapons bunkers in the process.[77] The attack was described by Lieutenant-Colonel Coward, the UN spokesman in Sarajevo, as "a significant military infrastructure target."[78] A second round of air strikes by NATO aircraft at Pale on 26 May destroyed six weapons bunkers.[79]

Although the effort was lauded by British and American officials, both the French and Russian foreign ministries condemned the action, maintaining that it produced "thoughtless risks" and was "misconceived."[80] Newly elected French President Jacques Chirac reissued warnings that the French would withdraw their troops if the United Nations continued to take inadequate steps to protect its peacekeepers. The rift in UN consensus regarding both the ultimatum and the consequent air strikes undermined not only UN credibility, but the capability of NATO to continue to wage an effective front. Motivated by their ability to defy UN demands, the Serbs retaliated by shelling five UN "safe havens" and conducting a massive bombardment of Tuzla in northern Bosnia-Herzegovina on the evening of 26 May.[81] In one of the worst atrocities of the war, 48 people were killed and more than 150 were injured.[82]

Exchange 13

On 11 July, Bosnian Serb forces captured the town of Srebrenica, a Muslim enclave and one of six UN-designated "safe areas." The assault began about five days earlier when close to 1,500 Bosnian Serb troops arrived in the city.[83] Two retaliatory actions/threats were issued in this exchange: a relatively weak NATO offensive designed to deter Bosnian Serb attacks, and a subsequent Bosnian Serb retaliatory threat to kill peacekeepers if the air strikes continued. The NATO offensive consisted of two relatively minor air strikes carried out by Dutch and U.S. aircraft, but a third sortie was abandoned when the Bosnian Serb military took peacekeepers as hostages. Unlike the NATO air strike threat, which lacked credibility once the third sortie was canceled, the threat to kill hostages satisfied all four prerequisites and succeeded in preventing further NATO air strikes at that time.[84] Srebrenica fell to the Bosnian Serbs shortly thereafter. On 24 July, Tadeusz Mazowiecki, the UN representative for human rights in the former Yugoslavia, resigned his post, citing what he called the international community's "hypocrisy" and the lack of resolve to deter insurgent forces from committing the atrocities in Srebrenica and Zepa.[85] The strongest reaction to the fall of Srebrenica came from French President Jacques Chirac, who chastised the UN for its military and political impotence in Bosnia, drawing parallels to the appeasement of Hitler in the 1930s.[86] With Srebrenica under Bosnian Serb control and Zepa already surrounded, the Bosnian Serbs moved to Bihac and Gorazde. Fighting continued and the war escalated.

Exchange 14 (a/b)

On 9 August, with the collaboration of French, German, Russian, British, and American efforts, the United States unveiled a new peace initiative based roughly on a 1994 proposal put forward by the Contact Group—the international body tasked with spearheading the West's approach to the situation in the former Yugoslavia and composed of the United States, the United Kingdom, France, Germany, Italy, and Russia. The plan outlined a territorial division designed to preserve the ratio of 49 percent of Bosnian territory for Serbs and 51 percent for a Muslim-Croat federation.[87] The Bosnian Serbs would be able to retain control of the recently acquired towns of Srebrenica (11 July) and Zepa (25 July), but the Muslims would be compensated with land around Sarajevo. The plan, introduced by Richard Holbrooke, then U.S. assistant secretary of state for European and Canadian Affairs, was gaining favor among the warring factions.[88] Hopes of an immediate peaceful resolution to the war, however, were shattered on the morning of 28 August when the Bosnian Serb military launched a single mortar shell near the Markale market in central Sarajevo, killing thirty-seven people and wounding approximately eighty other civilians.[89] The incident evoked memories of the Serbs' shelling of the same market in February 1994.[90]

Haris Silajdzic, the prime minister of Bosnia, set the stage for U.S.-led response by threatening to suspend his government's participation in the peace process until NATO clarified and reasserted its role in protecting Sarajevo as a UN-designated "safe area." Bosnian President Itzebegovic demanded that the UN establish a NATO-led rapid reaction force to respond to the "crime."[91] On 30 August, two days after the bombing, NATO launched a series of devastating air attacks on Bosnian Serb targets throughout Bosnia. Referred to as Operation Deliberate Force, the offensive amounted to the largest military operation undertaken by NATO since its formation in 1949.[92] Over a twelve-hour period, aircraft from five NATO countries (France, the Netherlands, Spain, the United Kingdom, and the United States) flew nearly 300 sorties.[93] Ninety radar, communication, missile, and artillery sites were hit across twenty-three target areas.[94] The strikes were part of an initiative to eliminate the capacity of the Bosnian Serbs to shell Sarajevo.

The U.S. State Department followed with a statement proclaiming that the Bosnian Serbs had "no military victory in sight for them."[95] French President Jacques Chirac echoed American sentiment the following day when he suggested that the bombing continue until "free access" to Sarajevo was guaranteed, and not just secured. In a statement issued on 30 August, Silajdzic described the NATO operations as "a very important step toward peace because it restored the *credibility* [emphasis added] of the international community."[96] Two days later, the Vatican gave support, in principle, to NATO bombing of Bosnian Serb targets in an effort to preempt further attacks on civilians.[97] On 10 September, the U.S. warship *Normandy* fired thirteen Tomahawk cruise missiles at Bosnian Serb targets. This was the first use of so-called "smart weapons" in the offensive and it received widespread media coverage.[98] In addition to international support, public interest and approval of the newest NATO assault strengthened allied resolve. By 13 September, NATO had carried out approximately 3,400 missions, including 850 bombing runs.[99]

On 14 September, nearly two weeks after its initial implementation, Operation Deliberate Force was suspended for three days following Bosnian Serb commitments to withdraw their heavy weapons from the twenty-kilometer exclusion zone around Sarajevo. The declaration was made by Karadzic and Mladic following negotiations in Belgrade, the Serbian capital. Russia, which had strongly condemned the resumption of NATO air attacks on 5 September, also announced its support for the latest deal. The sentiment was echoed by Russian Foreign Minister Andrei Kozyrev, who said the resolution offered "a quite realistic chance to overcome the stalemate over Sarajevo."[100] The first UN relief flight landed in Sarajevo on 15 September, and the following day, Serb forces began removing their heavy weapons (which Mladic had explicitly refused to do two weeks earlier).[101] By 21 September, the Serbs had removed some 250 heavy weapons from the "exclusion zone," and UN monitors were given unimpeded access to the area.[102] The fighting had stopped, and the peace process was well under way.

There were two stages to this particular exchange. Stage one (Exchange 14a) is unique in that it represents a failure of deterrence when all four conditions were met. Notwithstanding a series of devastating air attacks on Bosnian Serb targets (the largest military operation undertaken by NATO since its formation in 1949), Mladic refused to pull back. He was neither compelled to comply with NATO's key demands, nor deterred from committing further attacks in retaliation for the air strikes and bombing runs. Given failures during the previous four years of fighting, neither United States nor NATO had a very strong reputation for maintaining pressure on Mladic over the long run. Mladic, who at this point had very little to lose, assumed it was a matter of time before the air attacks would end, especially given Russian threats of intervention if the strikes continued.

Stage two (Exchange 14b) occurred when NATO resumed air strikes on 5 September, following a three-day delay to give Mladic time to comply with NATO demands. When those demands were not met, the attacks continued and were backed by artillery support from the Rapid Reaction Force and thirteen Tomahawk cruise missiles. The NATO assault received near universal acclamation, and on 14 September, the Bosnian Serbs capitulated to UN demands by withdrawing their heavy weapons from the twenty-kilometer exclusion zone around Sarajevo. A short-term deterrence failure in stage one, in other words, gave NATO an opportunity to demonstrate its resolve in stage two; how else would Mladic know whether the alliance was indeed committed to following through with the retaliatory threats? With all the prerequisites for deterrence and compellence met, the allied forces succeeded in ending nearly four years of war.

Three major events shifted the balance of power in the former Yugoslavia away from the Bosnian Serbs in 1995. First, the Krajina region was recaptured by Croatian and Bosnian government forces in one of the most significant losses by the rebel Serbs since the war began. The 200,000 refugees who are now relocating in Serb-controlled areas of Bosnia will further hamper any future Bosnian Serb military efforts.

Second, Karadzic lost his hold on power. He committed the biggest political blunder of his career by threatening to fire the Bosnian Serb general, Mladic, since few Bosnian Serbs shared his view of Mladic as a "psychopath" (at least none was willing to admit it in public). To make things worse for Karadzic, Milosevic joined the general in calling for the removal of the Bosnian Serb political leader, who had been criticizing Belgrade for not coming to the aid of Serbs in Krajina.

Third, General Mladic was no longer the invincible military tactician. In one week he managed to lose complete control over Krajina, give up the siege around the safe haven of Bihac, and was deterred from attacking Gorazde, thanks to a series of more credible threats of air strikes by NATO. Morale in the Bosnian Serb army fell, and the general struggled to contain his losses.

The most important lesson of the Bosnian war is that ethnic and religious divisions explained only why each side in the conflict was prepared to fight. But the actual level of violence in the region was a direct result of decisions by political and military officials. Mladic waged war with precise objectives in mind. Since these objectives depended on the likelihood of winning and losing particular battles, the Serb losses in Krajina forced the Bosnian Serb commander to begin thinking seriously about accepting the Contact Group plan presented at Dayton.

CASE STUDY: KOSOVO 1998–1999[103]

Exchange 1

Following a series of international condemnations and punitive sanctions against the Federal Republic of Yugoslavia (FRY) in the early months of 1998, international concern over growing violence in the province of Kosovo led to a more vociferous and threatening Western posture. At a meeting of European foreign ministers on 8 June, UK Foreign Secretary Robin Cook strongly hinted that Milosevic's continued aggression in Kosovo would not be without consequence: "I hope Milosevic is listening. This is the last warning. He should back off now."[104] Calls from the Contact Group for an immediate cease-fire, international monitoring, and talks toward a political solution followed shortly thereafter.

On 15 June 1998, as a result of mounting concern over the situation, NATO conducted major aerial exercises over Albania and Macedonia in a show of strength. Eighty-five aircraft from thirteen countries flew in Operation Determined Falcon, designed to "demonstrate that NATO is united in its commitment to seek a cease-fire and a cessation of hostilities [in Kosovo] and demonstrate its capacity to rapidly mobilize some very significant lethal capability,"[105] in the words of U.S. Defense Secretary William Cohen. Shortly after the exercises, Milosevic, following talks with Russian President Boris Yeltsin, agreed to meet with ethnic Albanian leaders, echoed a pledge to permit foreign diplomats to observe the situation, and promised Moscow (a traditional ally of the Serbs) that his government would try to assist the thousands of refugees generated by the crisis.[106] Later that month, U.S. envoy Richard Holbrooke—stating that the crisis was in a critical stage—failed to persuade Milosevic to reach a peaceful solution to the conflict. He mentioned, however, that NATO wasn't "bluffing" on its threat to use military force if the necessity arose.[107] On 24 June, UK Prime Minister Tony Blair warned that there remained the possibility of employing NATO air strikes against Serbia unless Milosevic withdrew from Kosovo as the alliance began to draft plans for the use of military force as a "final ultimatum." Nonetheless, reports from observers determined that NATO's show of force had little or no impact on the activities of Serbian security forces, who continued their crackdown on ethnic Albanians in the province.[108]

Although the demonstration of NATO airpower on 15 June was ample evidence of its capability to launch air strikes against the FRY, the Western powers only halfheartedly communicated real, credible threats to Milosevic. Furthermore, disagreement within the Contact Group over air strikes—namely from Russia—blunted the coherence of Western demands and their resolve, and thus the effectiveness of the threat of force in this exchange. At the end of the exchange, even while the violence continued in Kosovo, NATO air strikes were not considered by the Western powers as a serious option at that point in time.

Exchange 2

Escalating violence throughout the early months of 1998 broke out into an all-out Serb offensive against KLA separatists in June and July 1998. In early September it was evident that Serb military, paramilitary, and police units remained heavily engaged in "counterinsurgency" operations in Kosovo. Particularly distressing to the international community were reports of atrocities committed by Serb forces, including the razing of entire ethnic Albanian villages and a number of massacres that were forcing tens of thousands to flee their homes. As a result, on 23 September the UN Security Council adopted Resolution 1199, which demanded a cease-fire, condemned violence by "any party," and expressed "grave concern" over the "excessive and indiscriminate use of force by Serbian security forces."[109] The resolution invoked chapter 7 of the UN Charter, which hinted that further action was possible.

The threat of NATO intervention came soon afterward. The United States argued, contrary to Russian and Chinese claims, that NATO did not require further UN consent to use military force. Further, a number of NATO officials remarked that the alliance was completing plans for air strikes against Serbia. On 24 September the alliance approved an "activation warning" that authorized the Supreme Allied Commander Europe (SACEUR) to request the necessary forces to conduct military operations of a "limited" and more extensive "phased" nature against Serbia.[110] Later in the week, on 28 September, Milosevic announced that his forces were "victorious" in Kosovo and were returning to barracks. In response, U.S. Defense Secretary Cohen said there was no evidence that Serbia was beginning a strategic withdrawal or ending its military campaign against ethnic Albanian separatists. He warned Belgrade that failure to do so would result in NATO strikes.[111]

In early October, a massacre in which an estimated thirty-six ethnic Albanian civilians were killed by Serb forces resulted in further condemnation by the international community and shed doubt on Milosevic's claims that his forces were ending their operations in Kosovo. NATO faced a decision to commit to air strikes after UN Secretary-General Kofi Annan's report on the situation, and a number of officials made clear signals that the alliance was willing to use its considerable military strength in the region to affect an outcome. As the United States advised Americans to leave the FRY in anticipation of NATO military action, Secretary Cohen reportedly said that military strikes would begin soon. Secretary of State Albright mentioned that although the Western powers hoped for a negotiated solution to the crisis, the best way to press the issue was to back up diplomatic initiatives with the threat of force.[112]

On 6 October the Security Council reported that the FRY was not in full compliance with UN resolutions despite reports of a Serbian withdrawal from Kosovo. Furthermore, U.S. Special Envoy Richard Holbrooke reported continuing failure to persuade Milosevic to accept a political solution. At this juncture, U.S. President Bill Clinton made the most explicit statement of Western demands and threats thus far. Milosevic was required to unconditionally comply with Security Council demands by declaring an immediate cease-fire, pulling out Serbian security forces, allowing unhindered access to Kosovo for international relief organizations, and beginning negotiations with Kosovo Albanian rebels toward a political solution to the conflict. Clinton's statement that "NATO was prepared to act"[113] was reinforced by Secretary Cohen's statement that NATO possessed sufficient capability to inflict "substantial" losses on Yugoslav military capabilities from the air.[114] NATO Secretary-General Javier Solana further stated that the alliance stood ready to launch air strikes against the FRY in a matter of days, as the planning process was complete, and that an "activation order" would clear the way for the use of force. However, Solana refused to give a specific date for such an event. Last-ditch meetings between Holbrooke and Milosevic were reported to yield no progress, and Western countries began to advise their nationals to leave the FRY in advance of possible NATO action.

NATO's activation order came on October 13, which centralized NATO assets under the command of SACEUR and allowed for a limited program of strikes. (Although Italy and Germany—between governments at the time—had expressed their reservations about using force, their subsequent endorsement of the policy at the NAC meeting gave the order sealed alliance unity.) At the same time, however, the alliance announced a ninety-six-hour delay before launching air strikes. This came in the midst of confirmed reports that Milosevic was soon to agree on international requirements on the crisis in Kosovo, which were expanded to include allowing refugees to return to their homes as well as co-operation with the international war crimes investigators.[115] The next day an agreement was formally reached that called for the deployment of 2,000 unarmed observers under the aegis of the Organization for Security and Cooperation in Europe (OSCE) to verify Serb withdrawal, NATO reconnaissance overflights to supplement the OSCE mission, full refugee repatriation, and eventual negotiations between Milosevic and the ethnic Albanians, whose militant wing, the Kosovo Liberation Army (KLA), was committed to independence. The observers' safety and freedom of movement was also guaranteed. Milosevic responded by claiming that Serb units were withdrawing. He also told the Serbian public that military intervention had been averted and that the agreement would lead only to autonomy for Kosovo, not the full independence demanded by ethnic Albanian separatists. The threat of air strikes remained, however, as NATO gave Belgrade ninety-six hours to comply.

Despite the last-minute agreement between the FRY and the Western powers over the crisis, continuing violence and evidence of another Serb crackdown in Kosovo renewed NATO's threats to use force unless Milosevic came into full compliance. Western powers stated that they were not satisfied with the extent of Milosevic's withdrawal from Kosovo, and reminded Belgrade that NATO's activation order remained in force and gave it the authority to launch air strikes if it saw fit. SACEUR General Wesley Clark and U.S. envoy Christopher Hill gave Milosevic until 27 October to comply fully with the provisions of the agreement or risk NATO strikes.[116] Satisfied with Milosevic's "substantial compliance," NATO subsequently lifted the immediate threat of strikes on that date, but did not cancel it outright in order to "extend indefinitely the threat of strikes should Milosevic resume the campaign [in Kosovo]."[117]

NATO's activation order sent a clear signal to Milosevic that NATO's threat to use force was credible and resolute. The alliance's commitment to the threat of force to reinforce diplomatic initiatives succeeded in this case—albeit in a somewhat disjointed fashion—as Milosevic was given a clearly communicated set of coherent, realizable objectives, engaged by a credible threat of force from a highly capable military force, and faced with enough Western resolve (notwithstanding Russian objections) to sign on to the agreement brokered by Holbrooke. Although the situation lurched from crisis to crisis at first, steadily increasing and credible NATO resolve (to push Milosevic to the brink) and enough time and incentives to accept a political solution (to ensure that he did not step over the edge) assured that Belgrade would agree to the proposals on the table.

Exchange 3

Intensifying conflict between Serb forces and KLA rebels expanded into a crisis on 17 January after the discovery of the mutilated bodies of forty ethnic Albanians outside the village of Racak. The massacre and Serb attempts to hinder the verification mission resulted in swift international condemnation. More importantly, NATO held an emergency meeting to discuss any response to the massacre. It was identified as a clear violation of Serbia's commitments to NATO, and as such, the alliance demanded that the perpetrators of the massacre be brought to justice and permit war crimes prosecutors to conduct an investigation in addition to reiterating the provisions of the agreement struck between Serbia and NATO in October. The dispatch of two senior NATO generals and other officials to Belgrade soon after the massacre was intended to impress upon Belgrade the importance of living up to its commitments with NATO in addition to providing a "final" warning to both Milosevic and the increasingly unified and emboldened ethnic Albanian resistance.

The military option had thus been renewed: warnings that NATO would resort to air strikes to contain the situation and bring the Serbs into an acceptable level of compliance began to resound from various NATO and government officials. In addition to the statements made by Secretary-General Solana and Secretary of State Albright to the effect that the Serbs faced NATO action should Milosevic not comply with the October agreement, SACEUR noted after his meeting with Milosevic that the Yugoslav leader understood only the language of force, and thus it was upon the alliance to produce a credible military threat to the FRY.[118] As more NATO assets assembled in the region for possible use against targets throughout the FRY, the West ratcheted up the pressure on Milosevic, warning that his maneuverings to stay ahead of NATO air strikes left critical issues unresolved and risked the very action he was attempting to skirt.

At the same time, the situation was complicated by the growing strength and legitimacy of the KLA in Kosovo among ethnic Albanians. To engage this group of hard-line Kosovar separatists, the Clinton administration pressed them to support a realistic political settlement—one that gave Kosovo autonomy, not independence. Realizing that a political solution was necessary soon to avoid a deepening spiral of violence in Kosovo, the Contact Group struggled to bring the various parties to the negotiating table in France. To this end, threats of force were extended to the KLA as NATO warned both sides that they had "reached the limit."[119]

The turning point came on 29 January after two weeks of constant threats by NATO against both Belgrade and the KLA. The Contact Group gave the various sides three weeks (until 13 February) to reach a political solution to the conflict during talks at Rambouillet, France. They were then given another week to implement an agreement based on a Contact Group proposal calling for a "self-governing Kosovo" as well as demands that international verifiers and war crimes tribunal investigators be given full cooperation to maintain the cease-fire and answer questions about atrocities.[120] To that effect NATO issued an ultimatum consisting of a clear and direct warning of military intervention against both Serb and ethnic Albanian forces in Kosovo unless their respective negotiating parties came to an agreement on time.[121] The next day NATO removed the last constraints against military force to increase pressure on the warring parties. Soon after, both parties agreed to send high-level representatives to Rambouillet for talks, but Milosevic and several hard-line KLA officials refused to attend, sending aides to the negotiations instead. Despite this setback, however, a united front for urgent and comprehensive talks among the parties from the Contact Group and a credible, capable, and constantly communicated threat of force to reinforce the Contact Group's diplomatic pressure succeeded in bringing the various sides to the table.

Meanwhile, violence continued in Kosovo, as did Western threats of military intervention. Threats were especially leveled against Milosevic, who was under the most pressure to accept the Contact Group's proposals. Kosovo's autonomous status, the question of independence, and the deployment of an estimated 30,000-strong NATO implementation force remained the contentious issues. The latter was vigorously opposed by Milosevic, who categorically refused to permit foreign troops to operate on Yugoslav soil.[122] As the deadline for a solution neared, NATO stepped up threats to conduct military operations against the parties and backed them up by bringing more military assets into the region and planning for strikes. The United States in particular was pushing for immediate strikes should Belgrade block the agreement. The threats intensified as the deadline loomed and included direct warnings from Secretary-General Solana and President Clinton that strikes were imminent.[123] A clear signal was the evacuation of Western diplomatic and relief staff from the FRY.

Threats were effective at the very last minute: eleventh-hour progress at Rambouillet necessitated an extension of the deadline, and the threat of imminent strikes subsided. The two sides had agreed in principle to the other provisions of the accord, such as the plan for autonomy, but the Serbs continued to rebuff the military provisions of a NATO peacekeeping force. However, on 22 February the ethnic Albanian delegation failed to agree to the Contact Group proposals, essentially easing the pressure on Milosevic and negating the possibility of air strikes: NATO was unable to present a credible threat of compellence against Milosevic once the ethnic Albanian delegation had also rejected the proposed settlement. Although both parties eventually agreed to meet again in mid-March, only a rough, ambiguous "political framework" was established at

Rambouillet, which did not engage the question of NATO peacekeepers or the substantive questions surrounding autonomy. On 24 March NATO air strikes begin. On 9 April 1999, Kofi Annan made a statement establishing five conditions for an end to the conflict in Kosovo: an end to the violence; withdrawal of Yugoslav forces; deployment of peacekeeping force; return of refugees, and resumption of talks for a political solution. Finally, on 3 June the Serbian Parliament agreed to an international peace plan that committed Yugoslavia to withdraw all of its forces from Kosovo.

The credibility and resolve of the NATO threat to conduct air strikes was weakened to a certain extent by its extension to the KLA. Although threats of NATO action succeeded in bringing the various parties together, they had limited utility in successfully bridging the positions of the two sides during the negotiations. The intransigent positions of the respective parties—Milosevic's stance on NATO ground troops and the KLA's unwillingness to fully let go of independence—repeatedly frustrated Western efforts to bring the two sides together by joint diplomatic and coercive means. Although the capability of striking targets throughout the FRY was not questioned, the credibility of the threat and the resolve of the NATO allies to carry out that threat in the face of tortured yet recognizable progress toward an agreement was constantly challenged.

SUMMARY OF FINDINGS

As discussed in chapter 3, when the prerequisites for effective deterrence were satisfied, U.S., European, and NATO officials succeeded in mounting strong and credible threats of retaliation that controlled the fighting and produced cooperation on key demands in both Bosnia and Kosovo. When these prerequisites were absent or weak, the ability of NATO to control the fighting was weakened.

In general the findings indicate that deterrence and compellence, two abstract theories derived from the analysis of interstate relations in anarchy, continue to make important contributions to the study of international conflict, crisis management, and security policy in a post–Cold War world. With all of their faults, state-centric theories are as relevant to the study of ethnic conflict within states as they were to U.S.-Soviet relations since 1945. It would be dangerous, to say the least, to ignore the diagnostic and prescriptive qualities of deterrence and compellence theory if we are interested in managing or preventing the next ethnic war.

For example, decisions by FRY leaders to escalate the fighting in both Bosnia and Kosovo depended on the prospects of winning and losing particular confrontations. Whenever U.S. and European leaders mounted a prolonged and stable threat of retaliation (through NATO), backed by ultimatums, deadlines, and a clear commitment to punish, credibility was high and coercive diplomacy worked.[124]

Consistent with expectations, satisfaction of strategic requirements established the credibility of NATO threats and achieved immediate objectives. In Bosnia, when commitments were weak or ambiguous, the threats were challenged.

As failures mounted, the Serbs ignored subsequent efforts to stop the fighting until enough support was generated to mount the next clear retaliatory threat. In Kosovo, Milosevic showed even greater intransigence as he constantly probed for weaknesses in NATO's armor.

However, NATO's strategy in Kosovo was more successful than it was in Bosnia in part because the goal was also to demoralize the Serbian population and to demoralize the Serbian military through clearly defined and clearly articulated acts of compellence. An interesting question from the perspective of alternative strategies is whether a ground offensive would have achieved the same results since it would have much greater force on the ground to compel Milosevic to withdraw his troops. Consider the duration of a ground offensive against 40,000 troops in Kosovo, the collateral damage associated with that operation, the subsequent and far more costly (in terms of lives and money) operation against a few hundred thousand troops in Belgrade. This kind of compellance would certainly have taken longer than an eleven-week bombing campaign. (Consider also how long it was taking 40,000 Serb troops to get rid of a few hundred poorly equipped and poorly trained KLA troops.)

Consider the damage inflicted on Milosevic, the Serb military, Serb infrastructure, and the Serb people through the air campaign. That level of damage was sufficient in this case to compel Milosevic to cave in, so it serves as a fair representation of the critical point at which Milosevic calculated the costs of prolonging the conflict as too high. Using this level of damage as the critical benchmark (i.e., the point at which he decided that the costs of prolonging the conflict were too high), the key question is this: could any other strategy have produced the same cost calculus on the part of Milosevic, in the same period of time, without forcing NATO to suffer significant (and unacceptable) political and military costs in the process?

The claim that NATO failed to achieve its initial objectives because bombing didn't immediately result in the safe return of hundreds of thousands of refugees, or immediately stop the ethnic cleansing, or immediately resolve the conflict simply misses the point. A slightly more balanced assessment of the conflict shows that no strategy would have immediately achieved any of NATO's objectives. Similarly, a more balanced assessment of the situation would indicate that NATO achieved even its "initial" objectives: NATO prevented (and is preventing) more human suffering and more repression and violence against the civilian population of Kosovo; NATO curbed (and is curbing) the Serbs' capability of repressing the Kosovo Albanian population—and thus averted a humanitarian catastrophe.

The ground war option was unacceptable for several straightforward reasons, many of which are often ignored by critics of NATO's campaign. First, Milosevic would have "preferred" it—he needed a few hundred (if not a few thousand) little victories in the form of NATO casualties to sustain support for his fourth unsuccessful war in ten years. What better way to reinvigorate domestic support and morale levels in the military than by demonstrating that you aren't losing? If NATO's strategy ultimately worked by demoralizing the Serbian population, then sending in NATO ground troops would have had the exact opposite effect, by definition.

Milosevic would also have applied the lessons learned from the Bosnian war when contemplating responses to a NATO ground invasion. NATO's success at the end of the Bosnian conflict was helped in part by the fall of Krajina. This produced a mass exodus of approximately 250,000 Serbs from Krajina that overwhelmed the Bosnian Serb military. In addition to fighting Croats and Muslims, they had to deal with their own refugee problem. With that experience in mind, Milosevic would most certainly have attempted to create the same kind of problems for NATO during a ground offensive, forcing as many if not more Albanians to flee Kosovo and creating a humanitarian catastrophe that NATO would have to add to its problems. There is absolutely no reason to believe that a ground invasion would have resulted in any less of a humanitarian catastrophe; indeed, given the probability of collateral damage in a ground invasion, a far more compelling case can be made to suggest that the disaster would have been much worse.

There were also several tactical problems with the ground war option. In addition to gaining control of heavily fortified Serb centers in Preshtina, Dakovica, Srbica, and Decani, NATO presumably would have had to control villages held by the KLA. But how exactly was NATO supposed to deal with the KLA, successfully battle 40,000 well-armed and hunkered-down Serb troops, safeguard innocent Kosovars, and prevent ethnic cleansing, all while trying to limit collateral damage and NATO casualties? How many fewer targets would the air force have had if NATO troops had been deployed on the ground? How long would it have taken NATO to control all of Kosovo in preparation for invading Serbia and facing another 100,000 Serb troops? Political and military leaders were led to believe (based on the evidence available at the time) that air strikes were the least bad of several very bad options.[125]

With respect to the application of coercive diplomacy and NATO's use of communication and signaling, NATO military officials never promised that the air campaign would bring a "quick" acceptance of NATO's demands. Evidence from exchanges during the escalation phase of the Kosovo crisis (from January 1998 through 23 March 1998—that is, as the air strike option was being assessed, selected, threatened, and then used) indicates that the only comments coming out of the State Department, the Pentagon, European capitals, and NATO during this period were that this would be a long process, encompass three phases, and continue as long as required to achieve the stated objectives. Everyone was hopeful it would end quickly, but very few (if any) strategists predicted a quick outcome. Even fewer officials in the United States, NATO, Britain, France, Germany, or Canada accepted the assumption (or made the argument) that this would be an easy campaign. In fact, the reason NATO pursued the three-stage bombing campaign in the first place, beginning with attacking air defenses to gain air superiority (and not Serb troops in Kosovo), was precisely because Serbia (unlike Iraq or the Bosnian Serbs) was a formidable enemy. It was never treated as anything else. The target list was expanded in phase two as NATO established more secure air space over Kosovo, Serbia, and Montenegro. In the traditional spirit of planning for worst-case scenarios, NATO/U.S. military planners constantly referred to the fact that Serbia was a formidable enemy and that the campaign would have to be handled in that context.

Moreover, there were no "sharp" or meaningful divisions in NATO that would have given Milosevic misleading signals. A "sharp" division in NATO would have included a decision by one or more NATO allies to defect from the air campaign strategy. It didn't happen. A "sharp" division in NATO would have included a decision by one or more NATO allies to back off from their commitment and/or contribution to the air effort. It didn't happen. A "sharp" division would have included at least one statement by at least one NATO ally suggesting that the air campaign would fail or that using ground troops was the better option. None of this occurred. Even the British camp (the strongest supporters of ground troop mobilization) didn't break ranks regarding the utility of air strikes. The most impressive thing about the NATO campaign was the unanimity expressed by alliance members and the extent to which they stayed the course.

RESPONDING TO CRITICS

The critique of rational deterrence constitutes one of the most comprehensive and sustained attacks on a "theory" in the field of international relations, a theory that many still believe is a sound, parsimonious, policy-relevant explanation of both human-social and military-strategic behavior. The attempt to identify the theoretical problems that plague the theory's behavioral assumptions,[126] the methodological errors embedded within a great deal of deterrence literature,[127] and the practical problems associated with implementing deterrence as a strategy[128] encompass the main thrusts of the critique. As Fischoff (1987, 73) claims in his summary of the findings from this body of work, "deterrence emerges as a shabby parody of a scientific theory. Its fundamental behavioral assumptions are wrong. Its basic terms are ill-defined. It is used in inconsistent and contradictory ways. Commonly cited examples of effective deterrence are often based on flawed readings of history, sometimes reflecting ignorance, sometimes deliberate misrepresentation." Like Fischoff, many remain convinced that these findings provide more than enough evidence to discard deterrence as a weak, if not irrelevant, theory of crisis management behavior.

We have argued in this chapter that contrary to Fischoff, research programs dealing with deterrence and crisis management offer very useful illustrations of so-called "dominant concerns of the past" that critics claim are no longer useful for understanding "new" threats to peace and security. Since deterrence is a relatively abstract theory derived from analysis of states in anarchy, and since both anarchy and states are themselves becoming obsolete, state-centric, rationalist models such as deterrence cannot possibly offer any insight into post–Cold

War problems of intrastate and interethnic conflict. On the other hand, a very strong commitment to sovereign statehood remains a common objective for both old and newly developing states. Writing more than forty years ago, Arnold Wolfers concluded that "psychologically, nothing is more striking today than the way in which men in almost every part of the world come to value those possessions upon which independent national statehood depends . . . [and] are willing to make the most sweeping sacrifices of their own well-being as private individuals in the interest of their nation."[129] Furthermore, ethnic nationalist movements—often noted as increasingly important "non-state" actors—seek statehood, not transformation of the system. To claim that the Bosnian Serbs and Kosovo Albanians, for example, do not represent states in the conventional sense is true but misleading, especially within the context of crisis and war where these groups possess armies, political and military representatives, institutions of government (e.g., Bosnian Serb and Kosovo parliaments), and territorial claims. This is precisely why theories such as deterrence continue to be useful for describing, explaining, and perhaps even predicting events in the former Yugoslavia and Kosovo.

NOTES

1. Frank Harvey, "Rational Deterrence Theory Revisited: A Progress Report," *Canadian Journal of Political Science* 28 (September 1995): 403–436; Frank Harvey and Patrick James, "Nuclear Deterrence Theory: The Record of Aggregate Testing and an Alternative Research Agenda," *Conflict Management and Peace Science* 12 (1992): 17–45; "Nuclear Powers at the Brink: Toward a Multi-Stage Game of Crisis Interaction," *International Political Science Review* 17, no. 2 (1996): 197–214.

2. For example, NATO air strikes were used to deter the Bosnian Serb military from attacking peacekeepers and shelling UN-declared safe havens. Later in the crisis the Bosnian Serb military used UN peacekeepers as hostages (or human shields) to deter further NATO air strikes.

3. Carefully separating threat/counterthreat sequences to allow researchers to pinpoint aspects of behavior conforming to a direct or extended immediate deterrence or compellence encounter is difficult, if not impossible, to accomplish with any degree of empirical precision. Crises frequently encompass several different types of interactions.

4. A sample of cases must be alike in theoretical terms to be comparable. As Huth and Russett point out, "the fundamental differences in the policy instruments used by state A to deter, and the types of policy actions being considered by state B, suggest that theoretical propositions on success or failure in one class of cases cannot readily be applied to other cases. . . . State B may be vulnerable to military retaliation by state A but may not be vulnerable economically" (Huth and Russett, "Testing Deterrence Theory," 473). Gordon Craig and Alexander George provide a practical example of this complexity in their study of the 1973 Yom Kippur war in *Force and Statecraft: Diplomatic Problems of Our Time* (New York: Oxford University Press, 1990).

5. For an excellent discussion of these and other problems with aggregate tests of deterrence theory, see Jack Levy, "When Do Deterrent Threats Work?" *British Journal of Political Science* 18 (1988): 485–512; Robert Jervis, "Deterrence Theory Revisited,"

World Politics 31 (1979): 289–324; and Patrick Morgan, *Deterrence: A Conceptual Analysis* (Beverly Hills: Sage Publications, 1977). The controversy surrounding judgments about success and failure has received detailed treatment elsewhere (see references in note 1). See also the special issue of the *Journal of Social Issues* 43 (1987). The most apparent problem is the tendency to select cases that disprove the theory. Selection bias occurs because it is easier to identify deterrence failures, given the nature of the evidence required to establish that threats succeeded—challengers may never have intended on challenging in the first place, so the failure to mount a challenge cannot count as an instance of successful deterrence. On the issue of selection bias, see Christopher Achen and Duncan Snidal, "Rational Deterrence Theory and the Comparative Case Studies," *World Politics* 41, no. 2 (January 1989): 143–169.

6. Each research enterprise—aggregate data analysis, as applied by Huth and Russett, or structured, focused comparison, as used by Lebow and Stein—manifests the problems that will face any framework that focuses on success versus failure. For a discussion of research enterprises, see Patrick James, "Structural Realism as a Research Enterprise: Toward Elaborated Structural Realism," *International Political Science Review* 14 (1993): 123–148. For details on structured focused comparison, see Alexander George and Richard Smoke, *Deterrence in American Foreign Policy*.

7. Huth and Russett, "Testing Deterrence Theory," 475.

8. Although this distinction is useful, some exceptions should be noted. If state A threatens retaliation to contain the spread of violence in a crisis, does this constitute an attempt to deter escalation or compel compliance with demands to keep the fighting to a minimum? Similarly, does one deter a state from rejecting the latest peace proposal, or compel leaders to accept it? Did the United States threaten Serbia with economic sanctions in order to compel its leaders (Milosevic) to endorse the Vance-Owen plan, deter undesired actions in the form of Serbia's rejection of the accord, or compel Milosevic to deter Karadzic from escalating Bosnian-Serb attacks on Muslim enclaves? These questions are especially relevant in the case of the former Yugoslavia because the coercive threats attempted to accomplish more than one objective: deter escalation, particularly with respect to ethnic cleansing, through the creation of "safe havens" and "no-fly zones," and compel the Bosnian Serbs to accept Vance-Owen or at least return to the bargaining table. Even a straightforward threat linked to protection of safe havens is problematic. Were the Americans and Europeans (through NATO) trying to compel the Serbs to back away from territory bordering these "safe" areas, deter them from crossing the exclusion zone and/or shelling the city, or both? The issue becomes even more confusing when one considers encounters that constitute examples of successful deterrence but failed compellence, and vice versa. A major advantage of looking at crisis in terms of separate and distinct exchanges is that it offers an opportunity to look for both types of interaction in the same case, thus avoiding the need to make judgment about motives and intentions across the entire crisis.

9. The approach may bias case selection toward identifying failures, but if behavior in a crisis is consistent with expectations, notwithstanding this selection bias, that is all the more reason to accept the theory.

10. Audience costs affect the credibility of a retaliatory threat and are usually produced by (*a*) the act of signaling (e.g., "burning bridges," Spence 1973), and (*b*) the act of backing down (Fearon 1994). If a defender is expected to suffer enormous costs from backing down, the threat is likely to be more credible to the defender.

11. A few notes about "commitment" are in order. Rational deterrence theory stip-

ulates that the challenger will assess the costs and benefits of inaction versus action depending on, among other things, a critical judgment by the challenger of the defender's commitment to its threat. However, cases cannot be selected on the basis of whether there was a serious commitment by the defender to retaliate, because this would naturally bias the results in favor of successful deterrence. See Fearon, "Signaling Versus the Balance of Power and Interests," for an excellent discussion on this point. When assessing the defender's commitment to respond, a challenger will consider the severity of its challenge in terms of the defender's political and security interests. Consequently, challenges are often tailored in such a way that retaliation is deemed by the defender to be unnecessary, as demonstrated by the use of limited probes by the Bosnian Serbs to test NATO's resolve. Refer to George and Smoke, *Deterrence in American Foreign Policy*, for examples of limited probes in deterrence failures.

12. George and Smoke's (1974) excellent study of deterrence assesses the impact of several other factors from the perspectives of defender and challenger by focusing on their respective cost calculations. Included among variables tied to success are the initiator's belief that the *risks* of the challenge are calculable and controllable, and the challenger's comparison of the *costs* of a challenge versus the status quo. More often than not, however, these additional variables are embodied within deterrence strategies as different representations of the four core prerequisites specified here (a point discussed in more detail in the conclusion). Moreover, to the extent that there are other factors, they are usually considered "minor" in comparison (George and Smoke 1974: 530–532).

13. For current research on how post-1945 civil wars end, see Roy Licklider, ed., *Stopping the Killing* (New York: New York University Press, 1993); "The Consequences of Negotiated Settlements in Civil Wars, 1945–1993," *American Political Science Review* 89, no. 3 (1995): 681–690; and William Zartman, *Elusive Peace: Negotiating an End to Civil Wars, 1995–1996* (Washington, DC: Brookings Institution, 1995).

14. Dick Zandee, Disarmament, Arms Control, and Cooperative Security Section: Political Affairs Division, North Atlantic Treaty Organization, Brussels, letter to author (June 1995).

15. Alan Cowell, "NATO Jets to Enforce Ban on Illegal Bosnia Flights," *New York Times*, 12 April 1993, A8.

16. Paul Lewis, "Top Bosnian Serb Facing U.S. Action, Signs a Peace Plan," *New York Times*, 3 May 1993, A1, A10.

17. Keesing's Contemporary Archives reported on 4 December 1993 that fifty-six civilians were killed in a single shelling in Srebrenica, 39426–39427.

18. *New York Times*, 18 April 1993, A16.

19. This prompted speculation that U.S. officials were worried about the precedent a stronger statement would set for Israeli compliance with similar UN resolutions.

20. John Darnton, "Leader of Bosnian Serbs Remains Firmly Against Peace Plan, Despite UN Pressure," *New York Times*, 19 April 1993, A14.

21. Previously, on 2 April 1993, the Bosnian Serb Assembly rejected a UN resolution allowing for conditional acceptance of the Vance-Owen plan, with hard-line members dismissing as unacceptable the proposed allocation of only 43 percent of territory to Serbs, compared with 70 percent currently occupied (Keesing's, 4 April 1994, 39425–39426). Many analysts interpreted the Bosnian Serb decision as a calculated gamble that the West would remain tentative in their response and that there would be no direct international military intervention.

22. Stephen Kinzer, "Serbs Attack Muslim Stronghold in Northwest Bosnia," *New York Times*, 28 April 1993, A11.

23. Elaine Sciolino, "Bosnia Rivals Set New Talks as U.S. Weighs Action Plans," *New York Times*, 30 April 1993, A1, A7.

24. As Karadzic prepared for a new round of negotiations, the military continued to shell Sarajevo, Srebrenica, and Bihac. Michael Gordon, "Clinton Says U.S. Pressure Nudged Serbs Back to Talks," *New York Times*, 1 May 1993, A6.

25. George and Smoke, *Deterrence in American Foreign Policy*.

26. Thomas L. Friedman, "Bosnia Air Strikes Backed by Clinton, His Officials Say," *New York Times*, 2 May 1993, A1, A12.

27. Paul Lewis, "Top Bosnian Serb Facing U.S. Action, Signs a Peace Plan," *New York Times*, 3 May 1993, A1, A10.

28. Stephen Kinzer, "Serbs Reject Bosnia Pact, Defying Friends and Foes and Insist on Referendum," *New York Times*, 6 May 1993, A1, A16.

29. Frank J. Prial, "Resolution Establishes Safe Areas But Lacks Enforcement Provision," *New York Times*, 7 May 1993, A11.

30. "The White House was not in the grip of war planning and there (were) no special deployments of American aircraft or military personnel in preparation for action in Bosnia." Thomas L. Friedman, *New York Times*, 9 May 1993, A1.

31. *New York Times*, 8 May 1993, A4.

32. Major-General J. A. MacInnis, Land Force Atlantic Area Headquarters, Halifax, letter to author, November 24, 1994.

33. For details, see the Report of the Secretary-General Pursuant to Security Council Resolutions 982 (1995) and 987 (1995), United Nations, 5 May 1995.

34. Keesing's, July 1994, 39563–39564.

35. United Nations Human Rights Commission statement, Geneva, 8 July 1993.

36. Steven A. Holmes, "U.S. May Attack Serbs Even Without NATO," *New York Times*, 2 August 1993, A3.

37. Craig R. Whitney, "NATO to Join U.S. in Planning Air Strikes Against Serb's Forces," *New York Times*, 3 August 1993, A1.

38. Douglas Jehl, "U.S. Turns Bosnia Threat Into Near Ultimatum," *New York Times*, 4 August 1993, A1.

39. John F. Burns, "Dawn Brings a Ray of Hope to a Newly Silent Sarajevo," *New York Times*, 4 August 1993, A8.

40. Douglas Jehl, "Serbs Must Withdraw Promptly or Face Air Strikes, U.S. Insists." *New York Times*, 12 August 1993, A1.

41. David Binder, "U.S. Renews Warning to Serbs on Sarajevo Shelling," *New York Times*, 19 October 1993, A8.

42. According to Keesing's, 18 October 1994, 39695, Clinton publicly criticized his European allies for inaction.

43. R. W. Apple, "NATO Again Plans Possible Air Raids on Serbs in Bosnia," *New York Times*, 12 January 1994, A1.

44. Keesing's, 7 February 1994, 39870.

45. Ibid.

46. John Kifner, "Serbs Agree to Give Up Sarajevo Guns," *New York Times*, 10 February 1994, A14.

47. The large-scale withdrawal of Serb equipment, described by Lieutenant General Rose as "an exodus," began on 17 February, after Yeltsin's controversial decision to

send Russian troops to the region. His objective was to fill the vacuum left by Bosnian Serbs in the exclusion zone. Keesing's, 10–17 February 1994, 39871.

48. John Kifner, "U.N. Reports Serbs Are Pulling Back Around Sarajevo," *New York Times*, 18 February 1994, A1.

49. Stephen Cohen, *New York Times*, 20 February 1994, A1.

50. Bosnian Serb troops began bombarding the enclave in late March, stepping up the assault on 4 April, and breaching the Bosnian government front lines on 5 April when several villages were seized. Fighting resumed on 8 April after a twenty-four-hour cease-fire. On 10 April there was another Serb offensive involving tanks, infantry, and artillery bombardment on Gorazde. Keesing's, 4–8 April 1995, 39966.

51. Keesing's, 3 April 1995, 39966.

52. Paul Lewis, "U.N. Warns Serbs on Gorazde; Move Could Lead to Air Strikes," *New York Times*, 10 April 1994, A1.

53. Chuck Sudetic, "2 NATO Jets Bomb the Serbs Besieging a Bosnian Haven; U.S. Warns of More Strikes," *New York Times*, 11 April 1994, A1, A6.

54. Chuck Sudetic, "U.S. Planes Bomb Serbian Positions for a Second Day: Serbs Voicing Defiance," *New York Times*, 12 April 1994, A1, A10.

55. Michael R. Gordon, "The Bluff That Failed," *New York Times*, 19 April 1994, A1.

56. Keesing's, 25 April 1995, 39967.

57. Keesing's, April 1995, 40511.

58. Ibid.

59. Ibid.

60. Ibid., 40512.

61. *New York Times*, 18 April 1995, A25.

62. Since punitive strikes were ordered and NATO bombers failed to find any target, the condition was not met—NATO did not have the capability to carry out the threat. But such a conclusion would be misleading. After the first mission was aborted, there were no preparations for successive strikes. It stands to reason that if further strikes were ordered, there would have been substantial costs levied against the Bosnian Serbs (as was the case in previous offensives).

63. Keesing's, May 1995, 40565.

64. Ibid.

65. Ibid.

66. Ibid.

67. *New York Times*, 2 May 1995, A1, A3.

68. Keesing's, May 1995, 40563.

69. *New York Times*, 8 May 1995, A3.

70. Keesing's, May 1995, 40563.

71. Ibid.

72. Ibid.

73. Ibid.

74. This is the most striking case of allied fragmentation. Lieutenant-General Rupert Smith responded to Serb shelling of Sarajevo on 7 May with an order for punitive air strikes. But his order was countermanded by the UN special envoy, fearing the vulnerability of UN peacekeepers. A number of questions were raised concerning not only the logic of Akashi's decision, but the mandate of the UN as well. The controversy culmi-

nated in UN Secretary-General Boutros Boutros-Ghali's order for a fundamental review
of UN peacekeeping operations a week later.

75. Keesing's, May 1995, 40564.

76. *New York Times*, 25 May 1995, A14.

77. *New York Times*, 26 May 1995, A1.

78. Keesing's, May 1995, 40564.

79. Ibid.

80. Ibid.

81. Although the coding of this exchange is identical to the previous one, the encounter is of a different variety (because of its complexity). A series of NATO-led air
strikes struck an ammunition dump near Pale. Following retaliatory attacks by Serb forces
against five UN "safe havens," a second round of air strikes by NATO aircraft saw the
destruction of six weapons bunkers. Although the effort was lauded by British and American officials, both the French and Russian foreign ministers condemned the action.
France reissued its warnings that it would withdraw French troops. Obviously, little
resolve was demonstrated by the allied powers, and so this criterion was coded as "No."

82. Keesing's, May 1995, 40564.

83. Keesing's, August 1995, 40688.

84. Ibid.

85. Ibid.

86. Ibid.

87. Ibid., 40690.

88. *New York Times*, 18 August 1995, A4.

89. Keesing's, August 1995, 40690.

90. *New York Times*, 29 August 1995, A1.

91. Keesing's, August 1995, 40690.

92. Ibid., 40691.

93. Ibid.

94. Ibid.

95. Keesing's, August 1995, 40691.

96. Ibid.

97. *New York Times*, 1 September 1995, A10.

98. Keesing's, August 1995, 40735. In coordination with NATO, the UN Rapid
Reaction Force (comprising Dutch, French, and British units) fired hundreds of artillery
rounds on Bosnian Serb mortar emplacements and ammunition dumps around Sarajevo.

99. Ibid.

100. Ibid.

101. Ibid.

102. Ibid.

103. The authors would like to thank Hasit Thankey for his assistance in compiling
the information for these exchanges.

104. *Keesing's Record of World Events*, June 1998, 42356.

105. "NATO Demonstrates Firepower over Balkans," *CNN Interactive*, 15 June 1998,
<http://cnn.com/WORLD/europe/9806/15Ikosovo/index.html>. Accessed 14 February
1999.

106. "Milosevic Reportedly to Hold Talks with Kosovo Albanians," *CNN Interactive*,
16 June 1998, <http://cnn.com/WORLD/europe/9806/16fkosovo/index.html>, and *Facts
on File*, vol. 58, no. 3003, 25 June 1998, 440. The ethnic Albanians' rejection of Mil-

osevic's overtures to hold talks further destabilized the situation, leading to a tightening of Belgrade's grip on the region.

107. "Holbrooke Meets with Milosevic at Critical Moment," *CNN Interactive*, 23 June 1998, <http://cnn.com/WORLD/europe/9806/23Ikosovo/index.html>. Accessed 14 February 1999.

108. *Keesing's Record of World Events*, June 1998, 42356.

109. Ibid., September 1998, 42520.

110. "NATO Steps Towards Kosovo Action," *BBC Online Network*, 24 September 1998, <http://news.bbc.co.uk/hi/english/world/europe/newsid_179000/179156.stm>. Accessed 29 January 1999.

111. "U.S. Warns Milosevic: Follow Through on Troop Withdrawal," *CNN Interactive*, 28 September 1998, <http://cnn.com/WORLD/europe/9809/27~kosovo.html>. Accessed 18 January 1999.

112. "UN Condemns Kosovo Atrocities," *BBC Online Network*, 2 October 1998, <http://news.bbc.co.uk/hi/english/world/europe/newsid_184000/184698stm>. Accessed 29 January 1999.

113. "Clinton: 'Time Is Now to End Violence in Kosovo,' " *CNN Interactive*, 6 October 1998, <http://cnn.com/WORLD/europe/9810/06/kosovo.03/index.html>. Accessed 18 January 1999.

114. "NATO Strike Prospect Raised as Milosevic Refuses to Back Down," *CNN Interactive*, 6 October 1998, <http://cnn.com/WORLD/europe/9810/06/kosovo.03/index.html>. Accessed 18 January 1999.

115. "Countdown Begins to Kosovo Strikes," *BBC Online Network*, 13 October 1998, <http://news.bbc.co.uk/hi/english/world/europe/newsid_192000/92253.stm>. Accessed 29 January 1999.

116. "Milosevic: Yugoslavia Is Committed to Peace in Kosovo," *CNN Interactive*, 21 October 1998, <http://cnn.com/WORLD/europe/9810/21/kosovo.01/index.html>. Accessed 23 October 1998.

117. "NATO Lifts Air Strike Threat Against Yugoslavia," *Facts on File*, vol. 58 no. 3021, 29 October 1998, 764.

118. "U.S. to Push NATO to Issue Ultimatum to Milosevic," *New York Times on the Web*, 21 January 1999, <http://search.nytimes.com/search/daily/bin/getdoc-I-site+site_27171+59+2AAA+Kosovo>. Accessed 14 February 1999.

119. "West's Plan for Kosovo Talks Get Frigid Reception," *CNN Interactive*, 27 January 1999, <http://www.cnn.com/WORLD/europe/9901/27/kosovo.01/index.html>. Accessed 21 February 1999. The Contact Group was temporarily split on this matter, but the American position of extending the threat of force to both sides in order to compel negotiations won out in the end.

120. "Three Week Deadline over Kosovo," *BBC Online Network*, 29 January 1999, <http://news.bbc.co.uk/hi/english/world/europe/newsid_2000/265277stm>. Accessed 29 January 1999.

121. Ibid. See also "NATO Authorizes Airstrikes to Stop Kosovo Violence," *CNN Interactive*, 30 January 1999, <http://cnn.com/WORLD/europe/9901/30/kosovo.02/index.html>. Accessed 21 February 1999.

122. "Milosevic: No Foreign Troops," *BBC Online Network*, 17 February 1999, <http://news.bbc.co.uk/hi/english/world/europe/newsid_281000/281045.stm>. Accessed 20 February 1999.

123. "NATO Mobilizes Forces as Kosovo Deadline Nears," *CNN Interactive*, 18 February 1999, <http://cnn.com/WORLD/europe/9902/18/kosovo.03/index.html>. Accessed 21 February 1999. See also "Clinton Warns Serbs," *BBC Online Nework*, 19 February 1999, <http://news.bbc.co.uk/hi/english/world/europe/newsid_282000/282801.stm> Accessed 20 February 1999.

124. Thomas G. Weiss, "Intervention: Whither the United Nations," *The Washington Quarterly* 17 (1994): 109–128. Lincoln P. Bloomfield, "The Premature Burial of Global Law and Order: Looking Beyond the Three Cases from Hell," *The Washington Quarterly* 17 (1994): 157, makes a similar argument: "If the European powers (and the United States) had moved early to confront the latter-day vandals off Dubrovnik, or to actively protect relief supplies and UN peacekeepers at Sarajevo airport when first fired upon, or had consistently punished violations of their no-fly zones, things might have turned out differently."

125. Even if we accept critics' estimates of the low "kill" ratio of NATO bombs, the logical conclusion is that it took far less damage than expected to force Milosevic to cave in—all the more reason to applaud NATO's choice of strategies. Moreover, if Serb Mig fighters and tanks were kept hidden, the key tactical point the critics miss is that this equipment was rendered irrelevant to the war effort. All of these tanks and planes played a much smaller role in the fighting and ethnic cleansing than they did prior to NATO strikes, because the Serb military understood the risks of using and losing them. Some critics claim it would have been more "moral" for NATO to send in ground troops, but those who make that argument rarely (if ever) explain why it would have been more "moral" to lose more lives in a protracted war. No political leader should be prepared to accept civilian or military casualties simply for the sake of proving that they are prepared to accept casualties. If the best option (that is, the one most likely to achieve the stated objectives in the shortest period of time) also happens to be the one with the lowest risk of body bags, then it should be the preferred policy.

126. Many of the problems were illustrated in two symposiums in the *Journal of Social Issues* (1987) and *World Politics* (1989). The key question addressed in the latter was whether or not states behave in accordance with the logic stipulated in standard applications of rational deterrence theory. Achen and Snidal (1989, 143–169), relying almost entirely on the axiomatic (deductive) method borrowed from microeconomics, provided evidence that states generally do behave according to that logic. On the other hand, George and Smoke (1989), Jervis (1989), and Lebow and Stein (1989b), approaching the subject from an inductive perspective, provide convincing evidence from comparative case studies that rational deterrence is unrealistic, a conclusion that is reevaluated in this study.

127. The following are included among the works reviewed by Lebow and Stein: Russett (1963), George and Smoke (1974), Organski and Kugler (1980), Huth and Russett (1984, 1988), and Kugler (1984). Their criticisms, however, can be applied to a number of other aggregate studies of rationality and deterrence (e.g., Fink 1965; de Mesquita and Riker 1982; Weede 1981, 1983; Petersen 1986; and Betts 1987).

128. Key problems with testing deterrence theory, or implementing deterrence strategy, are covered in George and Smoke (1974), Jervis (1979), Jervis, Lebow, and Stein (1985), Levy (1988), Zagare (1990, 1996), Harvey and James (1992), Fearon (1994), and Zagare and Kilgour (1998).

129. Arnold Wolfers, "The Actors in International Politics," in *The Theory and Practice of International Relations*, ed. David McLellan, William Olson, and Fred Sonderman (Englewood Cliffs, NJ: Prentice-Hall), 8–19.

5

Predicting Success and Failure: States versus Institutions

INTRODUCTION

International institutions and individual states are under a great deal of pressure to manage and even resolve ethnic conflicts. This perceived responsibility for preserving human rights and political stability is unlikely to go away. A perceived long-term decline in the utility of unilateral interventions toward cost-effective multilateral preventive strategies creates the need to coordinate military actions with diplomatic communications, information, and analysis. This kind of cooperation is made difficult by a limited ability to demonstrate clear resolve and identify objectives, especially when the number of actors involved expands beyond a very few.

Yet there is no definitive evidence on when and under what conditions third parties (states or institutions) should intervene to prevent ethnic tensions from escalating out of control, or how to manage crises when they do. Nor do we clearly understand the conditions under which deterrent and compellent threats (or any form of coercive diplomacy, for that matter) will succeed or fail, or how credibility and resolve are influenced by (*a*) the *type of intervener*, (*b*) the *type of conflict*, or (*c*) the *stage* at which the intervention takes place.

Preventive strategies include a full range of political, diplomatic, and military instruments (Lund 1996). Primary goals should be to (*a*) act prior to the outbreak of armed violence; (*b*) encourage alignments based on interests other than ethnicity; (*c*) reduce conflict between groups; and (*d*) deter regional adventurism, which can result in interstate crisis.

With these points in mind, this chapter addresses two key questions: (1) are some third-party interveners more capable than others of deterring ethnic challenges, and (2) are some third-party interveners more capable than others of controlling violence and achieving key objectives if and when deterrence fails?

Answers to these questions are becoming crucial at a time when theory and policy on early warning and conflict prevention are being criticized for their lack of cumulation and their inability to overcome analytical gaps. With respect to deterrence theory and strategy, the most widely researched form of coercive diplomacy, there are few clear and consistent findings. Without an empirical base to evaluate the conditions under which coercive diplomatic strategies are likely to succeed, answers to pressing questions about the onset, escalation, and prevention of ethnic conflict and violence will remain elusive. This chapter provides evidence on (*a*) the success rate of different types of interventions, and (*b*) the impact of different types of conflict on the probability of successful intervention. The model is presented in the next section, followed by a discussion of assumptions and specification of propositions.

We argue that prevention is crucial in the management of today's conflicts but that there is rarely a collective political will to act prior to the outbreak of violence. On average, states are better equipped to respond to and prevent certain conflicts because they can overcome some problems related to political will. However, certain kinds of conflicts, specifically ethnic ones, make satisfying the prerequisites for successful deterrence difficult. When leaders are convinced that they cannot satisfy these prerequisites, they simply ignore early warnings of impending violence.

Apart from this introduction, the chapter unfolds in five sections. In the second section, we develop a model of operational conflict prevention based on insights from deterrence theory. In the third section we derive propositions from the model and place them in the context of intrastate and ethnic conflict. The fourth and fifth sections of the chapter explain our methodology and test the propositions against the quantitative evidence. The sixth section draws some conclusions and identifies areas for further research in the context of early warning and conflict prevention.

A MODEL OF DETERRENCE

John Ruggie (1993a, 1993b) developed a theory of deterrence to clarify the strategic dimensions of third-party military intervention. Addressing the problem within the context of UN activity in Bosnia, Ruggie argued that there is a need to fill the "doctrinal void" between peacekeeping and peace enforcement. Missions that involve goals clearly beyond those of traditional peacekeeping, such as seeking to neutralize local forces and push belligerent parties toward the negotiating table, require different strategies. Ruggie proposed that international forces be given the means and mandate to "deter, dissuade and deny" (D^3) the use of force by local protagonists (Ruggie 1993a, 1993b). If deterrence of violence fails, Ruggie argues, deployed forces can attempt to dissuade parties from continuing military activities. Failure on this level necessitates the use of force to deny any one side military victory in a conflict. Carment and Rowlands (1998), building on work by Ruggie, contend that by presenting a credible military threat, a third-party force seeks to convince all conflictual parties that violence will not succeed. International force is brought to bear to neutralize the local forces and to reduce the expected gains of continued fighting. The political objective is to prevent local force from becoming the successful arbiter of disputes and to persuade combatants that they have no viable alternative but to reach a third-party assisted negotiated settlement. The intended effect is to deny victory to any one group in order to create the military stalemate on which negotiated settlements often depend. To ensure credible effectiveness, coalition forces must not only decide whether to escalate their intervention, but also consider the degree of coercion to apply.

Whether the lead role is played by an institution or state actor, deterrence theory stipulates that a retaliatory threat will succeed if (A) leaders define the unacceptable behavior and communicate to challengers a commitment to punish violations, (B) the threatened punishment is severe enough to deny the challenger the objectives sought, (C) the deterring state possesses the means (capability) to do so, and (D) leaders demonstrate the resolve to carry through with the threat (Lebow and Stein 1989a, 1990).

Resolve is most effectively demonstrated through costly signals—that is, any action, statement, or condition that increases the political, economic, or military costs associated with the status quo while lowering the costs of responding to a challenger's probes. Resolve is enhanced in one or more of the following ways: *actions* (e.g., deployment of air, sea, or ground forces; evacuation of peacekeepers from safe havens, thus allowing a more decisive air-strike response to probes); *statements* (e.g., public announcements—promises—of impending retaliation; using explicit ultimatums and deadlines; public displays of unity among coalition members in support of response); *domestic support for retaliation* (e.g., public opinion; positive domestic and international press coverage). If these conditions (A–D) are satisfied, the expected net costs of the threatened sanction (to the challenger) should be greater than the expected net gain of noncompliance, because the punishment (if carried out) would prevent the challenger from achieving intended goals. If these requirements are met, but the behavior still occurs, that would constitute a case of failure, both in theory and strategy. On the other hand, if one or more of the conditions are not satisfied, the theory predicts failure in most cases. In other words, even clear and credible threats will fail if the challenger believes the challenge is worth the risks and political, military, or economic costs incurred by triggering the threatened response.

Our model builds on Regan's (1996a) study of utility estimates of challengers faced with a threat of third-party intervention. According to Regan, when contemplating a challenge, a typical challenger's preference ordering is

$$Us > Ubd > Ui$$

Where

Ubd = utility (payoff) to challenger for backing down in the face of third-party threat.[1]

Ui = utility (payoff) to challenger if intervention takes place.[2]

Us = utility for a successful challenge (with no intervention).

And z = probability that the third-party intervener will intervene if challenge takes place.

If $Ubd > z(Ui) + (1 - z)(Us)$ then the challenger is expected to back down and deterrence succeeds. Based on this preference order, Regan (1996a, 14) argues that the critical risk for the challenger is $z > Us\text{-}Ubd/Us\text{-}Ui$—"when the right hand side of the inequality is greater than z, the challenger will not be deterred by the threat (that is, violence will escalate); when the right hand side of the inequality is smaller than z, the challenger will succumb to the threat (deterrence succeeds)." By implication, the intervener can manipulate the challenger's critical risk on two dimensions: by increasing the utility to the challenger of backing down in the face of a threat (Ubd), thus decreasing the value of the numerator in the equation; or by decreasing the utility to the challenger of the intervention (Ui), thus increasing the value of the denominator.

We make two interrelated arguments in this context. First, the challenger's utility estimates are directly related to the *type of third-party intervener* (state versus international organization) and the *type of conflict* (intrastate versus interstate, ethnic versus nonethnic). Both of these factors have an impact on the challenger's utility estimates (and critical risk), because the prerequisites for successful deterrence are more or less present, depending on the type of intervener and dispute in question.

Second, in line with conventional wisdom, we argue that crises occur through phases (Kriesberg 1997; Dixon 1996; Lund 1996a). Although Regan's model is very useful for understanding a challenger's decision calculus during the onset phase (that is, before intervention takes place), a slightly different set of utility (and critical risk) estimates are likely to be made by the challenger once an intervention takes place, during the peak or crisis phase of the conflict. The revised preference order for the challenger, then, is

$$Usi > Us > Ubd > Ui > Ubdi$$

Where

Ubdi = utility to challenger for backing down in the face of third-party intervention.

Us = utility to challenger of a successful challenge without intervention.

Ui = utility to challenger of not backing down following third-party intervention.

psi = probability that third party will succeed in preventing escalation.

Usi = utility to challenger of successfully challenging third party.

Uui = utility to challenger of unsuccessful challenge.

The challenger will back down during the peak or crisis phase when Ubdi>
psi(Uui) + (1 − psi)(Usi).[3] The revised critical risk for the challenger following
intervention (based on the above preference order) is z>Usi-Ubdi/Usi-Uui. Once
again, there are two ways to improve the chances of deterrence success at this
stage of the crisis: (a) by increasing the numerator (that is, the utility of backing
down after intervention), and/or (b) by decreasing the denominator (that is, decrease the utility of an unsuccessful challenge).[4] As deterrence theory stipulates,
both of these can be accomplished if the third-party intervener satisfies key
prerequisites for successful deterrence as specified in the previous chapter. However, the ability to satisfy these conditions varies with the *dispute profile*—the
type of conflict and the *type of intervener*.[5] The next section outlines key assumptions and propositions derived from the model.

ASSUMPTIONS AND PROPOSITIONS

In order to compare the success rates of third-party state versus international
organization intervention into ethnic conflict, we begin with the following two
assumptions: (1) the probability of successful third-party intervention depends
on the ability of the third party to satisfy all four prerequisites for successful
deterrence: communication, commitment, capability, and resolve; and (2) states
are more capable than international organizations of satisfying more of these
prerequisites more often.

Successful intervention is measured with reference to controlling violence and
outcome. With respect to controlling violence, Regan (1996a, 17) makes a compelling case for why violence is an appropriate indication of success or failure:
stopping the violence usually is a key motivating factor for most interveners.
Decisions to intervene are often based on some perceived political need for
immediate results. Most declarations and public statements tend to focus on
stopping the violence, so we can assume that this is a common goal. The cessation of hostilities is usually required to initiate meaningful dialogue in an effort
to resolve a dispute.

Regan argues that in all interventions a single underlying goal is present: the
implementation of a strategy that will bring an end to hostilities: "[t]he key to
any intervention strategy is to alter the calculations by which the antagonists
arrive at particular outcomes . . . [t]he goal is to make it too costly for the combatants to continue fighting" (Regan 1996b, 341). Based on these assumptions,
and the basic tenets of deterrence theory, the following propositions about the
effectiveness of third-party intervention are tested:

Proposition 1: *Ethnic* crises are more likely than *nonethnic* crises to be violent.

Proposition 2: *Intrastate* crises are more likely than *interstate* crises to be violent.

Proposition 3a/b: States are more likely than IOs (international organizations) to control hostilities in both *ethnic* and *nonethnic* crises.

Proposition 4a/b: States are more likely than IOs to control hostilities in both *intra-* and *interstate* crises.

Proposition 5a/b: State and IO intervention is more likely than state-only or IO-only intervention to control hostilities in *ethnic* and *nonethnic* crises.

Proposition 6a/b: State and IO intervention is more likely than state-only or IO-only intervention to control hostilities in *intrastate* and *interstate* crises.

These propositions are not intended to be exhaustive. They serve only as a list of expectations derived from deterrence theory and the model outlined above. Moreover, the evidence is intended to be indicative rather than definitive. For example, empirical support for these propositions can help to estimate the probability of successful intervention across different conflict profiles.

Figure 5.1 is used to illustrate one possible rank ordering of conflict scenarios that could be produced through these tests. They are listed in order of probability of success. The logic associated with this particular rank ordering can be explained thus: If the conflict is interstate and, for example, based on territory, we would expect greater success, because clearly defined rules and procedures are in place to help states negotiate these kinds of settlements—that is, states are recognized actors with legal personality.

At the other end of the scale, intrastate ethnic conflicts are usually associated

Figure 5.1
Probability of Success

State intervention into interstate nonethnic conflict   ------ highest success

State intervention into intrastate nonethnic conflict,

IO intervention into interstate nonethnic conflict,

IO intervention into intrastate nonethnic conflict,

State intervention into interstate ethnic conflict,

State intervention into intrastate ethnic conflict,

IO intervention into interstate ethnic conflict,

IO intervention into intrastate ethnic conflict   ------ lowest success with ambiguous and indecisive results, such as compromise or stalemate, symbolizing an unresolved conflict. Subsequent crises and violence are anticipated by all adversaries. Ethnic conflicts are more difficult to deter than nonethnic conflicts, given restraints on satisfying the capability and communication prerequisites.

Not surprisingly, many of the ethnic conflicts examined by Brecher and Wilkenfeld (1997) have violent triggers. This points to the inherent problem in deterring any intrastate conflict—the clear lack of enforcement of any solution and the lack of restraints on violence (Lund 1996a). However costly and irrational it appears in human and material terms, violence is a means of regulating behavior, forging identities, creating a shared history, and safeguarding long-term political and economic outcomes. Therefore, commitment to a negotiated solution as opposed to violent measures is highly dependent on the problem of "agency." In ethnic disputes in particular, leaders must be convinced of a settlement's long-term viability and must also convince their followers of its merits.

Under such circumstances, third parties have a primary interest in stopping the killing and in containing and reversing the spread of internal unrest. Where consent is absent, violence is widespread, and groups are at risk, third-party force may come into play. Under such conditions, third parties are likely to be required to take on multiple functions, including peacekeeping and possibly peace enforcement. Missions that involve goals clearly beyond those of traditional peacekeeping, such as seeking to neutralize local forces and push belligerent parties toward the negotiating table, require different strategies and tactics. Using force entails a different kind of bargaining strategy with hostile militias. Such strategies are suited to relatively narrow time frames within each phase of a conflict (Lund 1996a). The receiving end needs to reflect on the action being undertaken and the costs associated with challenging that action.[6]

METHODOLOGY AND OPERATIONALIZATION OF VARIABLES

This study isolates the influence of three separate factors on the level of violence in a crisis: (1) the type of third party, (2) the presence of ethnic conflict, and (3) interstate/intrastate dimension. It relies on the actor level data from the International Crisis Behavior (ICB) project (Brecher and Wilkenfeld 1991, 1997). ICB data provide a wide range of cases and variables that permit an evaluation of crises rather than data that focus exclusively on violent events, most notably war. Indeed, many crises are managed successfully without recourse to violence. Among other important indicators, the data also provide the number of states involved, the nature of the threat, and issues over which the crisis arose. Such information is vital in determining whether the conflict is intrastate or interstate, ethnic or nonethnic.

A two-stage content analysis for each crisis was carried out. Each crisis was coded as either intra- or interstate respectively and ethnic or nonethnic respectively. In each case, the situation must include a foreign policy crisis for at least one state (please see Brecher and Wilkenfeld 1997 for coding procedure). The ICB project's definition refers to "a situation with three individually and collectively sufficient conditions, deriving from changes in a state's internal or external environment. All three perceptions are held by the highest-level decision-makers of the actor concerned: a threat to basic values, awareness of finite time for response to the value threat and a high probability of involvement in military hostilities" (Brecher and Wilkenfeld 1991).

In *Crisis, Conflict and Instability* Michael Brecher and Patrick James argue that intrastate conflicts are defined by political, economic, and social upheavals at the domestic level. In other cases "external crises have fueled the fires of internal disruption" (1989, 91). A conflict was deemed intrastate if (*a*) it involved a single crisis actor and the trigger to the conflict came from within that state, or (*b*) it involved multiple crisis actors and the trigger to the conflict came from within a single state.

Each crisis was also coded on the basis of whether ethnic conflict was deemed to be a salient factor in the conflict. Such conflicts may or may not involve the use of force and politically mobilized, well-organized, ethnic insurgency movements (see Brecher and Wilkenfeld 1997). The nonethnic conflict category consists of political, military, and ideological wars. There is some consistency in recent research to justify this separate category. For example, Licklider (1995) distinguished between identity civil wars and political/economic wars. Similarly, Regan (1996b), using three categories, separates religious wars from ethnic wars and ideological wars. Of course some ideological conflicts carry with them a heavy ethnic component, and not all ethnic conflicts are about differences in identity.[7]

The independent variable, type of intervener,[8] is identified by whether the highest crisis management technique was implemented by a state or by an international organization (regional or global).[9] The ICB variables that focus on global organization and regional organization involvement identify the content of UN or regional organizational (RO) involvement during an international crisis.[10] A similar coding was used to identify state involvement.

In this analysis, third-party involvement was taken to mean a perceptible form of action. Both Dixon (1996) and Regan (1996a, b) provide insight into the impact of the intervener's actions on the party against whom action is directed. Interveners were not judged to be involved if they simply expressed concern, raised the issue at the UN, or expressed verbal support or condemnation of one crisis actor.[11] More active forms of involvement were necessary. This included sending a mediation or investigative team (not necessarily a successful one), active participation in negotiations, sending troops, or overtly threatening to become involved if measures weren't taken.

It should be noted that a fair test of the propositions requires that we compare the relative effectiveness of different interveners (state versus international organization [IO], the independent variable) when one and/or the other is highly involved in the crisis. If we don't control for "high" intervention, it is difficult to know whether the variation on the dependent variable (cessation of violence or outcome) is the result of the intervener or the intervention (low, medium, high). By selecting only those cases in which the intervener is highly involved, it is much easier to make straightforward comparisons without having to deal with issues related to intensity. To determine which actor was most involved, the ICB profiles were assessed to get a sense of the level of UN/RO involvement. This coding was compared with the level of state involvement after reading the ICB case summaries and articles from *The Economist* relevant to the cases. Each crisis was assigned an intervener code based on which third party was judged to be most active in the crisis.[12]

With respect to the dependent variable success/failure, most studies have equated deterrence failure with the outbreak of war and other forms of violence. Although this is crucial for tests of deterrence, a greater role should be reserved for the achievement or denial of the intervener's and challenger's policy interests and objectives (Kugler 1984; Huth and Russett 1984, 1988, 1990). Clearly, if third parties manage to control violence by threatening intervention, but fail to (*a*) obtain policy objectives in that process, or (*b*) prevent the challenger from obtaining its goals, deterrence cannot be regarded as completely successful. As Huth and Russett (1990) argue, cases of successful deterrence should include instances in which the challenger did not resort to military force and did not coerce the third-party intervener into capitulating to its demands. Similarly, deterrence failures should include cases in which the challenger either attained its policy goals or resorted to the sustained use of force. In sum, it is not only the costs of "violence" that are considered in a decision maker's utility calculus, but the costs associated with overall "victory" and "defeat." Therefore, although the occurrence (or nonoccurrence) of war and major hostilities is an important indicator, valid testing requires a research design that specifies a range of dependent variables, including goal achievement, to determine whether interactions among states confirm the logic derived from the theory.

We use two indicators of success, *violence* and *outcome*, both operationalized using ordinal variables from ICB. Violence is assessed in terms of the intensity (or severity) from no or low clashes to full-scale war. For the purposes of this analysis we have dichotomized the severity of violence to identify those crises that managed to avoid severe violence and those that did not. With respect to outcome (i.e., achievement or nonachievement of goals and/or objectives in the crisis), "perceptual" measures are utilized. The intervener's level of satisfaction, upon termination of the crisis, is used to represent whether the disputants were either all or partially satisfied. Again the variable is dichotomized.

ANALYSIS OF DATA

We begin with the question of how third parties (interveners) control violence in different settings. Ethnicity and location can be viewed as later and separate factors in the model to help us establish how they affect violence, given that we also want to know how well third parties (the key variable) function in different settings.

Propositions one and two are supported by the data described in Table 5.1. When compared with nonethnic and interstate cases, the percentage of crises experiencing violence increases for disputes with ethnic or intrastate dimensions. Compared with the overall percentage of violent crises (58.3), the percentage of violent ethnic (69.0) and intrastate (86.4) disputes is higher, whereas the percentage of violent nonethnic (50.4) and interstate crises (53.9) is lower.

Change in Percentage of Violent Crises (from Table 5.1)

Conflict Type

Ethnic	10.7% higher
Nonethnic	7.9% lower
Intrastate	28.1% higher
Interstate	4.4% lower

Propositions three, four, and five also appear to be supported by the data (described in Tables 5.2 and 5.3). Consistent with expectations about the relative capacity of different interveners to deter hostilities, the number of violent crises is lower when states *and* IOs are involved together—35.5 (state and IO), 43.7 (state only), 77.3 (UN only) and 53.8 (RO only). The same trend is produced when controlling for conflict type (see Table 5.2), with the exception of intrastate cases. In these cases, RO intervention alone appears to be more likely to avoid violence than any other form of third-party involvement—79 percent (RO), 100 percent (UN only), 85.7 percent (state and IO), and 80 percent (state only).

Sole involvement by the UN is the least effective form of third-party intervention. Compared with state-only intervention, for example, the frequency of violent cases actually increases when the UN is the sole intervener—by 33.6 percent (from 43.7 to 77.3) across all crises, by 29 percent in ethnic crises, by 34 percent in nonethnic crises, by 20 percent in intrastate cases, and by 35 percent in interstate cases. On the other hand, when states join the UN in making a significant contribution to the peacekeeping/peacemaking effort, the frequency of violent conflicts tends to drop—by 41.8 percent (from 77.3 to 35.5) across all crises, by 27 percent in ethnic crises, by 49.9 percent in nonethnic crises, by 14.4 percent across intrastate cases, and by 44 percent in interstate disputes. The findings suggest that state involvement appears to add another, more credible and potent dimension to the deterrent threat. UN involvement alone is especially problematic for ethnic and intrastate cases. Protracted ethnic conflict in Bosnia

Table 5.1
Violence and Conflict Type

	All Crises	Ethnic	Non Ethnic	Intrastate	Interstate
Level of Violence:					
No Violence	41.7	31.0	49.6	13.6	46.1
	(265)	(83)	(182)	(11)	(251)
Violence	58.3	69.0	50.4	86.4	53.9
	(370)	(185)	(185)	(70)	(293)
Number of Crises	635	268	367	81	544

Notes: 1. Cell entries are percentages.
2. Numbers in parentheses show the number of observations.
3. All reported differences are statistically significant to at least the $\rho = 0.001$ level by Pearson's χ^2 test.

Table 5.2
Third-Party Involvement and Percentage of Violent Crises

	All Crises	Ethnic	Non Ethnic	Intrastate	Interstate
Third-party Most Involved:					
State and IO	35.5	54.2	23.7	85.7	29.6
	(62)	(24)	(38)	(7)	(54)
State	43.7	51.9	38.6	80.0	38.3
	(71)	(27)	(44)	(10)	(60)
UN	77.3	81.4	73.6	100.0	73.6
	(207)	(97)	(110)	(24)	(178)
RO	53.8	70.0	45.2	79.2	48.3
	(143)	(50)	(93)	(40)	(118)
Number of Crises	635	268	367	81	544
Measures of Statistical Association					
χ^2	53.42	14.47	39.45	5.57	49.09
ρ	0.0000	0.0059	0.0000	0.2340	0.0000

Notes: 1. Cell entries are percentages.
2. Numbers in parentheses show the number of observations.
3. The Pearson χ^2 is the reported measure of statistical association along with the corresponding level of statistical significance, ρ.
4. The total number of crises (635) includes both violent and nonviolent crises. Column observations refer only to violent crises.

Table 5.3

Percentage of Nonviolent Crises and Third-Party Involvement

Third-party Most Involved:	All Crises	Ethnic	Non Ethnic	Intrastate	Interstate
State and IO	64.5	45.8	76.3	14.3	70.4
	(62)	(24)	(38)	(7)	(54)
State	56.3	48.1	61.4	20.0	61.7
	(71)	(27)	(44)	(10)	(60)
UN	22.7	18.6	26.4	0.0	26.4
	(143)	(97)	(110)	(24)	(178)
RO	46.2	30.0	54.8	20.8	51.7
	(207)	(50)	(93)	(24)	(118)
No Third-party	47.4	37.1	56.1	18.8	50.7
	(152)	(70)	(82)	(16)	(134)
All	41.7	31.0	49.6	46.1	13.6
	(635)	(268)	(367)	(81)	(544)
Number of Crises	635	268	367	81	544
Measures of Statistical Association					
χ^2	51.50	13.32	37.73	47.83	5.56
ρ	0.0000	0.0050	0.0000	0.0000	0.1000

Notes: 1. Cell entries are percentages.
2. Numbers in parentheses show the number of crises for the given category.
3. The Pearson χ^2 is the reported measure of statistical association along with the corresponding level of statistical significance, ρ.

serves well to illustrate how the UN, and associated UN-Charter limitations, may (and often do) undermine efforts by external states to deter hostilities or resolve conflicts. When external states provide the military backing to support UN threats and resolutions, violence is less likely.

The next stage in the analysis compares zero-order correlation between type of intervener and outcome with the results produced when "ethnicity" and "type of conflict" are introduced as controls. We rely on Cramer's V and Goodman and Kruscal's gamma statistics, commonly used for drawing inferences about the relationship between nominal and ordinal variables, respectively. Cramer's V transforms χ^2 into a single measure between 0 and 1, which, although crude, offers a basic measure of association between type of intervener and violence. The gamma statistic represents the proportion (percentage) of errors reduced when predicting values on the dependent variable, violence, given information on the independent variable, type of intervener.

The results for both sets of statistics (outlined at the bottom of Table 5.3) are strong and significant across each category. A more meaningful assessment of

Table 5.4
Probability of Severe Violence Logit Regression Parameter Estimates

Control Characteristics	Parameter Estimates/ Standard Errors
Reference Crisis (Constant): (No Third-party, Interstate, Non Ethnic)	-0.3858* (0.1897)
Third-party Interveners: (Interstate, Non Ethnic)	
State & IO Mediated Crisis	-0.7296* (0.3296)
State Mediated Crisis	-0.3952 (0.3074)
UN Mediated Crisis	1.1299* (0.2423)
RO Mediated Crisis	0.0127 (0.2486)
Crises Characteristics: Intrastate Crises (No Third-party, Non Ethnic)	1.839* (0.3491)
Ethnic Crises (No Third-party, Interstate)	0.7666* (0.1823)
Number of Crises: Percentage of Correct Predictions:	635 68.32

Notes: 1. "*" denotes a parameter that is significant at the 5 percent level.
2. Numbers in parentheses are standard errors.
3. Control characteristics in parentheses denote the reference crises.
4. Mediated is used here to include coercive forms of intervention.

propositions three to five, however, can be obtained by observing the influence "ethnicity" and "conflict type" have on the strength and direction of the relationship between intervener and violence. The results indicate that third-party interventions into "ethnic" crises are more likely to function as standard applications of deterrence theory—the relationship between intervener and outcome (as predicted by the rank ordering on the independent variable) is stronger for "ethnic crisis" (gamma = .22; p < .005). In other words, state *and* IO intervention together is more likely than state-only or IO-only intervention to control violence, but more so when the crisis is characterized by ethnic conflict.

Table 5.5
Probability of Severe Violence Logit Regression Predicted Probabilities

Control Characteristics	Probability of Severe Violence (in Percent)
Reference Crisis (Constant): (No Third-party, Interstate, Non Ethnic)	41.0
Third-party Interveners: (Interstate, Non Ethnic)	
State & IO Mediated Crisis	25.1
State Mediated Crisis	31.8
UN Mediated Crisis	68.2
RO Mediated Crisis	41.3
Crises Characteristics:	
Intrastate Crises (No Third-party, Non Ethnic)	81.4
Ethnic Crises (No Third-party, Interstate)	59.9

zero order	gamma = 0.16	p<.0001
Nonethnic	gamma = 0.14	p<.0001
Ethnic	**gamma = 0.22**	**p<.005**
Interstate	gamma = 0.16	p<.0001
Intrastate	**gamma = −0.19**	**p<.1**

With respect to comparing interstate and intrastate crises, the results appear, once again, to support the proposition that intrastate crises are more difficult than interstate crises to manage according to standard application of deterrence. As we move from interstate to intrastate cases, our ability to predict violence levels based on the type of intervener actually increases, but in the opposite direction—we can eliminate 19 percent of the error when predicting violence levels if we reverse the rank ordering on the independent variable from the order specified by the deterrence model. Regional organizations (ROs) are likely to play a more productive role than external states or international organizations (IOs) when controlling intrastate violence. There may be a selection effect here.

Table 5.6
Logit Regression Estimated Change in Probability of Severe Violence

Control Characteristics	Change in Probability of Severe Violence
Reference Crisis (Constant): No Third-party, Interstate, Non Ethnic	0.0
Third-party Interveners: (Interstate, Non Ethnic)	
State & IO Mediated Crisis	-15.9
State Mediated Crisis	-9.1
UN Mediated Crisis	27.3
RO Mediated Crisis	0.3
Crises Characteristics: Intrastate Crises (No Third-party, Non Ethnic)	40.4
Ethnic Crises (No Third-party, Interstate)	18.9

Insofar as more violent disputes may be referred to the UN, it is possible that less intense disputes are those addressed by ROs, whereas the global organization is burdened by the weightier issues.

The crosstabs and correlations of each effect in isolation show the impacts of each factor to be fairly strong, but the analysis should not stop there. Since all the factors operate simultaneously to determine the level of violence, the influences might be confounded by the crosstabs. The *relative magnitudes of each effect* are hard to determine by examining only one factor in isolation. The third stage of our analysis applies logistical regression to compare probabilities of violence across categories of third-party intervention. The regression aspires to explain violence as the result of all influences operating simultaneously. In addition, the statistical strength of the relative influences can also be assessed.[13]

The results, specified in Table 5.4 and summarized in Tables 5.5 and 5.6, support the rank ordering stipulated in propositions three to five. The probability of violence is lowest, for example, when states and IOs intervene together, and highest when IOs are involved without significant state military or political intervention. The relative magnitudes of the parameters are of some interest.

The parameter estimates show that the factor most strongly associated with an increase in the level of violence is whether a crisis is internal or external. The characteristic most strongly associated with decreased levels of violence is joint mediation by both states and IOs. The significance levels indicate that state-mediated crises don't differ appreciably from unmediated crises, nor do RO-mediated crises.

Table 5.5 uses the logit parameters to make some inferences about the probabilities of severe violence in crises with certain characteristics, based on the following formula for converting the logit parameters into probabilities—that is,

$$\text{Prob of Violence} = 1/(1+e-^{(\text{constant}\ +\ \text{controls})}); \text{ where } e=2.7182.$$

For instance, for the reference crisis, the probability of severe violence would be

$$\text{Prob of Violence} = 1/(1+e-^{(-0.3658)}), \text{ or 41 percent}$$

For a state- and IO-mediated crisis, the probability of severe violence falls to 25.1 percent—$1/(1+e-^{(-0.3658\ -\ 0.7296)})$. An analogous series of calculations produced the other percentages, which reflect the signs and magnitudes of the logit parameters. Internal crises are strongly associated with violence, whereas state- and IO-mediated crises are more associated with nonviolent action.[14]

The percentages generated in Table 5.5 were used for Table 5.6. It shows the difference in the probability of violence for the various categories of crises relative to the reference case. We know the probability of violence for the reference crisis (unmediated, nonethnic, external) is 41.0 percent. And we also know the probability of violence for a state- and IO-mediated crisis is 25.1 percent. The increase in violence associated with moving from an unmediated (non-ethnic, external) crisis to a state- and IO-mediated (nonethnic, external) crisis is 41.0 − 25.1= 15.9 percent. This table most directly shows the relative influences of each factor.

Tables 5.7–5.8 were produced by controlling for ethnicity and location. The results, once again, are consistent with the rank ordering stipulated in the propositions. Internal and ethnic conflicts appear to be managed more effectively by states. In general, these logit runs are very helpful with respect to isolating the influence of three "separate" factors on the level of violence in a crisis: (1) which third party, (2) ethnicity, and (3) location. In this case, ethnicity and location are viewed as two separate factors in the model to help establish how each affects violence compared with, say, the type of intervener. Of course, an equally relevant and important question is this: how do third parties control violence in different settings? Put differently, we know the relative importance of, say, state and IO intervention compared with ethnicity (−0.7296 versus 0.7666)

Table 5.7
Probability of Severe Violence Logit Regression Parameter Estimates

Control Characteristics	Parameter Estimates				
	1	2	3	4	5
	All	External	Internal	Ethnic	Non Ethnic
Reference Crisis (Constant):	-0.3858*	-0.3526*	0.7431	0.3218	-0.3456
(No Third-party, Interstate, Non Ethnic)	(0.1897)	(0.1931)	(0.7755)	(0.2627)	(0.2275)
Third-party Interveners:					
(Interstate, Non Ethnic)					
State & IO Mediated Crisis	-0.7296*	-0.8494*	0.8028	-0.2775	-1.1154*
	(0.3296)	(0.3501)	(1.311)	(0.4927)	(0.4693)
State Mediated Crisis	-0.3952	-0.4414	0.3721	-0.4196	-0.3821
	(0.3074)	(0.3222)	(1.0774)	(0.4744)	(0.4026)
UN Mediated Crisis	1.1299*	1.062*	8.9882	0.9794*	1.2199*
	(0.2423)	(0.2464)	(32.8142)	(0.3716)	(0.3161)
RO Mediated Crisis	0.0127	0.0343	0.1480	0.2402	-0.1130
	(0.2486)	(0.2575)	(0.8566)	(0.4118)	(0.3165)
Crises Characteristics:					
Intrastate Crises	1.839*	-	-	1.9304*	1.8457*
(No Third-party, Non Ethnic)	(0.3491)			(0.6239)	(0.4326)
Ethnic Crises	0.7666*	0.7593*	1.1918*	-	-
(No Third-party, Interstate)	(.1823)	(0.1886)	(0.7578)		
Number of Crises:	635	544	81	268	367
Percentage of Correct Predictions:	68.32	65.63	86.42	69.58	67.40

Notes: 1. "*" denotes parameters significant at the 5 percent level.
2. Numbers in parentheses are standard errors.
3. Control characteristics in parentheses denote reference crises.

across "all cases," but we do not yet know the relative importance of state and IO intervention compared with, say, state-only intervention in "ethnic cases," regardless of how important ethnicity is to violence more generally. This requires analysis of the parameter estimates for each type of intervener when controlling for both ethnicity and location separately as specified in Tables 5.8–5.9.

In sum, the logit runs confirm that ethnic and internal conflicts are more difficult to deal with. State involvement, alone or with the UN, seems to be associated with less violence/escalation across all types of conflict. However, state-only intervention appears to be more effective than state and IO intervention together, and the UN appears to do especially poorly in these cases.

Table 5.8
Probability of Severe Violence Logit Regression Estimated Probabilities

Control Characteristics	Probability of Severe Violence				
	1	2	3	4	5
	All	External	Internal	Ethnic	Non Ethnic
Reference Crisis (Constant): **(No Third-party, Interstate, Non Ethnic)**	40.47	41.28	67.77	57.98	41.44
Third-party Interveners: **(Interstate, Non Ethnic)**					
State & IO Mediated Crisis	24.69	23.11	82.43	51.11	18.83
State Mediated Crisis	31.41	31.13	75.31	47.56	32.57
UN Mediated Crisis	67.79	67.03	99.99	78.60	70.56
RO Mediated Crisis	40.78	42.11	70.91	63.69	38.73
Crises Characteristics:					
Intrastate Crises **(No Third-party, Non Ethnic)**	81.05	-	-	90.48	81.76
Ethnic Crises **(No Third-party, Interstate)**	59.41	60.03	87.38	-	-

CONCLUSIONS

We postulated that relative to states, UN performance would be unimpressive because it lacks effective leverage relative to most adversaries and is poorly equipped to act as an interface between states and nonstate actors. The evidence confirmed our suspicions that the UN is a weak conflict manager. Others have found similar results (Diehl et al. 1996).

What was a little more surprising in the quantitative assessment was the finding that violence is more often prevented when ROs are involved. In the context of our deterrence model and in the Kosovo illustration, ROs are more likely than the UN to satisfy the four requirements and control violence. Regional organizations offer several advantages in pursuit of conflict prevention, most notably, familiarity with the history of the locale and with the parties to an impending dispute. These organizations often have the most at stake and therefore generally are more willing to get involved. By their proximity to a conflict, regional organizations almost inevitably are involved because their members must deal with refugee-related problems and other consequences. Finally, states that hesitate to refer a local dispute to the United Nations—for fear that it will no longer be under their control—may be more willing to see the matter addressed at a regional level.

Table 5.9
Logit Regression Estimated Change in Probability of Severe Violence

Control Characteristics	Change in Probability of Severe Violence				
	1 All	2 External	3 Internal	4 Ethnic	5 Non Ethnic
Reference Crisis (Constant): No Third-party, Interstate, Non Ethnic	0.00	0.00	0.00	0.00	0.00
Third-party Interveners: (Interstate, Non Ethnic)					
State & IO Mediated Crisis	-15.78	-18.17	14.66	-6.87	-22.61
State Mediated Crisis	-9.06	-10.15	7.54	-10.42	-8.88
UN Mediated Crisis	27.32	25.75	32.23	20.62	29.12
RO Mediated Crisis	0.31	0.83	3.14	5.72	-2.71
Crises Characteristics:					
Intrastate Crises (No Third-party, Non Ethnic)	40.58	-	-	32.50	40.32
Ethnic Crises (No Third-party, Interstate)	18.94	18.75	19.61	-	-

More generally the findings suggest that third-party interventions succeed and fail for reasons that can be linked to the central tenets of deterrence theory. Ethnic and intrastate conflicts leading to crises call for superior leverage and leadership that is capable of directing, containing, and reducing the level of violence and spillover. Only a few states posses these characteristics.

Our analysis set out a framework for understanding operational failure and success in today's conflicts. Alone, such analyses can never furnish any guarantee of success. Governments still carry the heavy burden of having to choose to act in a timely and responsible fashion in response to a perceived threat. Our findings, although certainly not conclusive, suggest that more work needs to be done in linking analysis to action with respect to the following.

First, with respect to early warning, does it really matter whether early warning capabilities are enhanced if managing conflict depends on who ultimately intervenes? Early warning is about anticipat and responding to prevent likely events from occurring (Adelman 1996, 32). Adelman argues that "humanitarian realism" is the appropriate frame of reference for developing and enhancing response to early warning. This perspective means that equal weight should be given to both state values and state interests in the formation of preventive policies. In the short run, more effective strategies may mean that international organizations will need to behave more like states.[15]

Second, major powers are not likely to become heavily involved in preventing ethnic conflicts until it is clear that substantial political, military, or humanitarian benefits will be gained from the intervention. This finding is consistent with Alexander George's (1991) argument that the essence of statecraft is to develop and manage relationships with other states in ways that will protect and enhance one's own security and welfare. Lund has argued that a state will act in a way that favors its own particular interests, and often a state may be unable to act until it has secured the support of its public and/or political elite (Lund 1996a). Thus, proposals on deterring conflict are often more farsighted than current circumstances permit. This is because the thinking of interested governments has yet to move far enough to reshape their approach to the many ways in which peace is sustained. In other words, to effectively anticipate and address impending conflicts, states need to consider not only revising the existing provisions and mechanisms for maintaining peace, but changing the attitudes of its users and public.

Third, most important among the immediate lessons taken from Kosovo and consistent with our quantitative assessment was that the United States and its allies needed to develop a policy of extended conventional deterrence based on a comprehensive set of guidelines to prevent ethnic violence from escalating out of control. This lesson is discernible in NATO's behavior toward the escalating violence in Kosovo. Since policy failures in Bosnia had a direct impact on the probability of success in Kosovo, establishing a strong and credible reputation for responding (without hesitation) to control the violence was a crucial factor in NATO's decision to use force in Kosovo.

Compounding this issue is the fact that most ethnically based civil wars are local affairs attracting little interest from extra-regional actors. The particularities of ethnic conflicts tend to make them self-limiting as a basis for undermining the sovereignty of other states. In the post–Cold War era, claims that give rise to ethnic violence have expanded across borders insofar as there are kindred groups who might be interested in providing support. In essence this means that most conflicts do not spread like "wild-fire."

Progress is possible only if prevention is nested in a broader set of policies and strategies. More specifically, sanctions and international condemnation may be necessary—but not sufficient—conditions for managing today's conflicts. It may be essential to augment these traditional approaches with deterrence strategies suited to the particularities of ethnic disputes.

NOTES

1. This is usually very low, unless there never was an intention to challenge, but this is a difficult thing to determine. It could be high if political leaders have a preference for demonstrating the military's weakness in an effort to purge the military of rogue

leaders and regain control over foreign policy. This, too, is difficult to isolate, since "no action" may or may not be interpreted as backing down, whereas some "actions" may or may not represent a decision to back down, depending on the provocation or the demands outlined in the third-party ultimatum.

2. This may be high or low, depending on the challenger's objectives, intentions, and capabilities. Bosnian Serb leaders actually preferred certain kinds of interventions by NATO, as long as they were limited. This gave them an opportunity to demonstrate successes against an international coalition of forces sponsored by NATO and the UN. The point is that Ui often depends on the type of intervention that is to take place, which is directly related to propositions regarding the relative success of state versus international organization intervention.

3. If the challenger backs down, the intervener receives a greater net benefit than had it initially intervened high. The problem is that the challenger is aware of this gap between credibility and capability and will attempt to force the issue by testing the third-party's commitment. The net result is a gradual escalation of the conflict until the point at which the belligerent has more to lose by continuing to fight. We are concerned with identifying conditions that facilitate this transfer point. The speed at which this occurs depends on the capacity of the intervener to increase the costs of a challenge. Once again, this varies, depending on the profile of the intervener and the type of conflict. Moreover, for the multilateral force to intervene high at the outset requires an estimation of the opponent's willingness to continue fighting. There are instances in which that willingness might be low (low expected gains) and some in which it might be quite high. That willingness is a function of not only the capabilities of the intervener but of the other ethnic group (i.e., Serbs versus Bosnian Muslims/Croatians). Therefore the capability of the belligerent determines its willingness to back down in addition to expected gains from continued fighting. There may be instances in which low capability plus low gains means that a multilateral force is effective in a low-intensity intervention, such as in Rwanda. The utility function of the challenger needs to include these factors. If the unilateral force is even more likely to control escalation (prevent a challenge) than is a multilateral force under the same "low capability/low gains" situation, then our expectations regarding the relative capacity of unilaterals and multilaterals to satisfy coercive diplomatic requirements would be supported. In any case, the utility function of the challenger (as noted above) does include these factors in the form of Ui and Ubd.

4. If we combine the utility estimates from each phase—that is, if we assume that a challenger's overall utility for backing down at the onset of the crisis is based on evaluation of both pre- and post-intervention scenarios—then the new expected utility model for the challenger's decision to back down during the onset stage is Ubd $>$ (z)(Ui) + (1-z)(Us).

5. Events in Bosnia identify the central problem for a third party in managing intrastate conflicts: the benefit of a negotiated outcome decreases for both actors when one of them decides to escalate. The further apart the two sides are on a negotiated settlement, the higher the costs associated with disagreement (or the higher the value of a negotiated settlement). An actor concedes, as the Bosnian Serbs did in late 1995, if the costs of enduring further escalation outweigh the benefits of giving in to the opponent.

6. Third-party coalitions usually begin the bargaining process by articulating proposals for a negotiated solution coinciding with a low-intensity mission. This proposal can be either accepted or rejected by the belligerent. This initial action requires no force

on the part of the third-party coalition. If one side accepts the terms for agreement, then both sides receive the benefits they associate with the proposed outcome. If an offer is rejected, then the bargaining process continues and neither player receives any benefits until one of the sides concedes to a demand. The problem facing both actors is to provide the opponent with an incentive to make concessions with limited costs to themselves. In general, the negotiation process is begun by one or both actors to reconcile their positions over some issue in dispute. In the case of intrastate conflicts, these consist of (*a*) control over territory, (*b*) power-sharing arrangements, and (*c*) a cease-fire (Regan 1996a; Diehl et al. 1996).

7. For the purposes of this chapter, political, military, and ideological conflicts are those in which groups refuse to recognize the existing political authorities, which can trigger a foreign policy crisis for the state in question. The result is an internal challenge leading to potential conflict, crisis, and war. Conflicts of either the ethnic or nonethnic variety and inter- or intrastate variety that have yet to produce international crises are not included in the analysis. The ICB collection is large enough, with sufficiently diverse spatial and temporal characteristics, to justify its use. Furthermore, given ICB's selection rules and procedures for identifying cases, it is highly improbable that any intense ethnic conflict would be overlooked during data assembly. This time frame covers the history of the UN from its inception to the transition into the post–Cold War era.

8. Crises with IO involvement almost always have state involvement as well, but we separate interventions into the following three categories. We are interested only in whether the IO or a state had the highest level of involvement. If we were unable to determine which had the highest level of involvement, we coded it as ambiguous and put it into category three:

3. IO with state involvement, mixed (UN peacekeeping and U.S./NATO air strikes later on)

2. no IO, only third-party state involvement (Chechnya)

1. no state, only IO involvement.

9. Esman (1995) defines UN intervention in ethnic conflict to include good offices, mediation, peacemaking, peacekeeping, protection of human rights, humanitarian assistance, and stigmatization of rogue governments. By Esman's standards, calls for condemnation by the General Assembly would fall under the rubric of intervention even though the UN need not take any follow-up action.

10. UN minor activity includes the following ICB categories: Security Council discussion without resolution, resolution without action, resolution with authorized members active, and General Assembly discussion only. Major UN activity includes fact-finding missions, good offices resolutions, mediation, sanctions, observer force, and emergency military force.

11. A correlation matrix for the logit runs was done to check for multicollinearity among independent variables. The matrix suggests that multicollinearity was not a problem. The few relatively high correlations (.3–.4 range) were between variables we would expect to be partially related—for example, UN-Active and State-Active. High UN involvement obviously requires some form of state involvement, but states can be involved in a crisis without UN backing.

12. The second form of the intervener variable focused exclusively on high involvement of third parties. In determining whether third-party involvement was high, the deployment of forces was the criteria for selection.

13. Significance levels, while informative, are not very meaningful when working with a universe of relevant cases, as we are doing in this study. Significance levels measure the probability that the results we obtain from our sample of cases were obtained by chance or measurement error. They also offer a preliminary indication of how likely it is that our results apply to the universe of cases under investigation. Since we are not using samples and are already looking at the universe of cases, significance levels should be specified with this qualification.

14. The raw parameter estimates of any logit regression are difficult to interpret directly. Parameter estimates show the increase in the log-of-the-odds ratio associated with a one-unit increase in a given regressor. (Suppose there is an 80 percent chance of winning a lottery. The odds ratio would be 4:1 or 4. One would take the log of 4 to find the log-of-the-odds ratio.)

15. Other possibilities would be to shift responsibilities to coalitions of the willing or possibly to develop a dedicated rapid reaction force capable of responding quickly and efficiently. There is a need to build regional capacity whereby a hub of states, presumably those with the most at stake, would take a lead in responding.

6

NATO and Postconflict Resolution in Bosnia and Kosovo

It has been more than four years since Bosnia's warring factions signed the Dayton Peace Accords. A particularly powerful image that still confronts visitors to the region is the distant beauty of fresh snow on the mountains near Sarajevo. Visitors to the city are shocked to find that the white blanket on some mountains isn't snow but thousands of fresh graves with white gravestones. The amount and kinds of destruction in Sarajevo (and Vukovar and Mostar as well) defy description. In defiance of any clear military strategy schools, homes, mosques, churches, marketplaces, apartments, and office buildings have been laid waste. Landmines, booby traps, and house fires now prevent people from coming home.[1]

INTRODUCTION

The purpose of this chapter is to assess the applicability of NATO postconflict peace operations in "out-of-area conflicts" in the context of ethnically based threats to regional security. This chapter argues that the moment is ripe for regional organizations to play a greater role in postconflict management and resolution. NATO's involvement in Bosnia and Kosovo demonstrates how a unified and expanded alliance can better utilize the political and military peacekeeping tools at its disposal as deterrents and sources of stability during peacetime. On one side of the ledger are those who argue that as intrastate security challenges ebb and flow, there will be conflicting opinions about NATO's role in managing tensions even at the highest levels, especially regarding areas outside NATO's sphere of influence. On the other side of the ledger are those who argue that NATO should concentrate on a combination of prevention and post-conflict peacebuilding. NATO charter law clearly favors the latter (and arguably less risky) approach.

For example, according to John Barrett, NATO has always had a number of conflict management mechanisms at its command.[2] Insofar as conflicts pertain to the security of member states, Articles 1 and 4 of the 1949 Washington Treaty commit NATO members to consult with each other when the territorial integrity, political independence, or security of any member is threatened.

However, NATO's role in "out-of area" peacebuilding and in long-term commitments to nonalliance members appears more problematic. The Washington Treaty considers only a political and legal obligation of member states to defend collectively against armed attack. The Washington Treaty specifically defines the limits of this responsibility in Article 5, which states that an armed attack against one or more members shall be considered an attack against them all. "Out-of-area" conflict management issues are not formally addressed as such in the treaty. Nevertheless, in the 1990s, NATO forces saw action in at least four "out-of-area" conflicts: Bosnia, Kosovo, the Gulf War, and Iraq (with Turkey's subsequent incursions into Kurdish-occupied areas of northern Iraq). With a minimum of three new members (Poland, Hungary, and the Czech Republic) under the NATO flag, the list of "problem areas" that NATO might be expected to address could expand even deeper into the Balkans, eastward into the Ukraine, or even northeastward toward the Baltic states.

On a more optimistic note, NATO's role as conflict manager *primus inter pares* seems assured at least in the short run. By 1998 the organization had successfully resolved the numerous problems inherent in the fledging Partnership for Peace (PfP) Programme through the inclusion of three new members in the alliance and through a special working relationship with Russia. At least for now, PfP will be seen as a legitimate stepping-stone for those states seeking NATO membership and not as the ambiguous halfway house it was only a few years earlier. At least for now, Russia will not seek to break its ties with NATO as long as it can be convinced that NATO expansion is not a direct threat to its regional interests in the Crimea and elsewhere. The fact that NATO has emerged as Europe's only substantial security organization—in the sense that it has the capacity to provide basic and fundamental security guarantees to countries and peoples in need—reinforces its post–Cold War stature. The only other security organizations that could realistically make this claim either lack the muscle required for peace support operations (as in the cases of the OSCE or West European Union [WEU]), or are clearly overstretched and overburdened (as in the case of the UN).

NATO's decision to expand its preventive as well as its postconflict peace support capabilities and to develop its own unique approach to peacekeeping operations signals an important change in the way the organization will likely approach future security issues.[3] Exemplary of NATO's capacity for quick adaptation is how its peacekeeping role expanded over the lifetime of the war in Bosnia and on into the Kosovo crisis. Initially, in June 1992, a ministerial decision placed NATO resources at the disposal of the OSCE and the UN, reflecting the alliance's decision to support, but not initiate, peace support operations. Until 1994 all NATO peace support operations fell within the scope of the UN-mandated operation UNPROFOR.[4]

By 1995, significant changes had taken place, initiated by NATO air strikes against the Bosnian Serb militia throughout the spring, then a relatively small deployment of a rapid reaction corps to quell Serb shelling in the late summer, then in the occupation of Bosnia by a 60,000-person peace implementation and stabilization force (IFOR and SFOR, respectively) mandated by the Dayton Accords in late 1995. SFOR strength now stands at about 30,000 personnel.[5]

NATO's Kosovo force (KFOR) is composed of about 50,000 personnel. Like SFOR, KFOR is multinational in nature. There remains, however, substantial NATO participation, with all NATO members with military forces contributing personnel. European countries currently contribute the bulk of KFOR troops (approximately 30,000 out of 50,000).[6] More than twelve non-NATO states have also contributed personnel.

NATO PEACE-BUILDING: A BOSNIAN TYPOLOGY

NATO's conflict management efforts pertain to both immediate and long-term strategies, such as the rapid deployment of a coalition of forces to respond to state failure and insurgencies on the one hand, and the provision of basic security guarantees for collapsed states on the other. Given that the former strategies have been laid out in the preceding chapters, this chapter focuses on NATO's postconflict roles in Bosnia and Kosovo. The evidence indicates that the organization has the capacity to carry out long- and short-term postconflict peace-building tasks.

NATO in Postconflict Bosnia

Various NATO operations in Bosnia represent examples in which immediate and long-term strategies were applied simultaneously rather than sequentially. These tasks are summarized in Table 6.1.

At the outset of the conflict in Bosnia (during Phase I as noted in Table 6.1), NATO's military efforts centered on spillover control, containment, and coercive diplomacy to reduce both the scope and intensity of violence.[7] For example, NATO operations Sharp Guard and Deliberate Force were examples of conflict containment in the service of specific UN resolutions.[8] In effect, NATO's strategy was to isolate the Bosnian Serb militia to drive a political wedge between them and their main line of support in Serbia. In turn, it is unlikely that without diplomatic pressure on Milosevic, a mediated settlement would have been pos-

Table 6.1
NATO's Tasks in Bosnia

military Phase I	Containing the scope and intensity of the violence through no-fly zones, embargoes and coercive military measures including a measured and appropriate use of force;
Phase II	separation of forces and military support for a range of political and humanitarian operations;
Phase III	observation of local forces, monitoring, disarmament, and de-mining
political stability Phase I, II and III	creation of a stable and secure environment to support negotiations by diplomatic and civil affairs personnel at strategic, operational, and local levels
displaced persons and refugee repatriation Phase III	provision of security guarantees to aid in the return and/or settlement of displaced persons and refugees
human rights Phase III	the monitoring and enforcement of basic human rights guarantees such as access to property, homes, and infrastructure
humanitarian assistance Phase II and III	assistance in the immediate provision of food, fuel, shelter, and medical care in order to save lives and alleviate suffering
law and order Phase II and III	the development of essential law and order structures such as support for civil and border police and the capture of persons indicted for war crimes
reconstruction/ rehabilitation Phase III	assistance in the rebuilding of infrastructure through civil-military cooperation
elections Phase II and III	assistance in policing and implementing post-conflict democratic elections
arms control/ disarmament Phase II and III	development of such measures as cantonments of heavy weapons and monitoring of militia activity to enhance the prospects for longer term stability

sible in so short a period. To escape the constraints imposed on Serbia (namely, sanctions and embargoes), Milosevic withdrew tangible support for the Serb breakaway leadership in Bosnia. In effect, the combination of sanctions and retaliatory measures sent unequivocal signals to Serbian leader Milosevic, who held a tight rein on Bosnian Serb leader Radovan Karadzic: he had to resolve the conflict through negotiations or face the consequences. On 20 November 1995 the Dayton Accord was signed and a cease-fire was obtained.

The second set of responsibilities (phase two of the military tasks and phase two of the other tasks) include establishing a stable and secure internal environment to create the conditions for a lasting peace. These tasks are generally consistent with traditional peacekeeping. Specific military operations include the denial of movement to local militia, which requires large and well-protected forces (ground and air); cargo aircraft; an increasing use of armor and substantial offshore facilities; protection of humanitarian relief through military operations; forceful separation of ethnic groups; and counterinsurgency activities.

The Dayton Mandate: IFOR and SFOR

The third and ongoing task for NATO forces in Bosnia (Phase III in Table 6.1) has been to prevent the outbreak of renewed hostilities among the warring factions in Bosnia. These efforts were undertaken to establish a secure basis for a sustained peacebuilding process once the parties began to demonstrate their commitment to the terms of the Dayton Accord. Under the implementation force (IFOR), NATO created a secure environment in a number of important ways, the most important being the maintenance of a permanent cease-fire, the cantonment of weapons, disarmament of the warring factions, the establishment of inter-entity boundary lines, and support for the gradual return of political power to a civilian government.[9]

The initial stages of IFOR concentrated on the transition of operational control from the UN Protection Force (UNPROFOR) to IFOR. Military support to relief activities and the disarming of factions continued throughout the transition. Latter stages consolidated the IFOR operation and concluded twelve months later when IFOR forces were deployed and operating effectively throughout Bosnia.

At this phase of the conflict, well-armed NATO forces provided a buffer between the warring factions. Under ideal conditions, the belligerents would comply with these basic principles of separation and the peacekeepers themselves would not be vulnerable to attack. Interposition is deemed necessary only to prevent further bloodshed.[10] However, conditions in Bosnia were far from ideal. In particular, the potential for renewed hostility between the warring factions as well as the potential for attacks on NATO forces called for robust measures on NATO's part.

To this end, IFOR's tasks were to supervise the selective marking of boundaries and the establishment of inter-entity boundary lines between the Republic of Srpska (RS) on the one hand, and the federation (Bosnian Croat [HdZ] and Bosnian Muslim forces [BiH]) on the other. These zones of separation (ZOS) between the parties included the removal of all heavy weapon cantonment sites that fell within ten kilometers of the boundary and the withdrawal of the three forces to their respective territories behind the ZOS. NATO also assumed control over Bosnian airspace and began to monitor the movement of military traffic on key ground routes. IFOR also established the Joint Military Commissions to serve as the central decision-making bodies for the warring factions. Finally, IFOR also had the difficult task of assisting in the withdrawal of UN forces not transferred to IFOR.[11]

NATO's 1996 follow-up mission in Bosnia, SFOR, was intended to build on the success of phase three IFOR tasks. Under SFOR, major efforts are being made to reduce NATO's military activity and assist civil authorities in exercising greater responsibility (for example, the 60,000-person force was cut back to

30,000 people). The final stages for NATO involvement in Bosnia would concern the reduction of SFOR forces, or the redeployment of some SFOR forces to KFOR, or the consolidation of KFOR and SFOR under one command. SFOR's mission in Bosnia will end only when Bosnian civilian control over the local police force is established and major NATO military operations are no longer required.

Although its main function has been to provide a continued military presence to deter renewed hostilities and to bring some stability to the entire region (through, for example, the monitoring of a regional arms control agreement), SFOR is also in Bosnia to consolidate the peace for the ongoing civil implementation plans. Thus, one of SFOR's primary objectives is to ensure respect for the cessation of hostilities and the inter-entity boundary lines so that its security function is no longer required.

Thus far, SFOR has strictly held the parties to compliance with the cantonment of heavy weapons and the demobilization of forces, and it has taken appropriate actions to prevent any new threats to the peace. As the Dayton Agreement states, other organizations are responsible for tasks related to nation building. These include conducting humanitarian missions, granting election security, police force duties, moving refugees, and implementing arms control and regional stability measures.

Whereas the military aspect of the IFOR mission was an integral part of the Bosnian peace process, SFOR's tasks have long-term political implications. Ideally, the deployment of SFOR should eventually create a secure environment that will facilitate the work of humanitarian organizations and the accomplishment of the nonmilitary aspects of the settlement well into this century. Although it is true that the overall intensity of violence in Bosnia has been reduced significantly, in large part because of SFOR's deterring presence in the region and the cantonment and control of weapons under SFOR's watchful eye, it is also true that sporadic violence still occurs and will likely continue for some time.[12]

Immediate and ongoing sources of insecurity include the return of thousands of displaced ethnic minorities to their homes in areas dominated by other ethnic groups. These minorities, whether Serbian, Croat, or Bosnian Muslim ("Bosniac"), are returning only to find their homes either occupied or destroyed by arson. Many, mostly the young and skilled, have chosen to stay away, preferring instead refuge in Germany or Italy, or in resort towns along the Adriatic coast where employment opportunities are better. The Federal Republic of Yugoslavia is home to some 200,000 internally displaced persons.

Equally problematic are the results of local elections in Bosnia; former residents, who were forced to flee their villages during the war, are encouraged to vote in municipal elections regardless of whether they intend to return to their homes. The net result can be as perplexing as the election of Serb councilors and mayors in Croat-dominated towns with a Bosniac police force. Given that Bosnia now has three very well-trained and well-equipped armies—the Republic of Srpska army (RS), the Bosniac (BiH), and Croat (HdZ)—the potential for renewed hostilities between these military forces cannot be underestimated. Indeed, the continual postponement of the decision regarding the political fate of Brcko on the border between the Republic of Srpska and Croatia—a tiny island of neutrality in a sea of hostility—is a case in point. SFOR troops train under chapter 7 of the UN Charter (which covers more robust rules of engagement) in anticipation that Brcko would be handed back to one of the warring factions. It has been widely anticipated that any concrete decision regarding Brcko will precipitate renewed clashes. To prevent this from happening, SFOR troops perform daily armed patrols in villages and towns, monitor all significant movements of the three armed forces (including training), and control their access to their heavy weapons. Ensuring the compliance of these fledgling armies under the Dayton Accord remains an essential task for SFOR and an important reason for staying the course.[13]

Also consistent with chapter 7 peace enforcement, SFOR has the difficult task of capturing persons wanted for war crimes, under the direction of the UN War Crimes Tribunal. Many observers are convinced that SFOR has a principled responsibility to stay in the region until this task is accomplished, whereas others suggest that the seizure of war criminals—especially Bosnian Serb leaders Karadzic and Mladic—would only aggravate the situation, particularly if spearheaded by SFOR troops. Unfortunately, neither the Bosnian civilian police force not the unarmed International Police Task Force, which is responsible for overseeing and training indigenous police, can do the job. The former lacks the credibility to perform anything but the most rudimentary policing functions, and the latter lacks both the mandate and capacity to take on SFOR's security role.

These are only a few of the many reasons it would be premature to conclude that SFOR's peacebuilding tasks are complete. Of course, with KFOR now firmly entrenched in Kosovo, NATO leadership knows that SFOR's presence in Bosnia cannot and should not be open-ended. It would be financially debilitating for NATO to have two open-ended occupying forces in the Balkans, let alone one. Therefore there will be a need for a clearly defined transition period associated with clear criteria of progress in both Bosnia and Kosovo in which authority and control is handed back to civilian authorities. Such a transition strategy would see SFOR's and KFOR's role reduced as support for, and trust in, civilian control broadens. On the one hand, most of SFOR's major military objectives as specified in the Dayton Accord have been met—clear demarcation and control of an inter-entity boundary line between Serb and federation (Bosniac and Croatian) forces, cantonment of heavy weapons, and the prevention of renewed warfare. On the other hand, it is still too early to tell if KFOR will achieve the same level of progress in Kosovo.[14]

KFOR in Kosovo

On 3 June 1999, the government of the Federal Republic of Yugoslavia and the Serbian parliament agreed to the international peace plan that committed

Yugoslavia to withdraw all of its forces from Kosovo. A day later on 4 June 1999, the North Atlantic Council provided the authority under the existing operations plan for General Sir Michael Jackson, commander of KFOR, to take operational control of the in-theater forces and to begin preparations for deployment to Kosovo. Two days later, FRY and NATO representatives began talks for the withdrawal of Serb troops from Kosovo. Russian military observers also participated in the meeting. Under an accord signed on 9 June 1999, NATO and Yugoslavia agreed to FRY troop withdrawal. The following day NATO announced a cessation of bombing and the deployment of KFOR forces under Operation Joint Guardian.[15]

The purpose of KFOR is to verify and enforce the terms of the accord; to establish a secure environment in which refugees and displaced persons can return home in safety; to establish a secure environment in which the international civil presence can operate, a transitional administration can be established, and humanitarian aid can be delivered; and to help achieve a self-sustaining, secure environment that will allow public security responsibilities to be transferred to appropriate civil organizations (including civil air traffic, policing, and so on).

More generally, KFOR has responsibilities similar in nature to SFOR and IFOR Phase I and Phase II operations noted in Table 6.1. KFOR's primary objective is to verify the withdrawal of FRY forces from Kosovo, as well as any nonlocal members of the KLA, and to provide appropriate control of the FRY borders in Kosovo (Albania and Macedonia) until the arrival of the civilian mission from the UN. KFOR also has the responsibility of deterring renewed hostilities, enforcing a cease-fire, demilitarizing the KLA, ensuring public safety and order for the interim, and establishing a safe environment for the return of refugees and so the international civil presence can operate. For example, immediately after the accord was signed, KFOR forces disarmed local KLA militia. And on occasion KFOR has been required to use threats supported by armored personnel carriers and attack helicopters to disarm members of the KLA. On other occasions NATO troops were required to use force to disarm KLA rebels who had undertaken reprisals (imprisonment and beatings) against Gypsies and Serbs. In addition, KFOR is responsible for establishing and monitoring the Air Safety Zone, defined as twenty-five kilometers beyond Kosovo's border into the FRY and the airspace above it, and the Ground Safety Zone, defined as a five-kilometer zone beyond Kosovo and into the FRY. KFOR may compel the removal, withdrawal, and relocation of forces and weapons and order the cessation of any activities that the commander deems a potential threat to KFOR or its mission.

Finally, KFOR is authorized and mandated to take "actions as are required," such as compelling the removal, withdrawal, and relocation of forces and weapons, which includes any use of necessary force, to ensure, for example, the compliance of the KLA to the demilitarization agreement. Consistent with SFOR, this kind of enforcement capability falls under chapter 7 of the UN

Charter and was adopted on 11 June 1999, when the United Nations Security Council accepted Resolution 1244 specifying the relationship between NATO (leading the military side) and the UN (responsible for civil implementation). This relationship continues the separation of the civil-military aspects of NATO and UN peacebuilding that was established under Dayton (and IFOR and SFOR).

Unlike SFOR, however, the occupation of NATO forces in Kosovo remains open-ended in terms of set dates for the transition to civil authorities. The UN Security Council requested that beginning in June 1999, KFOR remain in theater for an initial period of twelve months. KFOR's mandate could continue well afterward until the Security Council decides otherwise. Furthermore, the size of KFOR, when full capacity is reached (50,000), is more comparable to IFOR.

Apart from this basic difference, SFOR and KFOR operate quite similarly. Both are tasked with deterring the renewal of hostilities; with establishing, monitoring, and maintaining safety zones (known as inter-entity boundaries under SFOR); with creating fertile ground for an eventual turnover to civil authorities; and with reducing military presence by creating a secure environment for humanitarian organizations and civil society to take over. KFOR differs slightly in its mandate to ensure public safety and order.

LESSONS LEARNED

To what extent do Bosnia and Kosovo portend the future of NATO? The Bosnian crisis is, in the postwar European context, a rare example of complete state collapse. Kosovo is clearly not an example of state failure. Whereas the former is a situation in which armed groups operate outside the control of recognized political authorities and forcefully resist peacekeeping efforts for the duration of the conflict, the latter is more akin to conventional interstate warfare, with the victor becoming the occupying force. On the one hand, there is no reason to believe that the events that unfolded in Bosnia—and the way in which they unfolded—will be duplicated in the exact same sequence elsewhere. As Haglund and Pentland note,

In the first place, the Yugoslav conflict is unique in its multilateral, all-against-all, character. Most of the other potential ethnic flashpoints in Europe involve bilateral disputes which, regardless of the intensity they might attain, have limited potential to replicate the complex pattern of local tactical alliances and antagonisms among Serbs, Croats, and Muslims in Bosnia-Herzegovina. This complexity, and the direct linkage of the Bosnian conflict to parallel struggles in Croatia and elsewhere, make the Yugoslav situation uniquely unmanageable. Secondly, Yugoslavia's geographical location, size, and ethnic diversity mean that its internal conflicts have a particularly dangerous potential for regional spillover. Of the seven countries with which the former Yugoslav federation had borders, five have a more-than-passing interest in the fate of ethnic kin in Yugoslavia's successor states and warring regions, not least because their own internal equilibria and relations with other neighbors may be at risk. No other ethnic dispute in Europe has the same potential for explosive ramification. Hence the special importance and unusual difficulty of containing and managing the Yugoslav conflict in all its manifestations.[16]

On the other hand, there is also little reason to believe that another crisis similar in scope and intensity to Kosovo will not occur in the region. Kosovo was essentially a state of civil war between an ethnic militia and state forces leading to intervention by a multilateral force in an effort to support the weaker side—in this case the Kosovar Albanian population and its various political and military factions. Whether NATO, or any other regional organization, will be confronted by a conflict as complex as the one in Bosnia or as relatively "straightforward" as Kosovo is difficult to predict. However, regardless of the sources of the conflict, intrastate ethnic conflict—whether it be a Bosnia or a Kosovo—adds complexity to a mission in a number of ways. Therefore, although it remains to be seen whether the sources of the conflict in Bosnia or Kosovo will be duplicated elsewhere, these two cases hold three important lessons in the development of an effective NATO response to "out-of-area" ethnic conflicts.

First, the two situations show how extremely complex (and costly) peace support operations in ethnic conflicts can be. As noted in chapters 2 and 5 and Table 6.1, intervention in ethnic conflict tends to be protracted and long term, and the peace support tasks vary. As disunity within the ranks of the various factions makes it difficult for them and peacekeepers to engage in any purposeful form of conflict settlement, the occupying forces are themselves at risk of attack. This is especially true if ethnic leaders (especially those discredited by a military loss) lack the control and authority to make decisions or make concessions on behalf of their people. In essence, this kind of complexity is conditioned by varying levels of consent and the physical proximity of the belligerents to each other and to the peacekeepers. In situations where consent is unobtainable and where the belligerents are not easily separated, it would be extremely difficult to bring about stability without force.[17]

Complexity also relates to the number of actors in any given ethnic conflict as well as their diverse political and military interests. Both Kosovo and Bosnia have shown that outside actors can "muddy the waters" by threatening intervention (e.g., Russia in Kosovo). Since this kind of unilateral involvement occurs contemporaneously, a multilateral mission has the additional burden of ensuring that such involvement does not damage the prospects for peace. In the case of Kosovo, Russia was given a substantial role (through participation in KFOR), thus averting a situation whereby Russian efforts would counteract NATO's aims. In Bosnia, NATO was not so lucky (Serbian and Croatian intervention being unilateral, and UN and NATO intervention being multilateral). In Bosnia, for instance, multilateral intervention was motivated by the perceived need to restore a balance in the face of Serbia's support for the Bosnian Serbs. In Kosovo, NATO intervention had to find a strategy to ensure both a Serb withdrawal and limited Russian involvement. For obvious reasons NATO was not perceived as acting impartially by some outside actors.[18]

The second lesson (one that appears to have been applied in the Kosovo case) is the need for improved coordination between the UN and NATO. In the case of Bosnia, NATO and UNPROFOR missions included many competing objectives. These objectives included how to ensure humanitarian assistance to ordinary citizens in the midst of war, as well as activities guaranteeing them protection and freedom of movement while denying movement to Serb, Croat, and Bosniac militias. All this was done while Western political leaders attempted to address and resolve irreconcilable and competing visions of Bosnia's future. If, at the outset of a mission, the leaders of governments and international organizations are unclear on exactly how a mission is to achieve its goals and, more importantly, what those goals are, potential for failure is greater.[19] In contrast, coordination between NATO and the UN in Kosovo appears to be much smoother, at least with respect to the postconflict reconstruction phase where a clear demarcation exists between political peacebuilding activities under the UN's hat and military security objectives under NATO's.

The third lesson (noted in chapters 4 and 5 and repeated here) is that the use of force must be tightly linked to the mediation process. Coercive diplomacy is not an end in itself but rather a means to a political end. In essence, the inherent problem in negotiating any internal conflict is the lack of restraints on violence. Therefore there is a need to lay the political foundation through a proposal that clearly specifies responsibilities of the warring parties—before committing forces to any military operation. Once in place, forces are there to ensure that those groups that agree to the terms of settlement are supported, whereas those that do not are effectively removed.

A fundamental set of tasks for both policy makers and military strategists is to gain a better understanding of the underlying causes and phases of violent conflict and to relate this knowledge to conflict analysis training. Response needs to be linked with indicators of the escalation of conflict to full-scale violence. This approach is important in understanding not only when and how to respond to an escalating crisis situation but also when it is time to withdraw or pursue more passive, conciliatory strategies.

BEYOND BOSNIA AND KOSOVO: PREVENTING ETHNIC CONFLICT AND THE NATO ADVANTAGE

At the Rome Summit in November 1991, NATO's heads of state issued a Declaration on Peace and Cooperation, which recognized that the primary challenge to member states' security arose from the instability in newly emergent states. At the time, there was concern that NATO's military structure might obstruct involvement beyond the defined boundaries of NATO's area of responsibility. Despite the ongoing development of NATO peacekeeping doctrine, there remains a need to develop a doctrine of immediate and long-range conflict management based on a comprehensive set of guidelines to prevent intrastate ethnic violence from reaching the same levels in Bosnia and Kosovo. There are two areas of concern.

First, with respect to the question of strategies of immediate prevention, the ability to incorporate the lessons learned from Bosnia and Kosovo will have a direct impact on the probability of success in other regions and to some degree by other organizations in other parts of the world. It is obvious that to establish a strong and credible reputation it is first necessary to protect ordinary citizens and to control the escalation of violence. Kosovo was an important test case for NATO in this regard. If Bosnia showed how a failure to develop credible and consistent response to intrastate ethnic conflict can lead to even more conflict, then Kosovo shows how NATO needs to establish and maintain a stable and long-term deterrent threat (perhaps through a codified set of commitments within NATO peacekeeping doctrine) for the Balkans region.

Second, and related to this last point, these long-term strategies operate at the core level of NATO expansion. The basic logic of NATO expansion is to create long-term mechanisms for stability. Like any other regional organization, NATO offers several conflict prevention advantages for its own members, such as a knowledge of impending disputes. Because of their proximity to a conflict, it is often difficult for regional organizations to avoid involvement. This is particularly true if members are confronted with refugee-related problems and other consequences of spillover. Furthermore, now more than ever, NATO might also hesitate to refer a local dispute to the United Nations because of that organization's perceived lack of capability. NATO may be more willing to see the matter addressed at a regional level.

On the other hand, NATO involvement in out-of-area conflicts does have implications for its growing role in long-term conflict management in Europe and elsewhere. By virtue of its mandate, NATO cannot directly constrain actors from outside its regional boundaries. For example, disciplinary measures such as sanctions and embargoes and blockades are difficult to regulate. NATO was not entirely successful in the complete enforcement of sanctions against the warring factions in the former Yugoslavia. And, like other regional organizations, NATO has shown some reluctance to deploy its military forces abroad except on an ad hoc basis. In NATO's case the threat to regional security would have to be as intense as it was in Bosnia and Kosovo to justify another full-scale military intervention in out-of-area conflicts.

What is the path forward? In principle, NATO's Partnership for Peace Programme could serve as an important conflict prevention mechanism in two ways. First, commitments to PfP members in support of joint peacekeeping operations, such as IFOR, SFOR, and KFOR, are stabilizing influences through the integration of emerging states into multilateral structures.[20] Second, joint peacekeeping and peacebuilding operations with PfP states help prepare the latter as effective and reliable NATO partners. To date, NATO has pursued joint military planning, training, and exercises to establish and maintain strong linkages between the alliance and the Partnership for Peace nations.[21]

CONCLUSIONS

A basic problem in developing NATO's long-term peace support capacity is related to Europe's regional security and politics in general. Differences between regional actors who might want to intervene in ethnic conflicts for strategic, economic, or affective reasons need to be resolved as well. For example, Albania's connection to Kosovo is well known; Russia and Greece have both had a long history of relations with Serbia, and the Germans with Croatia. Although the threat of violence by one country against another has not disappeared, the sources and the manifestations of conflict in Central and Eastern Europe and elsewhere are changing. As noted in chapter 1, recent struggles within states, involving civil wars, local insurrections, or refugees and ethnic violence, have far outnumbered those stemming from external aggression or conflict between states. NATO has an important role to play to prevent, limit, and de-escalate these conflicts. However, NATO needs to focus on two important issues.

First, Kosovo notwithstanding, multilateral forces are still likely to be extremely hesitant to engage in costly interventionist strategies at the outset because they lack the sufficient "political will" and resources to fulfill their commitments. The inherent problem is that quick terminations of escalating violence require not only the military backing and political support of the major powers, but also long-term postconflict commitments. It is no longer sufficient to stop the violence. Refugees must be protected and returned; political control must be reinstated and economic development pursued. If interventions at the early stages of a conflict demand close coordination of military, diplomatic, and nongovernmental assets, then the postconflict phase requires an even more complex coordinated operation plan; one that engages global organizations and cuts across civilian and military control. In sum, considerable resources are required to foster development, intercommunal interdependence, and attitude change over a long time—perhaps generations. Few states, other than the major powers that are now part of NATO, are capable of providing this long-term support and commitment.

Second, proposals on making NATO more of a political alliance for conflict prevention are often more farsighted than current conditions allow. This is because the thinking of NATO's heads of state has yet to move far enough to reshape NATO's approach to the many new ways in which reconciliation and peace can be upheld and sustained. In other words, to effectively anticipate and address impending conflicts, NATO members need not only to consider a revision of existing provisions and mechanisms for maintaining peace and preventing conflict through military means, but to change the attitudes of their publics—who benefit from, but often decide not to support, outside efforts to establish peace and stability.

NOTES

1. Observations from travel through the region in March 1998. "Academics Visit Bosnia," in *The Maple Leaf* (DND HQ, May 1998, p. 3).

2. John Barrett, "Conflict Prevention and Crisis Management: The NATO Approach," in *The Art of Conflict Prevention*, ed. Werner Bauwens and Luc Reychler (London: Brassey's Atlantic Commentaries, 1994), 113–136.

3. In light of the peace Accord agreed upon in Dayton on 21 November 1995, the North Atlantic Council authorized on 1 December 1995 the Supreme Allied Commander Europe (SACEUR) to deploy enabling forces into Croatia and Bosnia-Herzegovina. All NATO nations with armed forces (Belgium, Canada, Denmark, France, Germany, Greece, Italy, Luxembourg, the Netherlands, Norway, Portugal, Spain, Turkey, the United Kingdom, and the United States) pledged to contribute forces to IFOR. Iceland has provided medical personnel to IFOR. The Peace Agreement (General Framework Agreement for Peace in Bosnia and Herzegovina) was formally signed in Paris on 14 December 1995. As of 19 January, the following sixteen non-NATO countries were considered for IFOR participation: Austria, Czech Republic, Egypt, Estonia, Finland, Hungary, Jordan, Latvia, Lithuania, Malaysia, Morocco, Poland, Romania, Russia, Sweden, and Ukraine.

4. In addition to the commanding role it assumed at the height of the conflict in 1995, NATO has since implemented various peace support and peace-building tasks at the request of the OSCE, the UN, the International Police Task Force, and various local and intergovernmental humanitarian agencies.

5. On 15 December 1995, the United Nations Security Council, acting under chapter 7 of the UN Charter, adopted Resolution 1031, which authorized the member states of NATO to establish the Implementation Force (IFOR) under unified command and control and composed of ground, air, and maritime units from NATO and non-NATO nations, to ensure compliance with the relevant provisions of the Dayton Peace Agreement.

6. In addition, in accordance with the agreement signed between NATO and the Russian Federation, Russia will supply a consistent proportion of troops as part of the KFOR. The total Russian deployment in Kosovo will not exceed five battalions, a total strength not exceeding 2,850 troops, plus up to 750 troops for the airfield and logistics base operation combined, plus sixteen officers. The level of Russian participation will be reduced in proportion to reductions in the overall size of KFOR.

7. See chapter 1 of *Peace in the Midst of Wars: Preventing and Managing International Ethnic Conflicts*, ed. David Carment and Patrick James (Columbia: University of South Carolina Press, 1998), for a full examination of the phases of conflict.

8. Among others, NATO announced on 22 April 1994 that if any Bosnian Serb attacks involving heavy weapons were carried out on UN-designated safe areas, these weapons and other Bosnian Serbs military assets, their direct and essential support facilities, fuel installations, and munitions sites would be subject to NATO air strikes in accordance with the procedural arrangements worked out between NATO and UNPROFOR following the council decisions of 2 and 9 August 1993. NATO Fact Sheets and Internet documents, various dates.

9. Key roles to be played by NATO and other third parties are assistance to the interim civil community, logistical efforts to establish cantonment sites, supervision of the handover of weapons and demobilization, ensuring the safe return of displaced populations, and training local cadres to clear the war zone of land mines.

10. In Bosnia, long-term political strategies encompass a package of incentives, policies, and techniques that encourage the deconstruction and demobilization of ethnic armies, and democratization processes that separate civilian from military control. Sources: SFOR Coalition Press Information Centres in Zagreb and NATO Fact Sheets. Portions of this analysis are based on David Carment's "NATO and the International Politics of Ethnic Conflict: Perspectives on Theory and Policy," *Contemporary Security Policy* 16, no. 3 (1995): 347–379.

11. On 18 February 1996 SACEUR reported to the secretary general of NATO the completion of the initial deployment of IFOR. Thirty-two nations had been part of the deployment, with some 50,000 troops provided by NATO nations and approximately 10,000 from non-NATO contributors. The movement of IFOR had involved more than 2,800 airlift missions, some 400 trains, and more than 50 cargo ships.

12. The close to 1,200-person Canadian contribution to NATO's Stabilization Force (SFOR) in Zgon, Drvar, and Velika Kladusa in the northwest area of operations has been instrumental in bringing stability, peace, and security to the Bihac corridor—one of the most hotly contested regions of Bosnia during the war and now a flash point for ethnic violence that threatens to spill over into areas under British, French, and U.S. control.

13. For example, Canadian forces are doing the best they can with outdated equipment. Every Canadian armored personnel carrier in Bosnia has ceramic tiles "Velcroed" to the outer skin—an odd but effective arrangement in ensuring additional protection for soldiers on patrol. Despite resources that are stretched thin and a comparatively small contingent, Canadian troops remain engaged and effective. There is little doubt that Canadian peacekeepers are widely respected in the region. This respect will pay dividends when it comes time for SFOR's security/military role to be superseded by a willingness of the Bosnian people to take control of their own lives.

14. Canadian SFOR forces are exemplary in the way they have chosen to approach the problem of transition. Unlike their U.S. counterparts, Canadian forces are directly engaged in civil reconstruction to a significant extent—rebuilding schools, hospitals, and bridges; training local troops in the art of detecting and removing an estimated 800,000 to 1,000,000 antipersonnel land mines still in the ground; and providing much-needed health care in areas that have no other source of medical support.

15. On 11 June 1999, a contingent of Russian troops rushed to Prishtina airport, denying access to NATO troops until negotiations between Russia and the United States produced terms about Russia's role in peacekeeping in the region that it found "acceptable."

16. David Haglund and Charles C. Pentland, "Ethnic Conflict and European Security: What Role for the EC and NATO?" in *Peace in the Midst of Wars: Preventing and Managing International Ethnic Conflicts*, ed. David Carment and Patrick James (Columbia: University of South Carolina Press, 1998).

17. Alan James, "Peacekeeping and Ethnic Conflicts: Theory and Evidence," in *Peace in the Midst of Wars*.

18. For example, Croat leader Tudjman took a calculated risk that would at once bolster his support at home and take advantage of a supportive international community: in 1993 and in 1995, Tudjman correctly predicted that attacks on Serb-held enclaves

would not be matched by reinforcements from Serbia. On 22 January 1993, Croatia's army launched an offensive to retake territory held by Serbs in southern Croatia's Krajina region. At issue was the important strategic role played by Krajina as the crucial overland link between the capital Zagreb and Dalmatia, on Croatia's Adriatic coast. *Globe and Mail*, 13 February 1993.

19. On the one hand, only armies are likely to have the resources necessary to save lives. On the other hand, peacekeepers may lack the sensitivity to and understanding of the local situation. If soldiers' personal safety depends on the cooperation of one of the warring factions, they have a strong motivation to collaborate with that faction, even if that is not in agreement with the international goals. Outside forces can become another party to the conflict, responding to the battlefield decisions of others rather than taking the initiative. For example, on 12 March 1994, after a mortar attack from Serb tanks against French Blue Helmet positions in the south of Bihac, the UN called for intervention by NATO aviation. However, at the last minute the attack was canceled. The UN explained that this was because of local atmospheric conditions and the fact that the Serb cannons had stopped firing. Such intervention would have been the first allied close air support action in favor of UNPROFOR. The NATO version is somewhat different. In Allied Forces Southern Command (AFSOUTH) headquarters in Naples, a spokesman pointed out that the attack had been canceled not because of bad weather but simply because UNPROFOR had not confirmed its request for an air strike. NAC Subcommittee on Defence and Security Cooperation Between Europe and North America, report entitled "NATO, Peacekeeping and the Former Yugoslavia," May 1994.

20. E. Gilman and Detlef E. Herold, eds., *Peacekeeping Challenges to Euro-Atlantic Security*, NATO Defense College, Monograph Series, No. 2, 1994; Charles L. Glaser, "Why NATO Is Still the Best: Future Security Arrangements for Europe," *International Security*, vol. 18 (1993), 1–52.

21. Cooperative programs in the fields of defense procurement and air defense represent examples of technical cooperation. Beyond technical assistance it is a priority for NATO to assist the PfP nations in establishing transparent and complementary defense planning, particularly in the area of peacekeeping. Joint exercises and participation in SFOR provide forums for cooperation and establish interoperability among PfP and NATO forces.

7

Evaluating Third-Party Efforts to End Intrastate Ethnic Conflict

INTRODUCTION

As we have argued in the preceding chapters, groups with a tendency to solve their political and ethnic differences through military means pose a danger to international order and to other groups in a number of important ways (Vayrynen 1997). As noted, noncombatants are at risk of large-scale violence, armed militias generally operate outside the purview of authority structures, and many internal conflicts spill over into the international domain, adding complexity to overburdened management strategies.

The preceding chapters have illustrated the cause, manifestations, and management of violent intrastate ethnic conflicts. Building on these insights, the purpose of this chapter is to develop basic knowledge on the effectiveness of third parties in the termination and resolution of intrastate ethnic conflicts (Lund 1996a; Hampson 1996; Licklider 1995). More specifically, the chapter has three interrelated objectives. The first is to identify the conditions associated with the ending of different types of intrastate conflicts. A second goal is to relate this knowledge to those strategies of third-party intervention that are thought to result in a stable and long-lasting peace. Third, and perhaps most challenging, is the search for conditions under which pacific forms of third-party intervention are likely to succeed.

The chapter unfolds in five sections. Sections two and three present general hypotheses relating to the characteristics of intrastate ethnic conflicts and third-party effectiveness, respectively. In the fourth section, the hypotheses are weighed against the evidence. In the fifth and final section, conclusions and directions for further research are presented.

UNDERSTANDING THE INTERNATIONALIZATION OF INTRASTATE ETHNIC CONFLICT

It is difficult to determine when and if an intrastate ethnic conflict will remain so. The reality is that few conflicts are not international in scope. Intrastate ethnic conflicts are those in which the triggers to widespread violence emanate from within the state but whose impact on the international system is indeterminate. Some ethnic conflicts have only a mild tendency to internationalize, whereas others slip easily from local conflict to full-scale interstate war.

For Vayrynen (1997) the identification of an "intrastate ethnic" conflict is made not by the actors involved or by their behavior but by the level of risk. An internally risky state is that which reflects a high degree of domestic disorder, which "enhances its proneness to opposition and rebellion." The degree to which that disorder fosters "non-compliance with the prevailing norms of international relations" is a measure of the risk to the international environment (Vayrynen 1997, 38).

Externally risky states are those whose intrastate ethnic conflicts spill over more directly into the international environment. Their internal ethnic behavior places them in a situation of repeated conflict with their neighbors. Consider, for example, the movement of displaced ethnic groups (through refugee flows or ethnic cleansing) to a neighboring state. Changes of demography, rapid and spontaneous, can drastically alter the ethnic balance in a neighboring state, thereby adding to regional instability. Viewed as high politics, ethnic conflict carries serious risks of internationalization through diffusion and vertical escalation. According to Lake and Rothchild (1996), diffusion can occur in four nonmutually exclusive ways: contagion, demonstration effects, information flows, and material and ideological support for diaspora. Under such conditions a perceived higher threat to core values would be anticipated (Carment and James 1997).

Escalation is distinguished from diffusion along a number of dimensions, but the most important difference is the level of the conflict's intensity, that is, whether the conflict leads to an interstate crisis. Theoretically, any one of the aforementioned dimensions of diffusion could be a precondition to escalation.

Whereas diffusion is a process that can persist in the absence of state-directed involvement, this is not the case for escalation. In other words, diffusion refers to the process by which ethnic conflict influences the behavior of neighboring ethnic groups in unpredictable and spontaneous ways (such as refugee flows and demonstration effects).

Escalation, in contrast, refers to a set of deliberate strategic interactions and processes by which the behavior of one state creates a crisis for one or more state actors who perceive a core threat to values. Escalation in this context is ethnic conflict leading to crisis, intervention, and possibly war.

More generally, intrastate ethnic conflicts are internationalized by

- the mobilization of political and ideological support from kindred groups in third countries, foreign government, and international or nongovernmental organizations;
- the establishment of sanctuaries in neighboring countries, particularly common where insurgent minorities are dispersed over two or more contiguous states (such as Kurds in Turkey, Iran, and Iraq);
- the spillover of violence into neighboring countries (Rwanda/Congo, Sri Lanka/India, and Afghanistan/Pakistan, among other examples);
- the spillover of terrorist violence into countries that are geographically distant from the initial locus of conflict (Irish terrorist operations on the European continent, Sikh terrorist operations in Europe and North America); and
- flights of refugees now numbering in the tens of millions, the vast majority of whom are displaced by ethnic conflicts.

All internationalized ethnic conflicts are, therefore, high-stake situations where the consequences are far reaching and long lasting. The essential problem is an "emerging anarchy" in which groups that lack many of the attributes of statehood must pay attention to the primary problem of their security (Posen 1993). The terms *security dilemma* and *conflict spiral* apply equally to situations where the pursuit of security by one group serves only to antagonize the other (Kaufman 1997; Posen 1993; Lake and Rothchild 1996). A general lack of trust about the other's intentions compels belligerents to pursue conflict through gradual escalation.

Decision-making theories and theories about preference formation would argue that discrepancies between preferences are more likely to inhibit aggressive domestic policies. Alternative perspectives might argue that any risky strategy could mobilize a counterelite (of a different ethnic group) or alternatively, lead to an uncontrollable situation of "outbidding." When social mobilization is high and political participation is high but there is institutional incompleteness, the capacity for the state to manage the demands made upon it are diminished. Weakened regimes lack the political capacity to carry out reforms peacefully and will rely extensively on coercive means to bring about economic and political change.

An important consideration when weighing these contributing factors is the degree to which they impede or enhance the prospects for a negotiated solution. Consider for example the size and number of groups as a potential impediment to conflict settlement. It is not unrealistic for as many as five or more "multiple sovereignties" to be engaged in a conflict at any given time. In some instances these groups, as noted in chapter 3, may be insurgent movements, representatives of legitimate political parties, or factions within ethnic groups or clans, allied on some issues and divided on others.[1]

As noted in chapters 3, 4, and 5, the fact that most intrastate ethnic conflicts involve both state and nonstate actors adds even greater complexity to the mix. As Ryan has argued, nonstate actors, such as ethnic minorities, lack the legal personality of states and therefore have difficulty relating to international norms and procedures that were designed exclusively for states.[2] Beyond traditional diplomacy and mediation, third-party intervention means developing mechanisms that give representatives of communal groups incentives to enter into internationally brokered negotiations and arrangements.[3]

A third mitigating factor, as noted in chapter 5, is the strategic attractiveness of violence. In essence, the inherent problem in negotiating any internal ethnic conflict is the clear lack of commitment to a negotiated solution. The continuation of violence is highly dependent on "agency." In ethnic disputes in particular, leaders must be convinced of a settlement's long-term viability and convince their followers of its merits. However costly and irrational it appears in human and material terms, violence is a means of safeguarding long-term political and economic outcomes.[4]

Failed states, such as Bosnia, occupy a special place in the pantheon of intransigent strategies. These are situations in which no side is willing to compromise. Since these quasi-states are incapable of providing basic control over political and economic space (Zartman 1995), they are prone to shifting power coalitions. Whenever the internal ethnic balance of power shifts, questions of control become preeminent. Mutually preferable settlements are unattainable because large well-armed groups are aware that they can make greater gains by holding out (Grant 1997).[5] The mistrust that develops increases the advantage for weaker groups to preemptively attack (Hardin 1995, 143).[6]

A final impediment to negotiating a settlement is the power imbalance between groups. It is usually the weaker side that is least likely to be convinced of the virtues of a negotiated solution. Without some significant act of good faith from the stronger side, the weaker side is unlikely to commit to a negotiated solution. There are several reasons for this.

First, getting to an agreed solution is a two-step process consisting of a series of "nested political games." If a less powerful group is to agree voluntarily to abide by a dominant group's rules, its interests also must be assured, including safeguards that the more powerful group cannot exploit it. According to Lake and Rothchild, it is the minority that ultimately determines the viability of any agreement between majority and minority. Unfortunately, the contractual agreements between minority and majority in many new states is so weak that minorities cannot be convinced that their interests are best served through accommodation (Lake and Rothchild 1996).

Groups that are prone to this kind of defection lack either information that would signal the true intent of their adversaries or a sufficient commitment from a third party that will credibly support their cause. Issues of information exchange become paramount in situations of mistrust. As Lake and Rothchild (1996), building on the work of Fearon, somewhat pessimistically conclude,

Where information failures can be mitigated by external mediators and problems of credible commitment offset, in part, by external guarantees of ethnic contracts, the ability of third parties to moderate the security dilemma is very limited. External actors can seek to raise the costs of using force, in general, and preemptive uses of force, in particular, by themselves punishing groups that strike first. Through early intervention and mediation, external actors may also be able to shape military doctrines and force structures in groups beginning to prepare for self-defense. Nevertheless, unless incentives to preempt are in place, there is little outsiders can do to mitigate the security dilemma. But they can do little to change the incentives to preempt that lead groups into the security dilemma.

Given the range of impediments in achieving conflict termination, it would be reasonable to conclude that internationalized ethnic conflicts do not end easily if at all. More specifically, ethnic conflicts should be more difficult to resolve through peaceful negotiation than their nonethnic counterparts.[7] This perspective appears to have support in the literature. For example, Licklider concludes that civil wars over political or economic issues are distinct from ethnic disputes by virtue of the relative ease with which they are terminated (Licklider 1995; Regan 1996a, 1996b; Brecher and Wilkenfeld 1997). It would also be anticipated that terminations are more ambiguous. Ambiguous terminations and resolutions are those resulting in *indecisive results*, such as compromise or stalemate, symbolizing an unresolved conflict. Subsequent crises and violence are anticipated by all adversaries.

The substance of the outcome, on the other hand, refers to the degree to which a political solution is *perceived* to be either ambiguous or definitive. For peace to be durable, it must be accepted by the opposing leaders and their followers. Lund has found that a key impediment to terminating a conflict quickly is a process into which the belligerents cannot put their faith and trust. For a settlement to hold, the participants must perceive that the negotiated solution is capable of maintaining a stable and lasting peace into the unforeseeable future (Lake and Rothchild 1996). A reasonable assessment of how intrastate ethnic conflicts end should include consideration of how the belligerents perceive the termination of the conflict and the form of that settlement. As Brecher and Wilkenfeld argue,

Whatever value is at stake in a particular crisis, ethnic adversaries do not identify its outcome in decisive terms: regardless of the outcome, the underlying conflict remains. . . . In this respect, as in many others, the impact of ethnicity is similar to that of protracted conflict. (Brecher and Wilkenfeld 1997, 172)

As a preliminary point of investigation into the termination of intrastate ethnic conflicts, it is anticipated that there are basic differences in both the form and substance of termination, such that: H_1 intrastate ethnic conflicts are more likely to (*a*) result in fewer definitive outcomes and (*b*) result in fewer formal outcomes.

THE EFFECTIVENESS OF THIRD PARTIES

It should be obvious from the preceding chapters that intervention is not just about mediating civil wars. Building on insights from chapter 6, it is important to understand how less intense forms of third-party intervention compare with other, more coercive strategies.

In theory, the primary responsibility of a third party is to prevent destructive conflict through a variety of noncoercive political channels and actions. This view is consistent with the principles of "preventive diplomacy" wherein the key strategic goal is the active participation of a third party to de-escalate an intrastate ethnic conflict before it becomes violent or to prevent the recurrence of such violence. Such an approach may prove ineffective after hostilities break out and violence is widespread.

In reality, there is little agreement within the discipline on the kinds of strategies necessary for the termination of intrastate ethnic conflicts. Critics have suggested that coercive and unilateral forms of intervention serve only to erode international norms of mutual restraint among states. Others, more provocatively, have argued that the quickest way to terminate an intrastate ethnic conflict with the fewest casualties is to favor the stronger side in any conflict (more often than not the state center) (Regan 1996b; Licklider 1995; see also this volume, chapter 4). Indeed, some ethnic conflicts produce interventions that appear to be motivated by intrastate ethnic struggles for power, as in Bosnia, whereas others, such as Kosovo, appear to be driven by humanitarian concerns.

As pointed out in chapters 4 and 5, there is a significant conceptual and theoretical problem of identifying the independent effects of individual strategies. For the purposes of this investigation, third parties, whether they are states or multilateral actors, are those that have an interest in creating a stable environment in which peace can be nurtured, and in developing a durable framework for a lasting negotiated settlement. These strategies differ from those identified in chapters 3 and 4 to the extent that the former, such as NATO, are essentially concerned with the recurrence, cessation, and prevention of violence. Of course, third-party strategies are not mutually exclusive. For example, as chapter 6 shows, initial mediation by the UN was complemented by UN peacekeeping and eventually NATO peace support activities.[8]

Given the limited knowledge on the effectiveness of third parties in the creation of long-lasting and durable settlements, hypotheses in this chapter are developed with respect to the type of intervener, its range of techniques, and its objectives. Each is considered in turn.

Consistent with the definition provided in chapter 5, the type of intervener refers to either an international/regional organization/coalition of states or an intermediary who is a representative of a state or an institution. As chapter 5 notes, third-party interventions are not limited to international and regional organizations. They may also include ad hoc coalitions of states, regional organizations, one or both of the superpowers, and even neighboring states. Of course, unilateral and multilateral forms of intervention often take place contemporaneously.

The fundamental question of whether individual states or organizations are more effective in terminating intrastate ethnic conflicts was examined in chapter 5. The key question addressed in chapter 5 was whether either would want to absorb the high costs of implementing a broad range of strategies when violence is at hand. It was found in chapter 5 (and chapter 3 and 4 as well) that regional organizations performed favorably in stopping the violence when compared with both individual states and the UN. In this chapter, however, the question is whether the same conclusion can be drawn when the focus is on achieving durable and long-lasting settlements.

There are several reasons to believe that a combination of state and international organizational strategies would prove more effective in the termination and resolution of ethnic strife.

First, faced with an intrastate conflict with regional consequences, third parties are likely to be extremely hesitant to engage in costly strategies at the outset because they lack the sufficient "political will" and resources to fulfill their commitments.[9] Slow escalation of violent conflict may evolve as a result of this unwillingness to "get involved." As the preceding chapters demonstrate, the termination of violence and the subsequent shift to long-term peacebuilding measures requires the military backing of major powers as well as their political support. Third-party interventions of this kind demand close coordination of military, diplomatic, and nongovernmental assets, a coordinated campaign plan, and considerable resources. Few states other than the major powers (such as those in NATO) are capable of providing these resources.

Second, settlements also require the stamp of institutional legitimacy upon which long-term measures depend. As Haas (1983) and Diehl et al. (1996) have shown, in areas where state interests converge, states have generally provided strong support for the application of institutionalized forms of conflict management. In the absence of cooperation among states, institutions, especially the United Nations, have proved far less effective. The most notable aspect of Haas's analysis is UN ineffectiveness when "metaissues" around which state interests coalesce (e.g., postwar decolonization and self-determination in Asia and Africa) are absent.

Turning now to the range of techniques, it is important to point out that intervention does not refer simply to the physical presence of a "managing agent" intent on using coercion to dissuade belligerents from using force to solve their differences (Dixon 1996, 358). Nor has intervention been confined to involvement by states or organizations through military means. Third-party intervention encompasses a broad range of techniques, although it is hard to find agreement on what these might be (Bercovitch 1996). For example, in his assessment of the United Nations' conflict management record, Esman (1995) defines intervention to include good offices, mediation, peacemaking, peacekeeping, protection of human rights, humanitarian assistance, and stigmatization of rogue governments. Esman's typology is analytically useful but far too broad in scope for the comparison of effective strategies. For example, calls for condemnation by the General Assembly would fall under the rubric of intervention even though the UN need not take any follow-up action. Intervention into intrastate ethnic conflicts involves at least some level of active engagement and is not simply a passive response to an issue at hand.

In the context of intrastate ethnic conflicts, rare is the intervention in which third parties have not relied on some form of coercive diplomacy (see chapters 3, 4, and 5) to bring the belligerents to the negotiating table. It is extremely unusual for a single strategy to be implemented over the life of any civil war. Thus it is important to understand when coercive and noncoercive strategies of third-party intervention are complementary and when they are not.[10]

An appreciation for pacific, but not necessarily impartial, forms of third-party intervention is consistent with contingency approaches to conflict resolution.[11] Fisher (1996), for example, draws a line between those strategies that are clearly pacific (such as conventional peacekeeping, track-two diplomacy, and consultation) and those that are not (such as peace enforcement).[12] He argues that the choice of third-party strategy is dependent on the nature of the strategies with which it must interact, and therefore there is no single best approach. If we are to properly understand the role of pacific third-party techniques in the ending of intrastate ethnic conflicts, it is important to understand their relative effectiveness.

For example, Dixon, drawing on the work of Skjelsbaek, provides a fairly comprehensive typology of conflict management principles based on different types of disputes. These principles range from public appeals to communication, observation, physical intervention, pure mediation, humanitarian aid, and adjudication. Dixon's typology is useful because of its comprehensiveness and for its important finding that pure mediation is the most likely strategy to succeed.[13] However, the inclusion of humanitarian assistance as a form of conflict management is somewhat problematic, given that only a handful of cases fit cleanly into this category. Using a similar set of assumptions, Haas (1983) distinguishes between large and small third-party interventions with conciliation, supervision, peacekeeping, and peace enforcement in the former category and investigation, fact finding, and pure mediation in the latter.

In their assessment of third-party effectiveness to terminate intrastate ethnic conflicts, Regan (1996a, 1996b), Vayrynen (1996), Lund (1996a), and Hampson (1996) argue that coalitional third parties will generally begin with lower-cost peaceful tactics such as mediation and condemnation. If those fail, the coalition may choose to escalate the intervention. Thus, intervention "progresses" in the following way: reassurance and preventive diplomacy, verbal appeals to not use force, inducements, deterrence, compellence, and preemption. Ultimately actions taken early on in the life cycle of a conflict are positive strategies (persuasion and rewards), whereas later negative strategies are more coercive in nature.

It is useful to think of intervention to end intrastate ethnic conflicts as a continuum or "spectrum of techniques." Different third-party techniques are set in motion at different points within a conflict (Lund 1996a). At one end of the interventionist spectrum is pure mediation, the facilitation of a negotiated settlement through persuasion, control of information, and identification of alternatives by a party that is perceived to be impartial.[14] Key elements in pacific forms of third-party intervention, such as mediation, are the nature of and level of consent and the level of coercion required to reach a settlement (Durch 1993): "Mediation is a voluntary, ad hoc, non-coercive, flexible, usually secretive mechanism for reducing uncertainty and risks between adversaries and whenever possible in managing a conflict (Bercovitch and Regan 1997, 188)."[15] Halfway up the spectrum is "mediation with muscle," or the deliberate and strategic use of rewards and punishments to bring the belligerents to the negotiating table.[16] Bercovitch, for example, distinguishes between third-party strategies such as communication, formulation, and manipulation on the one hand and tactics that are a function of those strategies on the other. Touval and Zartman use a similar approach; third-party strategies fall under the categories of communication, facilitation, formulation, and directive. All of these make up the range of techniques by third parties short of the use of force.[17] Focusing specifically on destructive conflicts, Bercovitch and Regan observe, "in the context of a detrimental relationship between long-standing rivals, directive strategies will not only be more frequently resorted to, but also more positively associated with a settlement" (1997, 192).

Finally, as shown in chapters 4, 5, and 6, in situations where consent is absent, violence is widespread, and groups are at risk, force comes into play. Under such conditions, third parties are likely to be required to take on a multiplicity of functions, including peacekeeping, humanitarian assistance, and possibly peace enforcement.[18]

Zartman argues that third parties can, in theory, induce negotiated settlements through the creation of hurting stalemates. With the prospect that one party might be eliminated (or at least have its power sufficiently reduced) by a third party, belligerents might be more open to a negotiated solution. Third parties can speed up the movement toward a settlement through the imposition of deadlines and other crisis-related strategies to decrease the perceived attractiveness of military options. Thus, the emergence of a resolving formula follows a readjustment of the belligerents' power relations and the elimination of alternative strategies through concerted effort by third parties.

Presumably under such circumstances, third-party success would be expected if intervention takes place after the belligerents have reached a hurting stalemate and not before. More specifically, there should be a relationship between deescalation, the point at which ripeness appears imminent, and more definitive outcomes. Hampson makes a similar but qualified point when he argues that in some cases the failure of peace accords to "stick" is because of a lack of "ripeness" (Hampson 1996). The settlement task is made easier, Hampson argues, if the groups have reached their own self-imposed "hurting stalemate." Absent a hurting stalemate, the tasks of the third party are simplified but less likely to prove fruitful. If no ripe moment exists, the purpose of the intervention can only be to separate the forces.[19]

On an abstract level, the objectives of the third-party intervention are very complex, ranging from the strengthening of international norms (Vayrynen 1997; Hampson 1996), to the reduction and elimination of armed violence (Licklider 1995), to the pursuit of larger geostrategic goals (Heraclides 1991).

On the other hand, it is important to measure the effectiveness of third parties in settling a conflict, not just ending the violence. Stable and long-lasting outcomes—as perceived through the eyes of the belligerent and the third party—are important for several reasons. Outcomes provide a reasonable indication of how "solid" a settlement is from the perspective of the belligerents. It tells us about the possibility of recurrence and the degree to which the conflict's underlying issues have been resolved. A decisive outcome is one in which the starting and end points are more autonomous. Crises are discrete and outcomes are clearer. Victory and defeat may be more readily identifiable and accepted as such (Brecher and Wilkenfeld 1997). Stable outcomes are those with definitive end points.

It is also important to measure effectiveness by the form of outcome achieved. Was a formal settlement achieved? Did one party impose a unilateral solution? Did the third party impose a solution, or did the crisis simply fade away only to recur again? Thus, outcomes can also be assessed objectively by their content. The form of the outcome refers to how the conflict was terminated, ranging from formal negotiated agreements to tacit understandings that a crisis will fade until the outbreak of the next crisis.

Thus,

H_2: definitive outcomes in intrastate ethnic conflicts are a result of

    a. a combination of pacific and nonspecific third-party techniques;
    b. a combination of state and IO involvement;
    c. de-escalation of the conflict,

and

H_3: formal agreements in intrastate ethnic conflicts are a result of

    a. a combination of pacific and nonspecific third-party techniques;
    b. a combination of state and IO involvement;
    c. de-escalation of the conflict.

GATHERING THE EVIDENCE AND MEASURING EFFECTIVENESS

As in chapter 5, this assessment of third-party intervention effectiveness uses actor level data taken from the International Crisis Behavior project for the period 1945–1994. As previously noted, there are several reasons for using crisis data. The data are very good for assessing the proposed relationships because they provide a range of internationalized intrastate ethnic conflicts as well as dependent and control variables far in excess of data that focus exclusively on war. Although crises are by definition conflicts, not all conflicts necessarily lead to war. Indeed, many crises are managed successfully without recourse to violence. Therefore the data capture a broad range of behavior, including that which falls short of war, but nevertheless reveal a significant level of conflict.

The crisis data focus specifically on both interstate and intrastate conflicts that have produced an international crisis. Similar to Vayrynen's definition of external riskiness noted above, ICB defines an international crisis as a disruption in process and a challenge in the structure of the international system. Cases that have yet to produce an international crisis are not included. Many prominent domestic conflicts are by definition excluded (Northern Ireland and Quebec separatism, for example).

One approach that might be useful, had it included measurements of internationalized intrastate ethnic conflicts, is the Overt Military Intervention File developed by Herbert Tillema. The file is designed to measure all authoritative military operations that directly involve a state in foreign combat or unilaterally and irrevocably commit regular military forces to combat should resistance be met (Tillema 1989, 181). The file contains data in excess of 591 instances of overt military intervention within more than 269 armed conflicts since World War II. On the one hand, the file is useful because of its breadth of coverage, including interventions that have ethnic strife as their source. For example, Tillema shows that 40 civil and regional conflicts attracted major foreign military intervention. Seven of the 40 conflicts were of national liberation by colonial peoples, and 16 of the 40 took place along intrastate ethnic or cross-border lines of "ethnopolitical" cleavage. Almost all of the countries that intervened in these 23 ethnic conflicts were Third World regimes (India, Libya, and Pakistan, for example).[20] Since the data are concerned only with overt military hostilities rather than the broader concept of internationalized conflict, comparative analysis is difficult. This fact, and the absence of comprehensive domestic variables, makes the data set useful only for developing intercoder reliability.

The ICB data set is not an exhaustive list of ethnic conflicts having an international dimension. However, the population size is large enough and the spatial and temporal characteristics representative enough to justify its utilization. For example, a comparison of the Overt Military Intervention File and the ICB data set shows that more than 67 percent of overt interventions are also found in the ICB data. Of the conflicts that include one or more foreign overt military interventions, which each sustain 100 or more combat fatalities (N=47), 95 percent are found in the ICB data. These positive results are a useful basis for external validation and indicate that the cases selected do have face validity.

Each case must fulfill the definition of a foreign policy crisis. A foreign policy crisis is defined as

[a] situation with three individually and collectively sufficient conditions, deriving from changes in a state's internal ethnic or external environment. All three perceptions are held by the highest-level decision-makers of the actor concerned: a threat to basic values, awareness of finite time for response to the value threat and a high probability of involvement in military hostilities. (Brecher and Wilkenfeld 1991)

A two-stage content analysis for each crisis was carried out to distinguish intrastate ethnic conflicts from interstate conflicts. In *Crisis, Conflict and Instability*, Michael Brecher and Patrick James argue that internal ethnic conflicts are defined by political, economic, and social upheavals at the domestic level. In other cases "external crises have fuelled the fires of internal ethnic disruption" (1989, 91). A conflict was deemed intrastate ethnic if (*a*) it involved a single crisis actor and the trigger to the conflict came from within that state, or (*b*) it involved multiple crisis actors and the trigger to the conflict came from within a single state. Of the 630 actor level crises, roughly one-third or 220 crises were coded as intrastate ethnic conflicts for the period 1945–1994.[21]

For the purposes of this chapter, political and ideological conflicts are those where groups refuse to recognize the existing political authorities, which can trigger a foreign policy crisis for the state in question. The result is an internal ethnic challenge leading to potential conflict, crisis, and war.

Two dependent variables are used to explain the way in which a conflict was terminated. Termination represents a decline in the intensity of threat perception and hostility and is measured by the type of outcome in substance and form. The form of the outcome is measured in four ways: formal agreements; unilateral acts; an "other" category, which includes imposed solutions and tacit understandings; and faded (no formal agreement or recognized termination point). The substance of the outcome refers to either ambiguous or decisive terminations (Brecher and Wilkenfeld 1997).

In the most optimistic of scenarios, the substance of conflict termination is understood as the extent to which violence has subsided as indicated by the acceptance of a "peace accord" and by the return to stable and peaceful relations among belligerents (Hampson 1996; Licklider 1995). Recognizing that there is never a guarantee against recurrence, most analysts ascribe a certain minimum period in which hostilities have ended to determine whether peace has been restored. For most analysts, success or failure is equated with outcome. A power sharing agreement in combination with an absence of hostilities over a five-year period is thought to be a good indicator of effective termination (Licklider 1995; Sisk 1996). For example, the extent of a third party's success is determined by the number of objectives reached (Kleiboer 1997).

The type of third-party intervener was identified as either an intermediary state or an international organization that actively participated in the management of the crisis. A category accounting for both state and organizational involvement was created to account for those cases in which both types of interveners were involved in the management and termination of the conflict.

Table 7.1
Outcomes of Ethnic vs. Ideological/Political Crises, 1945–1994

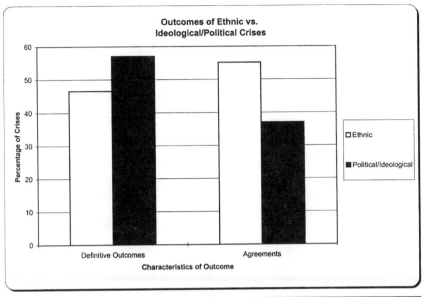

Type of Conflict:	Number of Crises	Percentage of Crises Resulting in:	
		Definitive Outcomes	Agreements
Ethnic	118	46.6	55.2
Political/Ideological	98	57.1	37.1

Measures of Statistical Association:
Somer's D	-0.10491
Gamma	-0.20863
Tau-b	-0.10491

As part of the testing, each crisis management strategy was assessed for its content and dichotomized by pacific and nonpacific strategies.[22]

To assess the timing of a crisis, phases for each crisis were identified. The first 20 percent of the crisis period from onset to peak point was allocated to escalation, 60 percent to the middle or peak period, and 20 percent to the de-escalation period.

The results from testing are provided in Tables 7.1, 7.2, and 7.3.

Hypothesis 1 tests for differences in outcome by type of conflict, the results of which are reported on the left side of Table 7.1. The results provide tentative support for H_{1a} with respect to the substance of outcomes in intrastate ethnic conflicts. Slightly more than 10 percent of the political/ideological conflicts resulted in definitive outcomes. Slightly less than half of all ethnic conflicts, on

Table 7.2

Third-party Technique and Substance of Outcome, 1945–1994

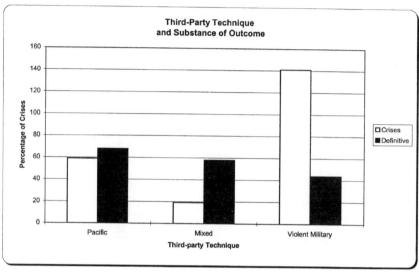

	Number of	Substance of Outcome:	
Crisis Management Technique:	Crises	Definitive	Ambiguous
Pacific	59	67.9	32.1
Mixed	19	57.9	42.1
Violent Military	141	44	56.0

Measures of Statistical Association:

Somer's D	-0.20306
Gamma	-0.39515
Tau-b	-0.20306

the other hand, resulted in outcomes that could be called definitive. This makes intuitive sense, since many ethnic conflicts are protracted disputes encompassing more than one crisis. We rely on *gamma* and *tau* statistics, both commonly used inferential statistics for ordinal variables. The gamma statistic is strong, implying that the "type of conflict" is related to outcome, although the numbers are more impressive for substance than form. Gamma measures the proportion (percentage) of errors we can reduce when predicting values on the dependent variable, given information on the independent variable. A gamma of .208 means we can reduce about 20 percent of the error when predicting values on the dependent variable. In the context of our study, for example, a gamma of 1.00 (or −1.00) means we would always be correct when predicting outcomes in a crisis if we knew the type of conflict.

Turning to H_{1b}, the results, as reported on the right side of Table 7.1, are

Table 7.3
Type of Third-party Interveners and Substance of Crisis Outcome, 1945–1994

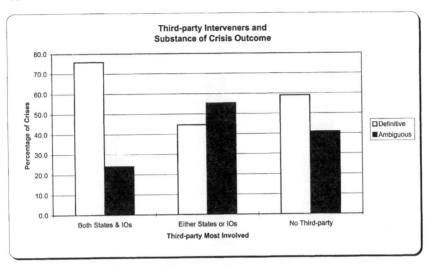

Third-party Intervener:	Number of Crises	Substance of Crisis Outcome:	
		Definitive	Ambiguous
Both States & IOs	29	75.9	24.1
Either States or IOs	148	44.6	55.4
No Third-party	39	59.0	41.0

Measures of Statistical Association:
Somer's D   -0.06153
Gamma   -0.12288
Tau-b   -0.06154

clearly counterintuitive. It had been anticipated that ethnic conflicts would involve a greater number of unilateral acts and fewer negotiated outcomes. The results show that a relatively large number of ethnic conflicts were terminated in a formal agreement as compared with political or ideological disputes (by a margin of almost 20 percent). Although this margin of difference is somewhat surprising, it is consistent with Licklider's results (Licklider 1995). He found that ethnic conflicts and political/economic wars were equally likely to end in a negotiated settlement. We can conclude from these mixed results, again consistent with Licklider, that although ethnic conflicts are more likely to end in a negotiated settlement, they are also more likely to be unstable outcomes. Insofar as negotiated outcomes involve some sort of power balancing and political trade-offs, this makes intuitive sense: parties to a conflict that are not eliminated

Table 7.4
Crisis Phases and Substance of Crisis Outcome, 1945–1994

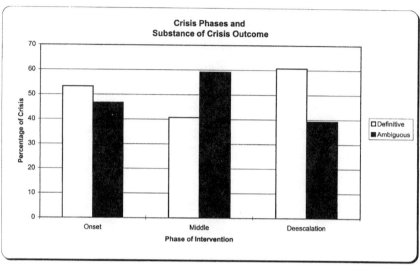

Phase of Intervention:	Number of Crises	Substance of Outcome:	
		Definitive	Ambiguous
Onset	135	53.3	46.7
Middle	49	40.8	59.2
Deescalation	28	60.7	39.3

Measures of Statistical Association:

Somer's D	-0.02401
Gamma	-0.04659
Tau-b	-0.02401

through unilateral solutions are more likely to challenge again. We did not examine in detail the differences between those negotiated ethnic conflicts that ended in renewed conflict and those unilateral conflicts that did, but it seems reasonable to assume that ethnic conflicts that are formally terminated are no more likely to be single crises.

Table 7.2 reports the results in testing H_{2a}. The general hypothesis is concerned with identifying those factors that result in definitive outcomes (regardless of conflict type). It was argued that more definitive outcomes should be associated with combinations of pacific and coercive strategies, mixed state/ organizational interventions, and points after which the crisis has "ripened" or approached termination.

Table 7.2 indicates that definitive outcomes are more likely when pacific strategies are applied, a result that is not unappealing, but is nevertheless in-

Table 7.5
Third-party Techniques and Form of Outcome, 1945–1994

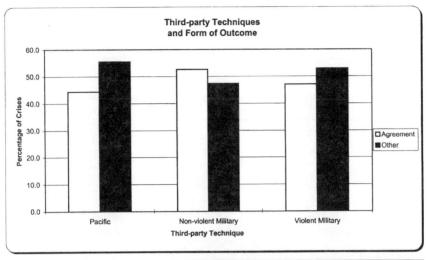

Third-party Technique:	Number of Crises	Form of Outcome:			
		Agreement	Unilateral Act	Other	Faded
Pacific	54	44.4	46.3	7.4	1.9
Mixed	19	52.6	36.8	5.3	5.3
Violent Military	140	47.1	41.4	7.1	4.3

Measures of Statistical Association:
Somer's D	-0.00065
Gamma	-0.00120
Tau-b	-0.00065

consistent with H_{2a}. It is important to note, however, that violent third-party techniques are least likely to result in definitive outcomes. Only 44 percent of those cases in which violent third-party techniques were applied resulted in definitive outcomes as compared with almost 68 percent under pacific techniques.

For H_{2b}, the results, reported in Table 7.3, are surprisingly strong. Definitive outcomes occur in more than 75 percent of the cases in which both states and IOs are involved as managers. This compares with 45 percent of cases where either a state or an IO intervened alone and 59 percent of cases where no third party was present.

Table 7.4 reports the results for testing H_{2c}. This hypothesis finds strong support. Definitive outcomes are most clearly associated with the latter stages of a conflict. Conversely, the peak point of crises are least likely to witness definitive outcomes by a margin of 13 percent.

Table 7.6

Type of Third-party Intervener and Form of Crisis Outcome, 1945–1994

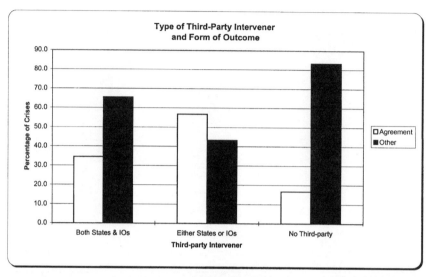

Type of Third-party:	Number of Crises	Form of Outcome:			
		Agreement	Unilateral Act	Other	Faded
Both States & IOs	29	34.5	62.1	0.0	3.4
Either States or IOs	148	56.8	32.4	8.1	2.7
No Third-party	36	16.7	66.7	8.3	8.3

Measures of Statistical Association:
Somer's D	0.13273
Gamma	0.23724
Tau-b	0.13365

Tables 7.5, 7.6, and 7.7 present the results for testing general hypothesis 3. Here the concern is identifying those factors associated with formal third-party-assisted negotiated outcomes. Some of the results are counter to those hypothesized.

In Table 7.5, H_{3a} finds mild support. Formal agreements are more likely when a combination of pacific and nonpacific techniques are applied (column two). Violent strategies appear to fare somewhat better than pacific strategies. Overall, third-party techniques appear to have a success rate of about 50 percent, regardless of the type.

Table 7.6 reports the results for H_{3b}. Formal agreements of intrastate ethnic conflicts are more likely to arise as the result of either state or IO involvement but not both. More than 50 percent of crises involving either states or IOs resulted in formal agreements, 17 percent of those cases in which no third party

Table 7.7
Crisis Phases and Form of Outcome, 1945–1994

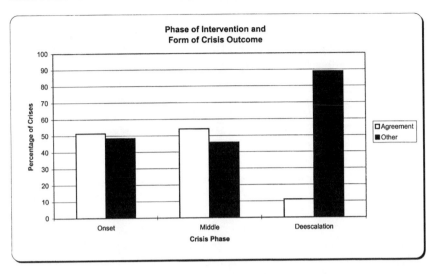

	Number	*Form of Outcome:*			
Crisis Phase:	*of Crises*	Agreement	Unilateral Act	Other	Faded
Onset	134	51.5	38.1	6.0	4.5
Middle	48	54.2	37.5	8.3	0.0
Deescalation	27	11.1	74.1	11.1	3.7

Measures of Statistical Association:
Somer's D	0.13876
Gamma	0.24438
Tau-b	0.13906

was involved resulted in a formal agreement, and 35 percent of those in which both states and IOs were involved led to formal agreement.

Many intervening factors could account for the differences summarized in Table 7.6. One possibility is that the type of conflict is having a confounding effect on the original relationship as noted in chapter 5. A second possibility is that when states (and organizations) are engaged independently of one another, they may have greater latitude in preventing the imposition of unilateral solutions by the stronger on the weaker. This may be especially true in those ethnic conflicts where third parties intervene not only to mediate but to prevent the destruction of their ethnic brethren. Although these results are mixed, it is clear that third-party intervention is more likely to lead to a formal outcome than when the disputants are left to negotiate on their own. Indeed unilateral solutions are most likely when no third party is present, which suggests that regardless of type, third parties do have a moderating and positive influence on the outcome.

Turning to H_{3c} the results in Table 7.7 show that more formal agreements arise early on in the life of a crisis. This finding in itself is surprising. It had been anticipated that formal agreements would come about only after the belligerents had reached a hurting stalemate, which presumably would come later in a conflict. Since hurting stalemates are by definition those situations where neither party is capable of imposing a unilateral solution, the fact that so many unilateral solutions come at the latter stages of a crisis is important. It means, as Licklider points out, that even after the parties are exhausted, at least one belligerent is capable of imposing its will.

In surveying these results it is important to consider varying levels of intensity among the crises examined. Not all of the cases in this analysis are violent nor are all equivalent to civil wars with a threshold of 1,000 battlefield fatalities. Some are resolved amicably and diffused at an early stage without recourse to violence. Taken together, these and other threats to validity suggest that more research and testing of a more complete set of interactions between type of conflict, the type of intervener, the timing, and the outcome are required.

A final observation on these findings relates to the differences between how a crisis termination is perceived in substance and in form. Third parties may be effective in reaching formal agreements, but this furnishes no guarantee that the parties to a conflict will perceive that settlement as definitive. Nor does it furnish any guarantee of recurrence.

CONCLUSIONS AND DIRECTIONS FOR FURTHER RESEARCH

Thus far the biggest impediment to strengthening peaceful approaches to winding down conflicts is a basic incongruity in today's international system. On the one hand, the end of the Cold War has made the possibility of the peaceful management of disputes seem more realistic (Hampson 1996). On the other hand, there has been a decided shift in conflict management approaches away from sponsoring proxy wars and toward the accommodation of contending interests. This approach has ramifications for the peaceful management of intrastate ethnic conflicts in three ways.

First, if the results from this research are taken at face value, it may not always be in the best interests of third parties to pursue formal agreements between belligerents. At the minimum, formal agreements do not signal the end of a conflict. In particular, ethnic conflicts ending in formal agreements are prone to recurrence. Although there are important reasons to believe that compromise is good, it may also lead to unresolved issues and renewed tensions. States and international organizations may have to be more discriminating about the sites and types of intervention they choose. Perhaps effectiveness should be defined not as resolution of conflict per se, but instead as the cessation of violence and the initiation of a process whereby adversaries can address underlying sources of hostility. Second, the amount of conflict in today's world is simply too much for the military forces of a few states to manage effectively. Consistent with chapter 5, the results of this chapter suggest that states and coalitions of states are as well equipped to wind down intrastate ethnic conflicts as are international organizational counterparts.

Finally, can we assume that it is always in the interests of a third party to intervene early and coercively if necessary, in order to obtain a negotiated settlement and to prevent unilateral action? This has been a key argument throughout the volume. Several alternatives should be considered before answering this question. Although more conflicts may result in formal agreements at the early stages of a crisis, it must be kept in mind that these agreements are not always perceived as "definitive" in the eyes of the belligerents. More ethnic disputes resulted in formal outcomes than did their nonethnic counterparts, but their outcomes were also decidedly ambiguous. Thus, although there is a greater chance for the formal settlement of ethnic conflicts within the early stages, there is also a greater chance of their recurrence.

If Licklider is correct in assuming that negotiated settlements are more likely to result in future conflict (1995, 687), then there is a basic dilemma for third parties. Early intervention may result in formal agreements and a cessation of violence, but these outcomes are not always likely to "stick." On the other hand, late interventions may result in unilateral solutions with the attendant dangers of genocide, state failure, refugee flows, and ethnic cleansing. For third parties, and the international community in general, it should be obvious that the former outcome is always preferable to the latter.

NOTES

1. Consider that during Sri Lanka's civil war no fewer than six insurgent movements were engaged in war with one another and the Sri Lankan state. In Somalia, fifteen clan groups were engaged in the negotiation process with UN representative Mohamed Sahnoun.

2. Consider Brecher (1993), who found that crises are more likely to escalate to violence when three or more actors are involved and they take place within a protracted conflict.

3. Basic principles determining classical UN Charter chapter 6 operations include impartiality, consent, and the use of force only for self-defense.

4. Since representing an ethnic group can provide specific benefits (such as prestige and military power), leaders may be more interested in prolongation and future escalation.

Licklider found that instances of genocide toward a group generally increase after that group is defeated in an identity-based civil war. The problem, as Licklider has shown, is that intrastate ethnic conflicts ending with a military victory are generally more stable than those that are negotiated (1995). The dilemma for the third party in this situation is, as Regan has demonstrated, whether to quickly terminate a conflict by favoring the stronger side or to protect the weaker side but also potentially prolong the conflict in doing so. Fearon (1995) argues that intrastate wars, specifically ethnic ones, result from a commitment problem that arises when two political communities find themselves without a third party that can guarantee agreements between them.

5. Some intrastate ethnic conflicts tend to be less protracted than conventional interstate wars precisely because they are more likely to end in a military victory by one side (Licklider 1995).

6. The inability of groups to uphold or negotiate ethnic "contracts" that would prevent a costly fight is higher when there is no external guarantor of security arrangements (Lake and Rothchild 1996). Under these circumstances, efforts to manage the conflict shift from the domestic to the international environment.

7. See Dixon (1996) for a fuller treatment.

8. For example, consider that during the life cycle of the Bosnian conflict third-party strategies included mediation, peacekeeping, peace enforcement, observation, and adjudication.

9. Adelman and Suhrke have suggested that one of the greatest problems in UN intervention is policy incoherence (Adelman and Suhrke 1996). The commensurate bureaucratic pulling and hauling within and between institutions stifles immediate response and leads to ambiguous half measures.

10. In their evaluations of a range of cases, Regan (1996a, 1996b), Bercovitch (1996), Dixon (1996), Tillema (1989), Haas (1983), and Carment and James (1997) conclude that in any given conflict, third parties will generally employ as many different strategies as possible, including economic and military initiatives. Regan's typology provides insight into how the status of the intervener and the party against whom action is directed impacts successful outcomes. He concludes that mixed strategies by powerful interveners on behalf of a government are more likely to lead to a cessation of hostilities.

11. At crisis onset, several traits distinguish the strategy of the third-party intervener. Three possible strategies are available: (1) forceful intervention, (2) efforts at mediation coupled with a low-intensity conventional peacekeeping mission, and (3) withdrawal. Each strategy involves risk. Doing nothing may precipitate undesirable outcomes as noted above in the Rwanda case. Forceful intervention may lead to further escalation and unnecessary costs for the intervener. Finally, low-intensity missions may not only produce undesirable results for the third party but may also lead to further gains for the belligerent. In this instance the intervener may be better off by not getting involved at all (Diehl et al. 1996, Carment and Rowlands 1998).

12. A third-party coalition intervenes against a protagonist on behalf of either a group or a state center to suppress or support the internal ethnic challenge (Regan 1996a, 1996b).

13. There may be an important selection effect here insofar as some states may be more predisposed to certain techniques than others. See G. A. Raymond, "Democracies, Disputes and Third-Party Intermediaries," *Journal of Conflict Resolution* vol. 38, no. 1 (1994).

14. The term *impartiality* implies that the third party is acting in the interests of all

the parties. Where pure mediation may imply the absence of bias toward the interests of the parties, it does not mean that the mediator is neutral or indifferent to outcome. Presumably mediators have an interest in seeing that a violent conflict end as quickly as possible.

15. For some observers, institutionalized forms of pure mediation do not exist in international politics (Touval 1996). Others have suggested that any form of institutionalized mediation is likely to violate the principles of pure mediation. Pure mediation, they argue, is found only in informal, non-power-based situations involving nonstate actors (Touval and Zartman 1996). We use mediation and intervention interchangeably. See Chapter 5.

16. In principle, any attempt to alter or disrupt the internal ethnic affairs of a state constitutes a form of intervention. It includes the calculated use of political, economic, and military instruments by an external actor to influence the domestic and foreign policies of another country. It is also possible to have both multilateral and unilateral intervention occur within the same theater of conflict. Bosnia illustrates this point with Serbian and Croatian intervention being unilateral, and UN and NATO intervention being multilateral.

17. The decision to pursue these goals through military escalation imposes costs on both the belligerents and third-party coalitions. The escalating actor suffers the costs associated with expending resources and risking lives, whereas the receiving actor suffers the costs of lost territory and lives and also a reduced chance of obtaining specific benefits at the bargaining table (Maoz 1990; Carment and Rowlands 1998).

18. Third-party coalitions usually begin the bargaining process by articulating proposals for a negotiated solution coinciding with a low-intensity mission. This proposal can be either accepted or rejected by the belligerent. This initial action requires no force on the part of the third-party coalition. If one side accepts the terms for agreement, then both sides receive the benefits they associate with the proposed outcome. If an offer is rejected, the bargaining process continues and neither player receives any benefits until one of the sides concedes to a demand. See Chapter 5.

19. Others following on Zartman's insight on the use of third parties as power balancers include Lake and Rothchild (1996), Fearon (1995), and Ruggie (1994). At this stage intervention requires territorial demarcation as well as some minimal agreement between enemies. Getting to the stage of a "hurting stalemate," however, requires third parties to wait on the sidelines of a conflict and endure the associated political and economic costs and risks (Carment and Rowlands 1998; Weiss 1994).

20. See Gurr (1990) for an analysis of the Tillema data.

21. Of the cases, slightly less than half (ninety-eight) were identified as political or ideological intrastate ethnic conflicts, with the remainder being ethnic conflicts. Of these, thirty-nine, or roughly one-fifth of the cases, did not involve a third party. Each crisis was then coded on the basis of whether ethnicity was deemed a salient factor in the conflict. For the purposes of this chapter, ethnic conflicts were identified as one of three kinds: secessionist, distributional, or irredentist. A secessionist conflict is the formal *and* informal aspects of political alienation in which one or more ethnic groups seek a reduction of control or autonomy from a central authority. A distributional conflict is one in which a group or groups seek redistribution of resources through political and military means. Such conflicts may or may not involve (*a*) the use of force and (*b*) politically mobilized, well-organized, ethnic insurgency movements. An irredentist conflict is one that triggers a foreign policy crisis for a state through an internal ethnic challenge supported by the redeeming state. The nonethnic conflict category consists of both political

and ideological wars. There is some consistency in recent research to justify this separate category. For example, Licklider (1995) equates all intrastate ethnic conflicts with civil wars and includes in that category both identity civil wars and political/economic wars. Similarly Regan (1996a, 1996b), using three categories, separates religious wars from ethnic wars and ideological wars. Of course some ideological conflicts carry with them a heavy ethnic component and, similarly, not all ethnic conflicts are about differences in identity.

22. International organizations were included with regional organizations. For organizations, pacific forms of involvement include: (a) discussion without resolution, (b) resolution without action, (c) resolution with authorized members active, (d) general assembly discussion only, (e) fact-finding missions, (f) good offices resolutions, and, (g) mediation. Nonpacific forms of involvement include: (a) sanctions, (b) observer force, and (c) emergency military force. For third-party states, pacific forms include: (a) negotiation, (b) adjudication, and (c) mediation, and nonpacific forms include: (a) multiple including violence, (b) nonmilitary pressure, (c) non-violent military pressure, and (d) violence only.

8

Conclusion: The Evolution of Ethnic Conflict

INTRODUCTION

We began this book with a search for the most meaningful causes and consequences of ethnic conflict in an effort to come to grips with this scourge of the 1990s and to better understand when, where, and how organizations such as NATO will be more effective in its prevention, management, and resolution. Along the way we have examined the precise role NATO and other third-party interveners can play in influencing the dynamics of ethnic conflict from onset to de-escalation to termination.

This chapter presents a brief summary of evolutionary co-adaptation involving ethnic groups and third parties. We evaluate the impact of co-evolutionary forces, namely the evolution of NATO peace operations as detailed in chapters 3, 4, and 6, to reestablish the predominance of environmental stimuli and, therefore, the utility of standard social scientific models when explaining ethnic conflict.

EVOLUTIONARY THEORY AND ETHNIC CONFLICT

The approach used in this volume has been an exploration of the relationship between third parties and the timing and intensity of ethnic violence. Changes in this relationship can be described as a co-evolutionary process. A few words on the distinction between "analogy" and "theory" are in order. Most applications of evolutionary theory in the social sciences (and, more specifically, international relations) attempt to explain behavior with reference to analogies derived from biological sciences. Contributions to a recent symposium on Evolutionary Paradigms in the Social Sciences,[1] for example, all use evolutionary processes of *selection, fitness,* and *adaptability* to explain (describe) everything from foreign policy decisions (Farkas, 1996), to the development of international institutions and norms (Florini 1996), to long-term economic growth (Hodgson 1996), and to the "economic evolution of national systems" (Gilpin 1996). Each is a detailed account of how both behavior and institutions get selected because they are more adaptive for individuals or groups within particular environments. Except in the most general sense of "survival of the fittest," there is no attempt to link this behavior to specific biological forces that compel individuals or groups to select one type of behavior over another. Modelski and Poznanski even acknowledge that the key question guiding the entire project was whether there are "conditions such that an evolutionary analogy is justified" (Modelski and Poznanski 1996, 316). The problem with analogies, as Barkow, Cosmides, and Tooby (1992, xvii) point out, is that they may indicate some general underlying historical or psychological processes, but they do not prove the existence of underlying biological or evolutionary forces.

Evolutionary psychology and sociobiology, on the other hand, are more explicit about the role of biology in the development of human social behavior. The approach explains behavior by reconstructing problems our ancestors faced in their primitive environments in order to identify specific problem-solving behaviors they developed to meet those particular challenges (Spriggs 1996). From these reconstructed problem-solving adaptations, "the science then attempts to explain how those common behavioral roots are manifested today in a variety of cultures, beliefs, and behaviors." The key difference between evolutionary analysis (analogy) and evolutionary theories is the belief that humans behave for reasons that have less to do with the environment, and more to do with biological forces that help individuals or groups adapt to local environments.[2] The research program is driven by the conviction that nothing moves us to act in particular ways more strongly than elements of our psyche of which we are completely unaware (Tooby and Cosmides 1992, xvi).

The vast literature on *cultural selection* is most relevant to this position and has developed along several different tracks: basic evolutionism (Lamarck 1809; Darwin 1869; Spencer 1873, 1876), social Darwinism (McDougall 1908, 1921) and its critics (Keller 1916), functionalism (Bock 1963; Radcliffe-Brown 1952), neo-evolutionism (Sahlins and Service 1960), diffusionism (Harris 1969), sociobiology (Wilson 1975), and so on. Many of these works explore the interaction between genetic and cultural selection (Durham 1991; Dawkins 1976) and have identified crucial similarities between biological and cultural evolution, examples of which are summarized by Fog (1996, 1):

People with certain life-styles or attitudes get more children on average than others, and if these life-styles are transmitted to the children, they are likely to spread more than other forms. Societies with certain religions have higher chances of winning wars and conquering new land than others, and consequently these religions are likely to spread. People with certain ideas or behavior patterns have higher chances than others of becoming leaders, teachers, or idols, and thereby transmitting their behavior patterns to a high number of cultural descendants. People who display success or prestige get imitated more than others. This also applies to traits which do not contribute to their success or prestige. Certain stories or discourses have a particularly high propensity for being told and passed on, because they appeal to certain feelings, because they are suited for working through psychological conflicts, because they serve as negative identification models, or because alternative discourses are hindered by cultural taboos or by incompatibility with existing preconceptions.

As Fog (1996, 4) points out, "these unconscious and 'automatic' selection mechanisms are particularly interesting to study because they are not planned and their consequences are not consciously intended or foreseen." With this in mind, the next question is whether the approach can help explain ethnic conflict.

Melotti's comprehensive review of research on in-group/out-group relations serves as an excellent source of information about the relationship between evolutionary processes and ethnic violence at particular points in time. Citing works by Spencer (1893) and Summer and Keller (1927), intergroup conflict often results from the interaction between two different genetic codes: a code of *amity* toward members of one's own group, and a code of *enmity* toward members of other groups" (Melotti 1986, 97). Codes are selected (in an evolutionary sense) depending on whether they confer a strong or weak selective advantage to individual or group survival. The question then becomes, When and under what conditions is one or the other strategy more or less likely to get selected? When the security, safety, and survival of the group is not an issue, *amity* (even among ethnic groups) is expected to be a more fit strategy, as was the case with the Serbs and Muslims prior to the outbreak of ethnic violence in 1990. Alternatively, when security is not assured, the survival of the individual, group, or state dictates that *enmity* is a more fit approach to social behavior, because it more effectively accommodates the group's interests and allows members to direct a larger pool of resources toward withstanding "other" individuals, groups, cultures, or states.

A similar argument is put forward by Grieco (1988, 1990) in his response to Keohane's observation (1984, 1986) that growing levels of global economic cooperation among states renders obsolete the traditional, state-centric "realist" paradigm. Grieco points out that a high level of mutual cooperation between states (or, by extension, ethnic groups) is not evidence that anarchy is no longer a defining characteristic of interstate (or intrastate) politics. Such high levels of cooperation are expected when security is not an issue. If security is scarce, however, cooperation becomes more difficult precisely because states (or ethnic groups), for security reasons, begin measuring benefits on the basis of relative, not absolute, gains. Under these circumstances states are more likely to reject cooperation, all else being equal, even if it produces absolute benefits, since an opponent may obtain a higher relative yield through defection.[3] Monod (1971) makes a similar argument in the context of evolutionary theory and intergroup conflict: "when man had more or less mastered the inimical forces of his . . . environment (such as hunger, cold, and predatory animals), war became the main selective factor in human evolution." Prior to that point, survival was dependent on cooperating to combat common enemies.

With respect to ethnic conflict in Bosnia and Kosovo, the changes in the former Yugoslavia around 1991–1992 (the decision by the European community, urged to recognize Slovenian and Croatian independence) may have created the conditions for a shift in strategy, making *enmity* a more fit alternative to *amity*. This also explains why ethnicity was readily politicized in 1991–1992 and not earlier, and why Bosnian Serbs and Muslims were persuaded, at that point in time, that the environmental stimuli—such as ethnic hatreds, religious division, economic disparities, a long history of ethnic cleansing, and genocide by both sides—were now relevant, when prior to that point the same environmental factors, signals, and stimuli were apparently irrelevant.

An equally convincing, although somewhat more sophisticated, evolutionary explanation for the timing of ethnic violence in the former Yugoslavia downplays the influence of environmental forces by re-evaluating their relative impact from the perspective of evolutionary theory. This explanation is derived from what Tooby and Cosmides (1992, 84) refer to as the *developmentally relevant environment*—"those particular aspects of the world that are rendered developmentally relevant by the evolved design of an organism's developmental adaptations." More specifically,

recurrent organization of the environment contributes a biological inheritance parallel to that of the genes, which acts co-equally with them to evolutionarily organize the organism throughout its life. Every time one gene is selected over another, one design for a development program is selected over another as well; by virtue of its structure, this developmental program interacts with some aspects of the environment rather than others, rendering certain environmental features causally relevant to development. So step by step, as natural selection constructs the species gene set (chosen from the available mutations) it constructs in tandem the species developmentally relevant environment (selected from the set of all properties of the world). (1992, 84)

The authors go on to question the almost automatic assumption held by proponents of the standard social scientific model "that traits and behaviors can be divided into genetically versus environmentally controlled sets, or arrayed along a spectrum that reflects the relative influence of genes versus environment." Behavior "is fully and equally co-determined by the interaction of the organism's genes (embedded in its initial package of zygotic cellular machinery) and its ontogenetic environments. . . . Natural selection actually adaptively organizes gene-environment interactions over time." In other words, "the environment is just as much the product of evolution as are the genes" (1992, 83–84).

With respect to ethnic conflict, then, we are all programmed to select both amity and enmity, but are preprogrammed to select the approach that best serves the individual or group under different sets of circumstances. In the case of the former Yugoslavia, for instance, the environmental stimuli used by elites following the breakup of Yugoslavia (economic divisions along ethnic lines, religious hatreds, memories of ethnic cleansing in World War II, and so on) were all present before and after the war. They were selected as the *developmentally relevant environment* (and stimuli) because at the time, this same information provided a better fit, under changing conditions, as an adaptive mechanism for group identity and survival. Beliefs, like genes, get selected because of their fitness, defined as adaptability to changing environmental circumstances such that the survival of the individual or group is enhanced. To the extent that ethnic hatred and violence (enmity) are more likely than not to help individuals cope, adapt, and survive, violence becomes a more acceptable behavioral trait.

OUTSIDE PARTIES AND EVOLUTIONARY FORCES IN ETHNIC CONFLICT

Using evolutionary theory as the sole explanation of ethnic conflict is as unwise as relying on primordialist explanations (examined in chapter 1). This argument becomes clearer when one considers the role and impact of co-evolutionary forces, namely, the role of outside parties in affecting the course of events in Bosnia and Kosovo. Cultural and biological traits rarely develop (i.e., get selected) in isolation, and these co-evolutionary forces can be mutually reinforcing, mutually exclusive, or mutually incompatible. As Modelski points out (1996, 339), "conditions that favour political evolution in turn depend on other evolutionary processes that are exogenous to it." There are multiple political, economic, cultural, and societal evolutionary processes that drive human social behavior, and they all play a role in some evolutionary system. Moreover, co-evolutionary processes can be constructive or destructive with respect to their fitness qualities. Tobacco and altruism are usually cited as examples—tobacco smoking has a positive fitness in cultural selection but a negative fitness in genetic selection. Altruism is both constructive to the group and destructive to the individual. Humans are social creatures with a long evolutionary history of living in groups. Thus, key psychological mechanisms evolved to meet the social needs of group living, and these mechanisms occasionally cause humans to put group loyalty above their own individual self-interests.

The same applies to cultural selection and ethnic conflict. Evolutionary processes associated with cultural selection take place alongside other evolutionary processes that themselves can either be destructive or constructive, depending on the environment, time, and circumstances.

In this view, the evolution of international organizations, such as NATO, affects the fitness of certain behaviors and the selection of ethnic violence as a strategy for securing ethnic group survival. Institutions and organizations do not just evolve structurally. Their reputations and credibility also change over time. Ethnicity and religion may have accounted for the mutual hatred underlying the fighting, but the war was waged with specific objectives in mind. Decisions by Serb leaders to escalate the fighting in Bosnia and Kosovo depended on the prospects of winning and losing particular battles. Whenever NATO leaders mounted a prolonged and stable threat of retaliation backed by ultimatums, dead-lines, and a clear commitment to punish, credibility was high and coercive di-plomacy worked. Weak threats, on the other hand, promoted violence.

Some of these co-evolutionary forces are specific to the Bosnian and Kosovo cases, but most are endemic to international politics in a post–Cold War world. The ability to generate the international consensus required to mount an effective response is becoming increasingly limited and difficult. But when consensus is reached, credibility and resolve are dramatically enhanced. For example, the evolution of NATO's reputation for responding to ethnic violence created a set of conditions that made escalation in the fighting unacceptable to all sides in the Bosnian dispute only after four years of sustained conflict in the region. In Kosovo the wide-scale violence was far shorter in duration, less intense, and involved far fewer casualties. In Bosnia when NATO was able to bypass the UN's "dual key" approach to crisis management, retaliatory threats were per-ceived by the Bosnian Serbs as credible and Mladic was deterred from fighting. The belligerents behaved exactly as one would expect under these conditions: they probed for weaknesses, attacked when they were apparent, and retreated only when NATO was able to mount a credible retaliatory threat.

Having learned from its bitter experiences in Bosnia, NATO demonstrated much greater resolve in responding to the violence in Kosovo. The organization did not waver from its threats to use force to expel FRY forces from Kosovo. The net result was a comparatively short campaign that succeeded in achieving most of the original objectives: stopping the violence, separating the belligerents, and providing a secure environment for the return of refugees.

In brief, the lesson learned from Bosnia and applied in Kosovo is simple: if an organization responds only when fundamental values and interests are threat-ened, then regardless of capabilities, it will generate a reputation for being res-olute. The organization's reputation may be enhanced, but the cost of being selective is a potential erosion of the norms that the organization sought to uphold in the first place. Similarly, if an organization always responds to a challenge regardless of its interests (perhaps because it has the capability to win every dispute), it, too, will generate a corresponding reputation. However, the immense cost in responding to every challenge could undermine the long-term effectiveness of the organization. Under these circumstances, there is an obvious and recurring dilemma for organizations when confronted by ethnic violence: the co-evolutionary organizational forces that work to stem violence cannot be in play everywhere and at all times. Until they are (if they ever are), the best we can hope for is to improve the quality of response through a better understanding of why prevention, management, and resolution succeeds and fails.

NOTES

1. *International Studies Quarterly* 40, no. 3 (1996).

2. This sociobiological position has often been misrepresented in a very pessimistic light because it is so fatalistic. It also explains why these views have so often been rejected as racist.

3. Others have tried to establish a middle ground between these two approaches, arguing that it is not necessarily the preference for absolute versus relative gains that marks the differences between realist and liberal internationalist theories of cooperation, but that states' preference for relative versus absolute gains are a product of "changes in the constraints facing the states" with respect to a war versus a status quo decision. For Powell (1990, 1304), "[A] state's utility depends solely on the absolute level of economic welfare it attains." This is in keeping with liberal institutionalism. But the states are trying to maximize their economic welfare within the constraints imposed by an anarchic international system in which the use of force, in keeping with realism, may be at issue.

Bibliography

Achen, Christopher, and Duncan Snidal (1989). "Rational Deterrence Theory and the Comparative Case Studies." *World Politics* 41, no. 2 (January): 143–169.

Adelman, Howard (1996). "Responding to Failed States." Unpublished manuscript.

Adelman, Howard, and Astri Suhrke (1996). "Joint Evaluation of Emergency Assistance to Rwanda." Vol. 2 on Early Warning. Norway Christian Michelson Institute.

Alan, Charles T. (1994). "Extended Conventional Deterrence: In from the Cold and Out of the Nuclear Freeze." *Washington Quarterly* 17: 203–233.

Amanpour, Christiane (1999). "KLA Recruits Race against Time." CNN. 12 May 1999. <http://cnn.com/WORLD/europe/9905/12/kla.camp/>.

Amnesty International (1998). *EUR 70/73/98: Federal Republic of Yugoslavia; A Human Rights Crisis in Kosovo Province*. October 1998. <www.amnesty.org>.

———— (1999). *EUR 65/03/99: Former Yugoslav Republic of Macedonia; the Protection of Kosovo Albanian Refugees*. May 1999. <www.amnesty.org>.

Apple, R. W. (1994). "NATO Again Plans Possible Air Raids on Serbs in Bosnia." *New York Times*, 12 January 1994, p. A1.

Azar, Edward E., P. Jureidini, and P. McLaurin (1978). "Protracted Social Conflict: Theory and Practice in the Middle East." *Journal of Peace Studies* 29: 41–60.

Azar, Edward, and John Burton, eds. (1986). *International Conflict Resolution*. Boulder: Lynne Rienner.

Barkow, James, Leda Cosmides, and John Tooby (1992). *The Adapted Mind*. New York: Oxford University Press.

Barrett, John (1994). "Conflict Prevention and Crisis Management: The NATO Approach." In *The Art of Conflict Prevention*, edited by Werner Bauwens and Luc Reychler. London: Brassey's Atlantic Commentaries.

Barth, F., ed. (1969). *Ethnic Groups and Boundaries: The Social Organisation of Cultural Differences*. Boston: Little, Brown.

Bauwens, Werner, and Luc Reychler, eds. (1994). *The Art of Conflict Prevention*. London: Brassey's Atlantic Commentaries.

BBC World News (1998). "Kosovo Separatist Group Threatens Revenge," BBC World News. 4 March 1998. <http://news2.thls.bbc.co.uk/hi/english/world/monitoring/newsid%5F62000/62042.stm>.

———— (1998). "US Opens Talks with Kosovo Guerillas," BBC World News. 28 June 1998. <http://news2.thls.bbc.co.uk/hi/english/world/europe/newsid%5F121000/121774.stm>.

———— (1998). "Last KLA Stronghold Falls to Serbs," BBC World News. 16 August 1998. <http://news2.thls.bbc.co.uk/hi/english/world/europe/newsid%5F151000/151950.stm>.

———— (1998). "KLA Calls Ceasefire in Kosovo." BBC World News. 8 October 1998. <http://news2.thls.bbc.co.uk/hi/english/world/europe/newsid%5F189000/189379.stm>.

———— (1998). "KLA Statement on the Belgrade Agreement." BBC World News. 18 October 1998. <http://news2.thls.bbc.co.uk/hi/english/world/monitoring/newsid%5F195000/195669.stm>.

———— (1998). "KLA Declares Civilian Rule." BBC World News. 6 November 1998.

———— (1999). "KLA Names Talks Team." BBC World News. 3 February 1999. <http://news.bbc.co.uk/hi/english/world/europe/newsid_271000/271528.stm>.

———— (1999). "Kosovar Albanians Announce Government." BBC World News. 24 February 1999. <http://news2.thls.bbc.co.uk/hi/english/world/europe/newsid%5F285000/285507.stm>.

———— (1999). "Kosovo Rebel Leader Quits." BBC World News. 2 March 1999. <http://news.bbc.co.uk/hi/english/world/europe/newsid_289000/289021.stm>.

———— (1999). "KLA: 'We Take Care of Refugees.' " BBC World News. 31 March 1999. <http://news2.thls.bbc.co.uk/hi/english/world/europe/newsid%5F308000/308660.stm>.

———— (1999). "KLA Launches Recruitment Push." BBC World News. 12 April 1999. <http://news2.thls.bbc.co.uk/hi/english/english/special_report/1998/kosovo/newsid_317000/317449.stm>.

———— (1999). "KLA Gives NATO Information on Yugoslav Forces." BBC World News. 16 April 1999. <http://news2.thls.bbc.co.uk/hi/english/world/europe/newsid%5F321000/321732.stm>.

———— (1999). "KLA Gaining Strength in Kosovo." BBC World News. 17 April 1999. <http://news2.thls.bbc.co.uk/hi/english/world/europe/newsid%5F21000/321741.stm>.

———— (1999). "Ibrahim Rugova: Pacifist at the Crossroads." BBC World News. 5 May 1999. <http://news.bbc.co.uk/hi/english/special_report/1998/kosovo/newsid_110000/110821.stm>.

Bell, Daniel (1975). "Ethnicity and Social Change." In *Ethnicity, Theory and Experience*, edited by Nathan Glazer and Daniel P. Moynihan. Cambridge: Harvard University Press.

Ben Dor, Gabriel (1997). "Intelligence and Early Warning: Lessons from a Case Study." In *Synergy in Early Warning Conference Proceedings*, edited by S. Schmeidl and H. Adelman. Conference held 15–18 March 1997, Toronto, Canada.

Bennett, Ruth, James Hanley, and John Orbell (1997). "Designing a Political Robot." Paper prepared for conference, *Evolutionary Theory and Its Critics: Toward a Greater Understanding of Ethnic Conflict*, 25–26 April 1997, Utah State University, Logan, Utah.

Benzon, William (1996). "Culture's Evolutionary Landscape: A Reply to Hans-Cees Speel." <http://www.newsavanna.com/wlb/CE/landscape.shtml>.

Bercovitch, Jacob (1993). "The Nature of the Dispute and the Effectiveness of International Mediation." *Journal of Conflict Resolution* 37 (4): 70–691.

———. (1996). "Understanding Mediation's Role in Preventive Diplomacy." *Negotiation Journal* 12 (3): 241–258.

Bercovitch, Jacob, and Patrick M. Regan (1997). "Managing Risks in International Relations: The Mediation of Enduring Rivalries." In *Enforcing Cooperation: Risky States and Intergovernmental Management of Conflict*, edited by Gerald Schneider and Patricia A. Weitsman. London: Macmillan.

Berdal, Mats (1994). "Fateful Encounter: The United States and UN Peacekeeping." *Survival* (1): 30–50.

Betts, Richard K. (1987). *Nuclear Blackmail and Nuclear Balance*. Washington, DC: The Brookings Institution.

Binder, David (1993). "U.S. Renews Warning to Serbs on Sarajevo Shelling." *New York Times*, 19 October 1993, p. A8.

Bloomfield, Lincoln P. (1994). "The Premature Burial of Global Law and Order: Looking Beyond the Three Cases from Hell." *Washington Quarterly* (17): 145–161.

Bock, Kenneth E. (1963). "Evolution, Function, and Change." *American Sociological Review* 28 (2): 229–237.

Boutros-Ghali, Boutros (1992). *An Agenda for Peace*. New York: United Nations, Department of Public Information.

Brams, S. J. (1985). *Superpower Games: Applying Game Theory to Superpower Conflict*. New Haven: Yale University Press.

Brams, S. J., and D. M. Kilgour (1987a). "Winding Down If Preemption or Escalation Occurs." *Journal of Conflict Resolution* 31: 547–572.

——— (1987b). "Threat Escalation and Crisis Stability: A Game Theoretic Analysis." *American Political Science Review* 81: 833–850.

Braumoeller, Bear F., and Gary Goertz (1997). *The Methodology of Necessary Conditions*. Unpublished manuscript.

Brecher, Michael (1993). *Crises in World Politics: Theory and Reality*. Oxford and New York: Pergamon Press.

Brecher, Michael, and Patrick James (1989). "Severity and Importance of Third World Crises: Middle East and Africa." In *Crisis, Conflict and Instability*, edited by Michael Brecher and Jonathan Wilkenfeld. Toronto: Pergamon Press.

Brecher, Michael, and Jonathan Wilkenfeld (1991). *International Crisis Behaviour Project Code Book*. Montreal and Baltimore: McGill University and University of Maryland.

——— (1997). "The Ethnic Dimension of International Crises." In *Wars in the Midst of Peace: The International Politics of Ethnic Conflict*, edited by David Carment and Patrick James. Pittsburgh: University of Pittsburgh Press.

Brecher, Michael, Patrick James, and Jonathan Wilkenfeld (1990). "Polarity and Stability: New Concepts, Indicators and Evidence." *International Interactions* 16, no. 1 (Winter): 49–80.

Brecher, Michael, Jonathan Wilkenfeld, and Sheila Moser (1988). *Crises in the Twentieth Century.* 2 vols. Oxford: Pergamon Press.

Brown, Ben (1998). "Weakening Refugees Face Winter's Threat." BBC World News. 12 October 1998. <http://news.bbc.co.uk/hi/english/special_report/1998/kosovo/newsid_191000/191367.stm>.

Bueno de Mesquita, Bruce, and William Riker (1982). "Assessing the Merits of Nuclear Proliferation." *Journal of Conflict Resolution* 26: 283–306.

Bugajski, Janusz (1998). "Blowup in the Balkans." *The World and I.* November 1998. <http://www.worldandi.com/archive/cinov98.htm>.

Burns, John F. (1993). "Dawn Brings a Ray of Hope to a Newly Silent Sarajevo." *New York Times.* 4 August 1993, p. A8.

Carment, David B. (1993). "The International Dimensions of Ethnic Conflict: Concepts, Indicators and Theory." *Journal of Peace Research* 30: 137–150.

——— (1994). "Ethnic Dimensions in World Politics: Theory, Policy and Early Warning." *Third World Quarterly* 15 (4): 551–582.

——— (1995). "NATO and the International Politics of Ethnic Conflict: Perspectives on Theory and Policy." *Contemporary Security Policy* 16 (3): 347–379.

Carment, David B., and Patrick James (1995). "Internal Constraints and Interstate Ethnic Conflict: Toward a Crisis-Based Assessment of Irredentism." *Journal of Conflict Resolution* 39 (March): 82–109.

Carment, David B., and Patrick James, eds. (1997). *Wars in the Midst of Peace: The International Politics of Ethnic Conflict.* Pittsburgh: University of Pittsburgh Press.

——— (1998). *Peace in the Midst of Wars: Preventing and Managing International Ethnic Conflicts.* Columbia: University of South Carolina Press.

Carment, David B., and Dane Rowlands (1998). "Three's Company: Evaluating Third Party Intervention in Intrastate Conflict." *Journal of Conflict Resolution* 42 no. 6 (October): 572–599.

Carment, David B., Patrick James, and Dane Rowlands (1997). "Ethnic Conflict and Third Party Intervention: Riskiness, Rationality and Commitment." In *Enforcing Cooperation: Risky States and Intergovernmental Management of Conflict*, edited by Gerald Schneider and Patricia A. Weitsman. London: Macmillan.

Carnevale, P., and S. Arad (1996). "Bias and Impartiality in International Meditation." In *Resolving International Conflicts*, edited by J. Bercovitch. Boulder: Lynne Rienner.

Chazan, Naomi, ed. (1991). *Irredentism and International Politics.* Boulder: Lynne Reinner.

Cohen, Lenard J. (1992). "The Disintegration of Yugoslavia." *Current History* 4 (November): 369–375.

Cohen, Roger (1994). "NATO Gives Serbs a 10-Day Deadline to Withdraw Guns." *New York Times*, 10 February 1994, p. A1.

Connor, Walker (1987). "Ethnonationalism." In *Understanding Political Development*, edited by Myron Weiner and Samuel P. Huntington. Boston: Little, Brown.

Cooper, Robert, and Robert Berdal (1993). "Outside Intervention in Ethnic Conflict." *Survival* 35 (1): 18–142.

Coser, Louis (1956). *The Functions of Social Conflict.* New York: Glencoe Free Press.

Cowell, Alan (1993). "NATO Jets to Enforce Ban on Illegal Bosnia Flights." *New York Times*, 12 April 1993, p. A8.

Cox, Robert (1992). "Towards a Post-Hegemonic Conceptualization of World Order: Reflections on the Relevancy of Ibn Khaladin." In *Governance without Government: Order and Change in World Politics*, edited by J. N. Rosenau and Ernst-Otto Czempiel. Cambridge: Cambridge University Press.

Craig, Gordon A., and Alexander George (1990). *Force and Statecraft: Diplomatic Problems of Our Time*. New York: Oxford University Press.

Crighton, Elizabeth, and Martha Abele MacIver (1991). "The Evolution of Protracted Ethnic Conflict." *Comparative Politics* 23: 127–142.

Darnton, John (1993). "Leader of Bosnian Serbs Remains Firmly Against Peace Plan, Despite U.N. Pressure." *New York Times*, 19 April 1993, p. A14.

Darwin, Charles (1869). *On the Origin of Species by Means of Natural Selection*. 5th ed. London: John Murray.

Davis, David, and Will Moore (1997). "Ethnicity Matters: Transnational Ethnic Alliances and Foreign Policy Behavior." *International Studies Quarterly* 41 (1): 171–184.

Davis, David, Keith Jaggers, and Will Moore (1997). "Ethnicity, Minorities and International Conflict Patterns." In *Wars in the Midst of Peace*, edited by David Carment and Patrick James. Pittsburgh: University of Pittsburgh Press.

Dawkins, Richard (1976). *The Selfish Gene*. Oxford: Oxford University Press.

——— (1993). "Viruses of the Mind." In *Dennett and His Critics: Demystifying Mind*, edited by Bo Dahlbom. Oxford: Blackwell.

Demars, William (1997). "Eyes and Ears? Limits of NGO Information for Early Warning." In *Synergy in Early Warning Conference Proceedings*, edited by S. Schmeidl and H. Adelman. 15–18 March 1997, Toronto, Canada.

Department of National Defense (1999). *Kosovo Historical Background*. <http://www.dnd.ca/eng/archive/apr99/Kosovo1_b_e.htm>.

Despres, L. A. (1967). *Cultural Pluralism and National Politics in British Guiana*. Chicago: Rand McNally.

Despres, L. A., ed. (1976). *Ethnicity and Resource Competition in Plural Societies*. Paris: Mouton Publishers.

Diehl, Paul F. (1993). *International Peacekeeping*. Baltimore: Johns Hopkins University Press.

Diehl, Paul F., J. Reifschneider, and Paul R. Hensel (1996). "United Nations Intervention and Recurring Conflict." *International Organization* 50 (4): 683–712.

Dion, Douglas (1997). "Evidence and Inference in the Comparative Case Study." *Comparative Politics* 30 (2): 127–158.

Dixon, W. J. (1996). "Third Party Techniques for Preventing Conflict Escalation and Promoting Peaceful Settlement." *International Organization* 50 (4): 653–681.

Durch, William J. (1993). *The Evolution of UN Peacekeeping: Case Studies and Comparative Analysis*. New York: St. Martin's Press.

Durham, W. (1991). *Coevolution: Genes, Culture, and Human Diversity*. Palo Alto, CA: Stanford University Press.

Elliot, Michael (1999). "The Nightmare: Special Report." *Newsweek*, 12 April 1999, 27–36.

Engelberg, Stephen, with Michael Gordon (1994). "Clinton Is Caught by Bosnian Dilemma." *New York Times*, 4 April 1994, p. A4.

Esman, M. (1995). "International Institutions and Ethnic Conflict." In *International Organizations and Ethnic Conflict*, edited by Milton Esman and Shibley Telhami. Ithaca, NY: Cornell University Press.

Farkas, Andrew (1996). "Evolutionary Models in Foreign Policy Analysis." *International Studies Quarterly* 40 no. 3 (September): 343–361.

Fearon, James D. (1994). "Signaling versus the Balance of Power and Interests: An Empirical Test of a Crisis Bargaining Model." *Journal of Conflict Resolution* 38 no. 2 (June): 236–269.

——— (1995). "Rationalist Explanations for War." *International Organization* 49: 379–414.

Fink, Clinton F. (1965). "More Calculations About Deterrence." *Journal of Conflict Resolution* 9: 54–65.

Fischoff, Baruch (1987). "Do We Want a Better Theory of Deterrence?" *Journal of Social Issues* 43: 73–77.

Fisher, R. J. (1996). "Pacific, Impartial Third Party Intervention in International Conflict: A Review and an Analysis." In *Beyond Confrontation*, edited by J. Vasquez et al. Ann Arbor: University of Michigan Press.

Florini, Ann (1996). "The Evolution of International Norms." *International Studies Quarterly* 40, no. 3 (September): 363–389.

Fog, Agner (1996). *Cultural Selection.* <http://announce.com/agner/cultsel/chapter3>. Copenhagen © 1996.

Fortmann, Michel, Pierre Martin, and Stéphane Rousel (1998). "Trial by Fire: International Actors and Organizations in the Yugoslav Crisis." In *Peace in the Midst of Wars*, edited by David Carment and Patrick James. Columbia: University of South Carolina Press.

Fox, Jonathan (1995). "Albanians in the Region of Kosovo." *Minorities at Risk.* <http://www.bsos.umd.edu/cidcm>.

Frei, Daniel, and Dieter Ruhoff (1989). *Handbook of Foreign Policy Analysis.* London: Martinus Nijhoff.

Friedman, Thomas L. (1993a) "Bosnia Air Strikes Backed by Clinton, His Officials Say." *New York Times*, 2 May 1993, pp. A1, A12.

——— (1993b). *New York Times*, 9 May 1993, p. A1.

Furnivall, J. S. (1948). *Colonial Policy and Practice.* London: Cambridge University Press.

Garfinkle, Adam (1991). "The Gulf War: Was It Worth It?" *World & I* 6: 70–79.

Geertz, Clifford (1973). *The Interpretation of Culture: Selected Essays.* New York: Basic Books.

Gellner, E. (1964). *Thought and Change.* London: Weidenfeld and Nicholson.

George, Alexander (1991). *Forceful Persuasion: Coercive Diplomacy as an Alternative to War.* Washington, DC: U.S. Institute for Peace.

George, Alexander, and Jane Holl (1997). "The Warning-Response Problem and Missed Opportunities in Preventive Diplomacy: Discussion Paper." *Carnegie Commission on Preventing Deadly Conflict.* Washington, DC: Carnegie Corporation of New York.

George, Alexander L., and Richard Smoke (1974). *Deterrence in American Foreign Policy: Theory and Practice.* New York: Columbia University Press.

——— (1989). "Deterrence and Foreign Policy." *World Politics* 41: 170–182.

Gilligan, Andrew (1999). "RAF Admits It Failed in Kosovo." *Ottawa Citizen*, 25 July 1999, p. A7.

Gilpin, Robert (1996). "Economic Evolution of National Systems." *International Studies Quarterly* 40, no. 3 (September): 411–431.

Glaser, Charles L. (1993). "Why NATO Is Still Best: Future Security Arrangements for Europe." *International Security* 18: 5–50.

Glenny, Misha (1993). "What Is to Be Done?" *New York Review of Books* 27 (May): 14–17.

Goertz, Gary (1996). "(Enduring) Rivalries and the Study of Deterrence." Paper prepared for conference, Deterrence in Enduring Rivalries, September 1996, Monterey, California.

Gompert, David (1994). "How to Defeat Serbia." *Foreign Affairs* 73: 30–47.

Gordon, Michael R. (1993). "Clinton Says U.S. Pressure Nudged Serbs Back to Talks." *New York Times*, 1 May 1993, p. A6.

——— (1994). "The Bluff That Failed." *New York Times*, 19 April 1994, p. A1.

Gould, S. J. (1985). "Not Necessarily a Wing." *Natural History* (October): 12–13.

Grant, Alison (1997). "Ethnic Conflict in the Former Soviet Union: Explaining Minority Intransigence." Master's research essay, Carleton University, Ottawa, Ontario.

Grieco, Joseph (1988). "Anarchy and the Limits of Cooperation: A Realist Critique of the Newest Liberal Institutionalism." *International Organizations* 42: 485–507.

——— (1990). *Cooperation Among Nations*. Ithaca: Cornell University Press.

Guerin, Orla (1999). "Serbs Find KLA 'Arms Cache'." BBC World News. 3 February 1999. <http://news.bbc.co.uk/hi/english/world/europe/newsid_271000/271063.stm>.

Gupta, Dipak (1997). "An Early Warning About Forecasts: Oracle to Academics." In *Synergy in Early Warning Conference Proceedings*, edited by S. Schmeidl and H. Adelman. Conference held 15–18 March 1997, Toronto, Canada.

Gurr, Ted Robert (1970). *Why Men Rebel*. Princeton: Princeton University Press.

——— (1990). "Ethnic Warfare and the Changing Priorities of Global Security." *Mediterranean Quarterly* 1 (Winter): 82–98.

——— (1992). "The Internationalization of Protracted Communal Conflicts since 1945: Which Groups, Where and How." In *The Internationalization of Communal Strife*, edited by Manus I. Midlarsky. London: Routledge.

——— (1994). "People Against States: Ethnopolitical Conflict and the Changing World System," *International Studies Quarterly* 38: 347–377.

——— (1996). "Early Warning Systems: From Surveillance to Assessment to Action." In *Preventive Diplomacy: The Therapeutics of Mediation*, edited by Kevin M. Cahill. Proceedings of a conference at the United Nations, New York, 23–24 April 1996.

Gurr, Ted Robert, ed. (1980). *Handbook of Political Conflict: Theory and Research*. New York: Free Press.

Gurr, Ted Robert, and Michael Haxton (1996). "Minorities Report 1, Ethnopolitical Conflict in the 1990s: Patterns and Trends." College Park: Department of Government and Politics, University of Maryland, College Park, and Minorities at Risk Project Center for International Development and Conflict Management.

Haas, Ernst (1983). "Regime Decay: Conflict Management and International Organizations, 1945–1981." *International Organizations* 30, no. 21 (Spring): 189–256.

Haglund, David G, and Charles C. Pentland (1998). "Ethnic Conflict and European Security: What Role for the EC and NATO?" In *Peace in the Midst of Wars*, edited by David Carment and Patrick James. Columbia: University of South Carolina Press.

Hampson, Fen Osler (1996). *Nurturing Peace*. Washington, DC: USIP Press.

Hardin, R. (1995). *One for All: The Logic of Group Conflicts*. Princeton: Princeton University Press.

Harff, Barbara, and Ted Robert Gurr (1988). "Toward Empirical Theory of Genocides and Politicides: Identification and Measurement of Cases since 1945." *International Studies Quarterly* 32: 359–371.

Harris, Marvin (1969). *The Rise of Anthropological Theory*. London: Routledge & Kegan Paul.

Harvey, Frank (1995). "Rational Deterrence Theory Revisited: A Progress Report." *Canadian Journal of Political Science* 28 (September): 403–436.

——— (1997a). "Deterrence and Ethnic Conflict: The Case of Bosnia-Herzegovina, 1993–1994." *Security Studies* 6 no. 3 (Spring): 181–209.

——— (1997b). "Deterrence and Compellence in Protracted Crises: Methodology and Preliminary Findings." *International Studies Notes* 22 no. 1 (Winter): 12–23.

——— (1998). "Rigor Mortis or Rigor, More Tests: Necessity, Sufficiency, and Deterrence Logic." *International Studies Quarterly* 42 (4): 675–707.

Harvey, Frank, and Patrick James (1992). "Nuclear Deterrence Theory: The Record of Aggregate Testing and an Alternative Research Agenda." *Conflict Management and Peace Science* 12: 17–45.

——— (1996). "Nuclear Powers at the Brink: Toward a Multi-Stage Game of Crisis Interaction." *International Political Science Review* 17 (2): 197–214.

Hechter, M. (1975). *Internal Colonialism: The Celtic Fringe in British National Development, 1536–1966*. Berkeley: University of California Press.

——— (1986). "Theories of Ethnic Relations." In *The Primordial Challenge: Ethnicity in the Contemporary World*, edited by J. F. Stack, Jr. New York/London: Greenwood Press.

Hedges, Chris (1999). "Kosovo's Next Master?" *Foreign Affairs* 78 (3): 24–42.

Helsinki Watch (1992). "Letter to Milosevic." 21 January 1992.

Heraclides, Alexis (1991). *The Self-Determination of Minorities in International Politics*. Portland, ME: Fank Cass.

Hirsh, Michael, and John Barry (1999). "How We Stumbled into a War." *Newsweek*, 12 April 1999, 38–40.

Hislope, Robert (1997). "Evolutionary Theory as Analogy, Not Ontology: Understanding Ethnic Politics." Paper prepared for conference, *Evolutionary Theory and Its Critics: Toward a Greater Understanding of Ethnic Conflict*, Logan: Utah State University, 25–26 April 1997.

Hodgson, Geoffrey (1996). "An Evolutionary Theory of Long-Term Economic Growth." *International Studies Quarterly* 40, no. 3 (September): 391–410.

Holl, Jane, et al. (1997). *Carnegie Commission on Preventing Deadly Conflict: Final Report*. Washington, DC: Carnegie Corporation of New York. Web-based text available at <http://www.ccpdc.org/frpub.htm>, chapter 3.

Holmes, Steven A. (1993). "U.S. May Attack Serbs Even Without NATO." *New York Times*, 2 August 1993, p. A3.

Holsti, Kalevi J. (1985). *The Dividing Discipline: Hegemony and Diversity in International Theory*. Boston: Allen & Unwin.

——— (1989). "International Theory and Domestic War in the Third World: The Limits of Relevance." Unpublished manuscript, University of British Columbia.

Horowitz, Donald L. (1985). *Ethnic Groups in Conflict*. Berkeley/London: University of California Press.

———— (1991). "Irredentas and Successions: Adjacent Phenomena, Neglected Connections." In *Irredentism and International Politics*, edited by Naomi Chazan. Boulder: Lynne Rienner.

Human Rights Watch (1999). *Kosovo Human Rights Flash*, numbers 1–51 (25 March 1999–2 July 1999). <http://www.hrw.org/campaigns/kosovo98/index.htm>.

Huth, Paul, and Bruce M. Russett (1984). "What Makes Deterrence Work? Cases from 1900 to 1980." *World Politics* 36: 496–526.

———— (1988). "Deterrence Failure and Crisis Escalation." *International Studies Quarterly* 32: 29–45.

———— (1990). "Testing Deterrence Theory: Rigor Makes a Difference." *World Politics* 42: 466–501.

IFOR Coalition Press Centres (1995). NATO Headquarters. See <www.nato.int>.

Ignatieff, Michael (1993). *Blood and Belonging*. Toronto: Penguin.

International Alert (1993). "Preventative Diplomacy." Recommendation of a Round Table on Preventative Diplomacy. London, January 1993, pp. 28–30.

International Crisis Group (1998a). "Serbia: The Milosevic Factor." 24 February 1998. <http://www.crisisweb.org>.

———— (1998b). "Kosovo Spring Report." 20 March 1998. <http://www.crisisweb.org>.

———— (1998c). "Slobodan Milosevic's Manipulation of the Kosovo Dispute." 6 May 1998. <http://www.crisisweb.org>.

———— (1999a). "Kosovo Briefing." 17 February 1999. <http://www.crisisweb.org>.

———— (1999b). "Kosovo, the Road to Peace: Critical Implementation Issues and a 'Who's Who' of Key Players." 12 March 1999. <http://www.crisisweb.org>.

———— (1999c). "Let's Learn from Bosnia." 17 May 1999.<http://www.crisisweb.org>.

———— (1999d). "Statement: ICG Voices Concern over Kosovo Peace Plan." 11 June 1999. <http://www.crisisweb.org>.

———— (1999e). "The New Kosovo Protectorate." 20 June 1999. <http://www.crisisweb.org>.

———— (1999f). "Back to the Future: Milosevic Prepares for Life After Kosovo." 28 June 1999. <http://www.crisisweb.org>.

———— (1999g). "ICG Kosovo Briefing: Who Will Lead Kosovo Albanians Now? Making Sense of Kosovo's Feuding Factions." 28 June 1999. <http://www.crisisweb.org>.

International Studies Quarterly (1996). Special issue on evolutionary theory.

Isaacs, Harold (1975). *Idols of the Tribe: Group Identity and Political Change*. New York: Harper & Row.

James, Alan (1998). "Peacekeeping and Ethnic Conflict: Theory and Evidence." In *Peace in the Midst of Wars*, edited by David Carment and Patrick James. Columbia: University of South Carolina Press.

James, Patrick (1991). "Rational Retaliation: Superpower Response to Crisis, 1948–1979." *Public Choice* 68: 117–135.

———— (1993). "Structural Realism as a Research Enterprise: Toward Elaborated Structural Realism." *International Political Science Review* 14: 123–148.

Jehl, Douglas (1993a). "U.S. Turns Bosnia Threat Into Near Ultimatum." *New York Times*, 4 August 1993, p. A1.

———— (1993b). "Serbs Must Withdraw Promptly or Face Air Strikes, U.S. Insists." *New York Times*, 12 August 1993, p. A1.

Jervis, Robert (1979). "Deterrence Theory Revisited." *World Politic* 31: 289–324.

——— (1989). "Rational Deterrence: Theory and Evidence." *World Politics* 41: 183–207.

Jervis, Robert, Richard N. Lebow, and Janice G. Stein (1985). *Psychology and Deterrence*. Baltimore: Johns Hopkins University Press.

Johnson, Gary (1986). "Kin Selection, Socialisation, and Patriotism: An Integrating Theory." *Politics and the Life Sciences* 4: 127–154.

——— (1987). "In the Name of the Fatherland: An Analysis of Kin Term Usage in Patriotic Speech and Literature." *International Political Science Review* 8: 165–174.

——— (1997). "The Evolutionary Roots of Patriotism." In *Patriotism in the Lives of Individuals and Nations*, edited by Daniel Bar-Tal and Ervin Staub. Chicago: Nelson-Hall.

Jones, Bruce, and Janice Gross Stein (1997). "NGOs and Early Warning: The Case of Rwanda." In *Synergy in Early Warning Conference Proceedings*, edited by S. Schmeidl and H. Adelman. 15–18 March 1997, Toronto, Canada.

Journal of Social Issues 43 (1987). Special issue.

Judah, Tim (1999a). "The KLA: Out from the Shadows." BBC World News. 24 March 1999. <http://news.bbc.co.uk/hi/english/special_report/1998/kosovo/newsid_271000/271860.stm>.

——— (1999b). "Inside the KLA." *New York Review of Books* 46 (10): 19–24.

Kaplan, Robert D. (1994). "The Coming Anarchy." *Atlantic Monthly*. February.

Kaufman, Stuart (1998). "Preventing Ethnic Violence: Conditions for Successful Peacekeeping." In *Peace in the Midst of Wars*, edited by David Carment and Patrick James. Columbia: University of South Carolina Press.

Keesing's Contemporary Archives: 4 December 1993, 39426–39427; 7 February 1994, 39870; 4 April 1994, 39425–39426; July 1994, 39563–39564; 18 October 1994, 39695; April 1995, 40512, 40511, 39966; May 1995, 40564, 40563; August 1995, 40691, 40735, 40690, 40688; June 1998, 42356.

Keller, Albert Galloway (1916). *Societal Evolution*. New York: Macmillan.

Keohane, Robert (1984). *After Hegemony: Cooperation and Discord in World Political Economy*. Princeton: Princeton University Press.

Keohane, Robert, ed. (1986). *Neorealism and Its Critics*. New York: Columbia University Press.

Kifner, John (1994a). "Serbs Agree to Give Up Sarajevo Guns." *New York Times*, 10 February 1994, p. A14.

——— (1994b). "U.N. Reports Serbs Are Pulling Back Around Sarajevo." *New York Times*, 18 February 1994, p. A11.

Kinzer, Stephen (1993a). "Serbs Attack Muslim Stronghold in Northwest Bosnia." *New York Times*, 28 April 1993, p. A11.

——— (1993b). "Serbs Reject Bosnia Pact, Defying Friends and Foes and Insist on Referendum." *New York Times*, 6 May 1993, pp. A1, A16.

Kleiboer, Marieke (1997). *International Mediation*. New York: Lynne Rienner.

Kline, Edward (1994). "The Conflict in Chechnya." 27 November 1994. <http://www.wdn.com/asf/chechbp.html>.

Kolsto, Pal (1993). "The New Russian Diaspora: Minority Protection in Soviet Successor States." *Journal of Peace Research* 30, no. 2 (May): 197–217.

Kriesberg, Louis (1998). "The Phases of Destructive Communal Conflicts: Communal Conflicts and Proactive Solutions." In *Peace in the Midst of Wars*, edited by D. Carment and Patrick James. Columbia: University of South Carolina Press, 1998.

Kugler, Jacek (1984). "Terror Without Deterrence." *Journal of Conflict Resolution* 28: 470–506.

Lake, D. A., and Rothchild, D. (1996). "Containing Fear: The Origins and Management of Ethnic Conflict." *International Security* 21 (2): 41–75.

Lamarck, Jean-Baptiste de (1809). *Philsophie Zoologique*. Paris.

Leatherman, Janie, and Raimo Vayrynen (1995). "Structure, Culture and Territory: Three Sets of Early Warning Indicators." Paper presented at the International Studies Association 36th Annual Convention. 21–25 April 1995, Chicago.

Lebow, Richard Ned (1981). *Between Peace and War: The Nature of International Crises*. Baltimore: John Hopkins University Press.

Lebow, Richard N., and Janice G. Stein (1987). "Beyond Deterrence." *Journal of Social Issues* 43: 5–71.

——— (1989a). "Rational Deterrence Theory: I Think, Therefore I Deter." *World Politics* 41: 208–224.

——— (1989b). "When Does Deterrence Succeed and How Do We Know?" Paper presented at the Annual Meeting of the International Studies Association, 22–25 February 1989, Washington, DC.

——— (1990). "Deterrence: The Elusive Dependent Variable." *World Politics* 42: 336–369.

Levy, Jack (1988). "When Do Deterrent Threats Work?" *British Journal of Political Science* 18: 485–512.

Lewis, Paul (1993). "Top Bosnian Serb Facing U.S. Action, Signs a Peace Plan." *New York Times*, 3 May 1993, pp. A1, A10.

——— (1994). "U.N. Warns Serbs on Gorazde; Move Could Lead to Air Strikes." *New York Times*, 10 April 1994, p. A1.

Leyne, Jon (1999). "Funding the KLA." BBC World News. 24 March 1999. <http://news2. thls.bbc.co.uk/hi/english/special%5Freport/1998/kosovo/newsid%5F296000 /296004.stm>.

Licklider, Roy (1995). "The Consequences of Negotiated Settlements in Civil Wars, 1945–1993." *American Political Science Review* 89 (3): 681–690.

Licklider, Roy, ed. (1993). *Stopping the Killing*. New York: New York University Press.

Lieber, Robert (1994). "Constraints on American Foreign Policy in the Post–Cold War Era." Paper presented at the XVI World Congress of the International Political Science Association, August 1994, Berlin.

Lieberman, Eli (1994). "What Makes Deterrence Work? Lessons from the Egyptian-Israeli Enduring Rivalry." Paper presented at the Annual Meeting of the American Political Science Association, New York.

Lund, M. S. (1996a). *Preventing Violent Conflict: A Strategy for Preventive Diplomacy*. Washington DC: United States Institute of Peace Press.

——— (1996b). "Early Warning and Preventive Diplomacy." In *Managing Global Chaos*, edited by Fen Osler Hampson and Chester A. Crocker. Washington, DC: USIP.

Lungescu, Oana (1998). "The KLA: A Dilemma for the West." BBC World News, 30 June 1998. <http://news2.thls.bbc.co.uk/hi/english/world/europe/newsid%5F123000 /123544.stm>.

Lustick, Ian S. (1986). "Writing the Intifada: Collective Action in the Occupied Territories." *World Politics* 31, no. 3 (April): 560–594.

Luttwak, Edward N. (1999). "Give War a Chance," *Foreign Affairs* 78, no. 4: 36–44.

Luvtrup, S. (1987). *Darwinism: The Refutation of a Myth*. Beckingham, UK: Croom
Helm Ltd.

MacInnis, Major-General J. A. (1994). Letter to authors, 24 November 1994. Land Force
Atlantic Area Headquarters, Halifax.

Maoz, Zeev (1990). *National Choices and International Processes*. Cambridge, UK:
Cambridge University Press.

Marcus, Jonathan (1999). "Analysis: NATO's Kosovo Options." BBC World News. 19
February 1999. <http://news2.thls.bbc.co.uk/hi/english/special%5Freport/1998/
kosovo/newsid%5F282000/282532.stm>.

Marshall, Monty G. (1997). "The Societal Dimensions of 'Human Nature' and the Dynamics of Group Conflict: Violence, Diffusion and Disintegration in the Middle
East." In *The International Politics of Ethnic Conflict: Theory and Evidence*,
edited by David Carment and Patrick James. Pittsburgh: University of Pittsburgh
Press.

Mason, David T. (1994). "The Ethnic Dimension of Civil Violence in the Post–Cold
War Era: Structural Configurations and Rational Choices." Paper presented at the
annual meeting of the American Political Science Association. September 1994,
New York.

Masters, R. D. (1989). *The Nature of Politics*. New Haven: Yale University Press.

McCarthy, Mary O. (1997). "Potential Humanitarian Crises: The Warning Process and
Roles for Intelligence." In *Synergy in Early Warning Conference Proceedings*,
edited by S. Schmeidl and H. Adelman. 15–18 March 1997, Toronto, Canada.

McDougall, William (1908). *An Introduction to Social Psychology*. London: Methuen &
Co.

––––––– (1921). *The Group Mind*. Cambridge: Cambridge University Press.

Melotti, Umberto (1986). "In-group/Out-group Relations and the Issue of Group Selection." In *The Sociobiology of Ethnocentrism*, edited by V. Reynolds, V. S. S.
Falger, and I. Vine. Athens: University of Georgia Press.

Michod, Richard E. (1999). *Darwinian Dynamics: Evolutionary Transitions in Fitness
and Individuality*. Princeton: Princeton University Press. <http://eebweb.arizona.
edu/michod/Books/dd/synopsis%20of%20book.htm>.

Midlarsky, Manus (1997). "Systemic War in the Former Yugoslavia." In *Wars in the
Midst of Peace*, edited by David Carment and Patrick James. Pittsburgh: University of Pittsburgh Press.

Midlarsky, Manus, ed. (1992). *The Internationalization of Communal Strife*. London:
Routledge.

Mivat, St. George (1996). *On the Genesis of Species*. London: Macmillan.

Modelski, George (1996). "Evolutionary Paradigms for Global Politics." *International
Studies Quarterly* 40, no. 3 (September): 321–342.

Modelski, George, and Kazimierz Poznanski (1996). "Evolutionary Paradigms in the
Social Sciences." *International Studies Quarterly* 40, no. 3 (September): 315–
319.

Monod, Albert (1971; reprint 1916). De Pascale a chateaubriand. New York: Franklin.

Moore, Will, and Gurr, T. R. (1997). "Assessing Risks of Ethnopolitical Rebellion in the
Year 2000: Three Empirical Approaches." In *Synergy in Early Warning Confer-*

ence Proceedings, edited by S. Schmeidl and H. Adelman. 15–18 March 1997, Toronto, Canada.

Moreno, Rafael, and Juan Jose Vega (1994). "Lessons from Somalia." *Peacekeeping and International Relations* 23 (3): 11–12.

Morgan, Patrick (1977). *Deterrence: A Conceptual Analysis*. Beverly Hills: Sage Publications.

Morrison, Alex (1998). "International Action and National Sovereignty: Adjusting to New Realities." In *Peace in the Midst of Wars*, edited by David Carment and Patrick James. Columbia: University of South Carolina Press.

Moses, Joel (1997). "Regionalism in the Former Soviet Union: Russian Kaliningrad and Ukrainian Odessa, 1991–1996." Paper prepared for conference, Evolutionary Theory and Its Critics: Toward a Greater Understanding of Ethnic Conflict. 25–26 April 1997, Utah State University, Logan.

Most, Benjamin, and Harvey Starr (1989). *Inquiry, Logic and International Politics*. South Carolina: University of South Carolina Press.

Moynihan, Daniel Patrick (1993). *Pandemonium*. Oxford: Oxford University Press.

Muller, Edward N., and Erich Weede (1990). "Cross-National Variation in Political Violence: A Rational Action Approach." *Journal of Conflict Resolution* 34: 624–651.

NAC Subcommittee on Defence and Security Cooperation Between Europe and North America (May 1994). Report entitled "NATO, Peacekeeping and the Former Yugoslavia."

Nadler, John (1999). "NATO Continues to Fight Kosovo's Hidden Foes." *Ottawa Citizen*, 25 July 1999, p. A7.

Nagel, Joane, and Susan Olzak (1982). "Ethnic Mobilisation in New and Old States: An Extension of the Competition Model." *Social Problem* 30: 127–143.

NATO Fact Sheet. 18 January 1996. Brussels: NATO Headquarters.

Neilson, François (1985). "Toward a Theory of Ethnic Solidarity in Modern Societies." *American Sociological Review* 50: 133–149.

Neilsson, Gunnar P. (1985). "States and Nation Groups: A Global Taxonomy." In *New Nationalisms of the Developed West*, edited by Edward A. Tiryakian and Ronald Rogowski. Boston: Allen & Unwin.

Organski, A. F. K., and Jacek Kugler (1980). *The War Ledger*. Chicago: University of Chicago Press.

O'Sullivan-See, Katherine (1986). *First World Nationalism: Class and Ethnic Politics in Northern Ireland and Quebec*. Chicago: University of Chicago Press.

Olzak, Susan (1983). "Contemporary Ethnic Mobilisation." *Annual Review of Sociology* 9: 355–374.

Partos, Gabriel (1999). "Analysis: KLA Rides Out the Storm." BBC World News, 12 April 1999. <http://news2.thls.bbc.co.uk/hi/english/special%5Freport/1998/kosovo/newsid%5F315000/315832.stm>.

Petersen, W. J. (1986). "Deterrence and Compellence: A Critical Assessment of Conventional Wisdom." *International Studies Quarterly* 30: 269–294.

Posen, Barry (1993). "The Security Dilemma and Ethnic Conflict." *Survival* 35 no. 1: 27–47.

Powell, Robert (1990). *Nuclear Deterrence Theory: The Search for Credibility*. Cambridge: Cambridge University Press.

Prial, Frank J. (1993). "Resolution Establishes Safe Areas but Lacks Enforcement Provision." *New York Times*, 7 May 1993, p. A11.

Radcliffe-Brown, Alfred R. (1952). *Structure and Function in Primitive Society*. London: West.

Ramet, Sabrina P. (1992a). *Nationalism and Federalism in Yugoslavia, 1962–1991*. 2d ed. Bloomington: University of Indiana Press.

——— (1992b). "War in the Balkans." *Foreign Affairs* 71 (Fall): 79–98.

Raymond, G. A. (1994). "Democracies, Disputes and Third-Party Intermediaries." *Journal of Conflict Resolution* 38 (1): 24–42.

Record, Jeffrey (1993). "Defeating Desert Storm (and Why Saddam Didn't)." *Comparative Strategy* 12: 125–140.

Regan, Pat (1996a). "Interventions into Intense Intrastate Conflicts: Minimizing the Uncertainty in the Decision Process." International Studies Association Paper, San Diego.

——— (1996b). "Conditions for Successful Third Party Intervention in Intrastate Conflicts." *Journal of Conflict Resolution* 40 (2): 336–359.

"Report of the Secretary-General Pursuant to Security Council Resolutions 982 (1995) and 987, (1995)," 5 May 1995, United Nations.

Reychler, Luc (1994). "The Art of Conflict Prevention: Theory and Practice." In *The Art of Conflict Prevention*, edited by Werner Bauwens and Luc Reychler. London: Brassey's Atlantic Commentaries.

Reynolds, V., S. E. Falger, and I. Vine, eds. (1986). *The Sociobiology of Ethnocentrism*. Athens: University of Georgia Press.

Ross, L., and Stillinger, C. (1991). "Barriers to Conflict Resolution." *Negotiation Journal* 7 (4): 389–404.

Rothchild, Donald, and Naomi Chazan (1988). *The Precarious Balance: State and Society in Africa*. Boulder: Westview Press.

Rothschild, Joseph (1981). *Ethnopolitics: A Conceptual Framework*. New York: Columbia University Press.

Ruggie, John Gerard (1993a). "Wandering in the Void: Charting the UN's New Strategic Role." *Foreign Affairs* 72 no. 5, November/December: 26–31.

——— (1993b). "The United Nations: Stuck in a Fog Between Peacekeeping and Enforcement." In *Peacekeeping: The Way Ahead*, edited by William H. Lewis. Washington, DC. McNair Paper 25.

Ruggie, J. (1994). "The New U.S. Peacekeeping Doctrine." *Washington Quarterly* 17 (4): 175–184.

Rupesinghe, Kumar (1995). "Towards a Policy Framework for Advancing Preventive Diplomacy." Paper presented at: Towards a Common Agenda for Conflict Prevention. May 1995. Oslo.

Russett, Bruce M. (1963). "The Calculus of Deterrence." *Journal of Conflict Resolution* 7: 97–109.

Ryan, Stephen (1998). "Preventative Diplomacy, Conflict Prevention and Ethnic Conflict." In *Peace in the Midst of Wars*, edited by David Carment and Patrick James. Columbia: University of South Carolina Press.

Sahlins, Marshal D., and Elman R. Service, eds. (1960). *Evolution and Culture*. Ann Arbor: University of Michigan Press.

Saideman, Stephen M. (1997). "Explaining the International Relations of Secessionist Conflicts: Vulnerability versus Ethnic Ties." *International Organization* 51 (4): 721–753.

Salter, Frank (1997). "Ethnic Infrastructures: An Ethnological Approach to Ethnic Competition." Paper prepared for conference, Evolutionary Theory and Its Critics: Toward a Greater Understanding of Ethnic Conflict. 25–26 April 1997, Utah State University, Logan.

Schelling, Thomas C. (1960). *Strategy and Conflict*. Cambridge: Harvard University Press.

Schneider, Gerald, and Patricia A. Weitsman (1995). "Eliciting Cooperation from 'Risky' States." In *Enforcing Cooperation: Risky States and Intergovernmental Management of Conflict*, edited by Gerald Schneider and Patricia A. Weitsman. London: Macmillan.

Schneider, Gerald, and Patricia Weitsman, eds. (1995). *Enforcing Cooperation: Risky States and Intergovernmental Management of Conflict*. London: Macmillan.

Sciolino, Elaine (1993). "Bosnia Rivals Set New Talks as U.S. Weighs Action Plans." *New York Times*, 30 April 1993, pp. A1, A7.

Sciolino, Elaine, and Ethan Bronner (1999). "How a President, Distracted by Scandal, Entered Balkan War." *New York Times*, 18 April 1999, Section 1, pp. 1, 11–14.

Sebak, Nened (1998). "The KLA—Terrorists or Freedom Fighters?" BBC World News. 28 June 1998. <http://news2.thls.bbc.co.uk/hi/english/world/europe/newsid%5F121000/121818.stm>.

Shalom, Stephen R. (1999). "Reflections on NATO and Kosovo." *New Politics* 7 no. 3 (Summer) <http://www.wilpaterson.edu/~newpol/issue27/shalom27.htm>.

Shih, Cheng-Feng (1991). "A Multivariate Model of Ethnic Diversity and Violent Political Behaviour." Ph.D. dissertation, Ohio State University.

Silverman, I., and D. Case (1997). "Ethnocentrism vs. Pragmatism in the Conduct of Human Affairs." In *Indoctrinability, Ideology and Warfare: Evolutionary Perspectives*, edited by I. Eibl-Eibesfeldt and F. K. Salter. Oxford, UK: Berghahn.

Sisk, Timothy (1996). *Power Sharing and International Mediation in Ethnic Conflict*. Washington, DC: USIP.

Smith, Anthony D. (1981). *The Ethnic Revival in the Modern World*. New York: Cambridge University Press.

———— (1986). "The Suppression of Nationalism." *International Journal of Comparative Sociology* 31: 1–31.

Smith, M. (1965). *The Plural Societies in the British West Indies*. Berkeley: University of California Press.

Speel, H.C.A.M. (1997). "A Short Comment from a Biologist." *Journal of Social and Evolutionary Systems* 20 (3): 309–322.

Spence, A. M. (1973). "Job Market Signalling." *Quarterly Journal of Economics* 87: 355–374.

Spencer, Herbert (1873). *The Study of Sociology*. London: Williams & Norgate.

———— [1876] (1969). *Principles of Sociology. Vol 1*. Reprint, edited by S. Andreski. London: Macmillan.

———— [1893] (1969). *Principles of Sociology. Vol 2*. Reprint, edited by S. Andreski. London: Macmillan.

Spriggs, W. A. (1996). "Evolutionary Psychology and the Origins of Bigotry and Prejudice." <http://www.evoyage.com:80>.

Stack, John (1997). "The Ethnic Challenge to International Relations Theory." In *Wars in the Midst of Peace*, edited by David Carment and Patrick James. Pittsburgh: University of Pittsburgh Press.

Stack, John, ed (1981). *Ethnic Identities in a Transnational World*. Westport, CT: Greenwood Press.

——— (1986). *The Primordial Challenge: Ethnicity in the Contemporary World*. New York/London: Greenwood Press.

Stedman, S. J. (1995). "Alchemy for a New World Disorder: Overselling Preventative Diplomacy." *Foreign Affairs* 76, no. 3 (May/June): 14–20.

Sudetic, Chuck (1994a). "Serbs Pound Sarajevo Again and Bosnian Counterattack." *New York Times*, 12 January 1994, p. A8.

——— (1994b). "2 NATO Jets Bomb the Serbs Besieging a Bosnian Haven; U.S. Warns of More Strikes." *New York Times*, 11 April 1994, pp. A1, A6.

——— (1994c). "U.S. Planes Bomb Serbian Positions for a Second Day: Serbs Voicing Defiance." *New York Times*, 12 April 1994, pp. A1, A10.

Suhrke, Astri, and Lela Garner Noble, eds. (1977). *Ethnic Conflict and International Relations*. New York: Praeger.

Sumner, William Graham, and Albert Galloway Keller (1927). *The Science of Society*. Vol. 2. New Haven: Yale University Press.

Swedish Ministry of Foreign Affairs (1997). *Preventing Violent Conflict: A Study*. Stockholm: Norstedts Tryckeri AB.

Taylor, Charles L., and David A. Jodice (1983). *World Handbook of Political and Social Indicators*. 3d ed. New Haven: Yale University Press.

Taylor, Donald M., and Fathali M. Moghaddam (1988). *Theories of Intergroup Relations: International Social Psychological Perspectives*. New York: Praeger.

Tenet, George J. (1999). Statement of the Director of Central Intelligence, George J. Tenet, As Prepared for Delivery Before the Senate Armed Services Committee Hearing on Current and Projected National Security Threats. 2 February 1999. <http://www.odci.gov/cia/>.

Tillema, Herbert K. (1989). "Foreign over Military Intervention in the Nuclear Age." *Journal of Peace Resolution* 26 (2): 179–193.

Tooby, John, and Leda Cosmides (1992). "The Psychological Foundations of Culture." In *The Adapted Mind*, edited by J. H. Barkow, Leda Cosmides, and John Tooby. New York: Oxford University Press.

Touval, Saadia (1996). "Lessons of Preventative Diplomacy in Yugoslavia." In *Managing Global Chaos*, edited by Fen Osler Hampson and Chester A. Crocker. Washington, DC: USIP.

Touval, Saadia, and William Zartman (1996). "International Mediation in the Post Cold War Era." In *Managing Global Chaos*, edited by Fen Osler Hampson and Chester A. Crocker. Washington, DC: USIP.

Troebst, Stefan (1999). "Conflict in Kosovo: Causes and Cures—an Analytical Documentation." In *The Southeast European Challenge: Ethnic Conflict and the International Response*, edited by Hans-Georg Ehrhart and Albrecht Schnabel. Baden-Baden: Nomos Verglagsesellschaft.

United Nations Human Rights Commission statement, Geneva, 8 July 1993.

United States Information Agency. *NATO Briefings Summaries*. 23 September 1998–2 June 1999. <http://www.usia.gov/kosovo/texts/archive.htm>.

Valdez, Jonathan (1994). "Ethnic Militia and Identity-Based Violence in the Former Yugoslavia." Unpublished manuscript, DEAITC workshop on ethnic conflict, McGill University.

van den Berghe, Pierre L. (1981). *The Ethnic Phenomenon*. New York: Elsevier.

Van Evra, Stephen (1994). "Hypotheses on Nationalism and War." *International Security* 18: 5–39.

Vayrynen, Raimo (1996). "Toward Effective Conflict Prevention: Comparison of the Usability and Impact of Different Instruments." In *Preventive and Inventive Action in Intrastate Crises*, edited by J. Leatherman, W. De Mars, P. Gaffney, and R. Vayrynen. Manuscript under review. Presented as a paper at the ISA annual meeting. 16–20 April 1996, San Diego.

———— (1997). "Risky States and the Enforcement of Norms." In *Enforcing Cooperation*, edited by G. Schneider and P. Weitsman. London: Macmillan.

von Muller, Albrecht, and David Law (1995). "The Needs of Researchers: Crisis Management and Conflict Prevention in a Historic Transition Period." *Information Technologies and International Security* 30: 27–38.

Waltz, Kenneth (1979). *Theory of International Politics.* Reading, MA: Addison-Wesley.

Warnecke, A. M., R. D. Masters, and G. Kempter (1992). "The Roots of Nationalism: Non-Verbal Behavior and Xenophobia." *Ethnology and Sociobiology* 13: 267–282.

Weede, E. (1981). "Preventing War by Nuclear Deterrence or by Detente." *Conflict Management and Peace Science* 6: 1–18.

———— (1983). "Extended Deterrence by Superpower Alliance." *Journal of Conflict Resolution* 27: 231–253.

Wehling, Fred, ed. (1995). *U.S. Intervention in Ethnic Conflict.* University of California IGCC Policy Paper No. 12, 1995.

Weiner, Myron (1971). "The Macedonia Syndrome: An Historical Model of International Relations and Political Development." *World Politics* (July): 665–683.

———— (1992). "People and States in a New Ethnic Order?" *Third World Quarterly* 13 (2): 317–333.

Weingast, Barry (1995). "Understanding Ethnic Conflict." Unpublished manuscript. Stanford, CA: Hoover Institution.

Weiss, Thomas G. (1994). "Intervention: Whither the United Nations?" *Washington Quarterly* 17: 109–128.

Whitney, Craig R. (1993). "NATO to Join U.S. in Planning Air Strikes Against Serbs' Forces." *New York Times*, 3 August 1993, p. A1.

———— (1999). "Serbs Press Sweep of Kosovo; Refugees Keep Fleeing." *New York Times*, 18 April 1999, p. 11.

Wilson, Edward O. (1975). *Sociobiology: The New Synthesis.* Cambridge, MA: Belknap.

———— (1978). *On Human Nature.* Cambridge, MA: Harvard University Press.

Wolfers, Arnold (1959). "The Actors in International Politics." In *The Theory and Practice of International Relations*, edited by David McLellan, William Olson, and Fred Sonderman. Englewood Cliffs, NJ: Prentice-Hall.

Woodward, Susan (1995). *Balkan Tragedy.* Washington, DC: Brookings Institution.

World Politics (1989). Vol. 41 Special issue.

Zagare, Frank (1990). "Rationality and Deterrence." *World Politics* 42: 238–260.

———— (1996). "Classical Deterrence Theory: A Critical Assessment." *International Interactions* 21:365–87.

Zagare, Frank, and D. Marc Kilgour (1998). "Deterrence Theory and the Spiral Model Revisited." *Journal of Theoretical Politics* 10: 59–87.

Zald, Mayer N., and John D. McCarthy, eds. (1987). *Social Movements in an Organizational Society: Collected Essays.* Oxford: Transactions Books.

Zartman, I. William (1989). *Ripe for Resolution: Conflict and Intervention in Africa.* 2d. ed. New York: Oxford University Press.

—— (1990). "Negotiations and Prenegotiations in Ethnic Conflict: The Beginning, the Middle, and the Ends." In *Conflict and Peacemaking in Multiethnic Societies,* edited by Joseph V. Montville. Lexington, MA: Lexington Books.

—— (1992). "Internationalization of Communal Strife: Temptations and Opportunities of Triangulation." In *The Internationalization of Communal Strife,* edited by Manus I. Midlarsky. London: Routledge.

—— (1995). *Elusive Peace: Negotiating an End to Civil Wars, 1995–1996.* Washington, DC: Brookings Institution.

ADDITIONAL WORLD WIDE WEB SOURCES:

Agreed Points on Russian Participation in KFOR (18 June 1999). <http://www.nato.int/kosovo/docu/a990618a.htm>

Allied Forces Southern Europe: Operation Joint Guardian. AFSOUTH Public Information Office. (pio@afsouth.nato.int) <http://www.afsouth.nato.int/kfor>

BBC News. <http://news.bbc.co.uk/hi/english/world/europe>

Canadian Department of National Defense, Press Room. <http://www.dnd.ca/eng/archive/apr99/Kosovo1_b_e.htm>

CNN Interactive. <http://cnn.com/WORLD/europe>

Human Rights Watch, Kosovo Flash Reports. <http://www.hrw.org/hrw/campaigns/kosovo98>

Military Technical Agreement between the International Security Force ("KFOR") and the Governments of the Federal Republic of Yugoslavia and the Republic of Serbia. (9 June 1999). <http://www.nato.int/kosovo/docu/a990609a.htm>

NATO's Role in Relation to the Conflict in Kosovo (updated 15 July 1999). <http://www.nato.int/kosovo/history.htm>

New York Times. <http://search.nytimes.com/search/daily/>

Operation Joint Guardian (updated 14 July 1999). <http://www.nato.int/kosovo/jnt-grdn.htm>

South European Division, DFAIT, July 1999: Chronology of Events: <http://www.dfait-maeci.gc.ca/foreignp/kosovo/text/chrono-e.asp>

Undertaking of Demilitarization and Transformation by the UCK (20 June 1999). <http://www.nato.int/kosovo/docu/a990620a.htm>

United States Information Agency, Kosovo Timeline. <http://www.usia.gov/kosovo/timeline.htm>

Index

About the Authors

DAVID CARMENT is a NATO Fellow and Associate Professor of International Affairs at the Norman Paterson School of International Affairs, Carleton University, Ottawa, Canada. Professor Carment has published extensively in the field of ethnic conflict and conflict prevention. His latest books are *Peace in the Midst of Wars* and *Wars in the Midst of Peace*, with Patrick James.

FRANK HARVEY is a NATO Fellow and Associate Professor of Political Science at Dalhousie University and the Centre for Foreign Policy Studies, Halifax, Canada. His books include *The Future's Back* and *Conflict in World Politics*, with Ben Mor.